Lord Francis Garden Gardenstone

Miscellanies in Prose and Verse

Second Edition

Lord Francis Garden Gardenstone

Miscellanies in Prose and Verse
Second Edition

ISBN/EAN: 9783744689403

Printed in Europe, USA, Canada, Australia, Japan

Cover: Foto ©Thomas Meinert / pixelio.de

More available books at **www.hansebooks.com**

MISCELLANIES

IN

PROSE AND VERSE;

INCLUDING REMARKS ON

ENGLISH PLAYS, OPERAS, AND FARCES,

And on a Variety of other

MODERN PUBLICATIONS.

BY THE HONOURABLE LORD GARDENSTONE.

DULCE EST DESIPERE IN LOCO.

THE SECOND EDITION, CORRECTED AND ENLARGED.

EDINBURGH:

PRINTED BY J. ROBERTSON, SOUTH BRIDGE-STREET.

MDCCXCII.

PREFACE.

THE Remarks on Engliſh Plays, and thoſe other Remarks on Modern Publications which are printed next after them, in this volume, are tranſcribed from the library of the Honourable Lord Gardenſtone, kept open for the amuſement of Travellers, at the Inn of his village of Laurencekirk. It is his Lordſhip's practice to inſert his Critical Obſervations on the margins of the reſpective books, and to interline with his pen ſome of the moſt remarkable paſſages. This explanation may be neceſſary, to enable the reader to underſtand ſome of his Lordſhip's expreſſions which refer to theſe circumſtances.

The firſt Edition of this Miſcellany was not intended for Sale; but a ſecond having been deſired by the Public, the Editor has exerted his attention to render it as correct as poſſible. A variety of Articles have likewiſe been added, which are, perhaps, not unworthy of preſervation.

EDINBURGH, *January* 1. 1792.

POETICAL ESSAYS.

THE PROGRESS OF VIRGINITY:

A TALE.

In days of old, as ancient poets ſing,
There reign'd in Greece, a certain jealous king;
Who, leaſt her bloom a lover ſhould deflower,
Shut up his daughter in a loneſome tower.
The walls were lofty, and the gate was ſtrong,
There pin'd the poor young lady all day long.
No more in balls our princeſs led the van,
With each warm glance to fire the outward man;
Nor in her chariot roll'd about the town,
To cheapen lace, and ſhow the laſt new gown;
No ſcandal heard, no captive ſwain might ſee,
No ſoul to ſhare her ſolitary tea.
Herſelf as fair a girl as could be ſeen,
Was not a ſecond leſs than ſweet ſeventeen.
And well you may ſuppoſe, that ſuch a cage,
Agreed but badly with her amorous age;
She fondly fancied, that ſuperior charms
Would bring ſome fearleſs rover to her arms;
And, as all maidens in the faſhion bred,
Think every hour five hundred, till they're wed;
So ſhe, reluctant, bore *the loſs of time*,
And ſaw her beauty languiſh in the prime.
She panted for the height of human bliſs,
To pour her tranſports in a balmy kiſs;
And that ſublimer joy we bluſh to name,
Which vanquiſh'd virgins feel the victor claim.
A wicked dream would likewiſe now and then,
Remind her females were but made for men.
Thus, nor awake, nor tortur'd into ſleep,
Could mournful Miſs forbear to wiſh and weep;

The fruit was ripe, but there appear'd no hand
To crop the harvest of her promis'd land.
No fond assailant dar'd provoke his fate,
All night nine mastiffs howl'd before the gate;
Through the long day she saw the king alone,
Who lov'd, admir'd, and plagu'd her as his own.
For, as our parents in the present days
Hear with disdain what honest nature says,
Spurn from the heart what manly feeling springs,
And but inquire what cash the fellow brings;
So this wise prince no proffer would content;
He claim'd a father's title to torment.
But Venus soon, that Nymph who rules the skies,
Roll'd on the dungeon her indignant eyes;
And first her lovely cheeks were flush'd with red,
As when poor Mars and she lay shackled on her bed;
A cuckold's vengeance Vulcan chose to boast,
And laughter shook the pleas'd celestial host.
Then thus her silence to her sire she broke,
The Monarch's pulse beat harder while she spoke.
" What horrid doings in the world below!
" What blest rewards on beauty to bestow!
" Forgive me, dear Papa; who would not wail,
" A buxom virgin buried in a jail.
" Go!—if your thunder has not stunn'd your brains,
" If yet one spark of fire invigorates your veins,
" For injur'd innocence your pity prove,
" And storm, at once, yon sweet recess of love."
'Twas thus her will, the wanton Queen express'd;
And Jove rejoic'd at such a filthy jest.
His throne deserting down the skies he flew,
But near the prison, when the Thunderer drew,
His shape he alter'd, as the story's told,
And through the roof shot in a shower of gold.
Yet soon his form resum'd; and (strange to tell!)
Her royal highness bore her wrongs so well;
With such intrepid patience Hopeful prest,
Juno's chaste husband to her generous breast;

That old Squire Padlock found himſelf beguil'd,
And ſaw, full ſoon, his pretty maid with child.
Here let us pauſe; and in a moral ſcale,
Survey the merit of this famous tale.
Whoe'er would rob a woman of her will,
Muſt, ſoon or late ſucceed but very ill.
Their native cunning, the ſly ſex refines,
And fate, we ſee, will ſecond their deſigns.
Are love's advances with neglect repaid?
The frozen Dotard muſt be diſobey'd:
He fawns, he lectures, and he bolts in vain;
Inſulted nature burſts the tyrant's chain.
A thouſand furies fire his frantic ſpouſe;
A thouſand horns are ſprouting on his brows.
By Jove's device, the Muſe would make it known,
That gold, like hunger, breaks through walls of ſtone.
Nay, ſurly ſailors ſoften at the ſight;
And every ſoldier ſwears you party right;
And like a man of honour, ſpills his blood,
While one poor farthing in an hour's allow'd.
So when the Sage of Macedon aſſail'd
The citadels of Greece, he thus prevail'd:
And fire and ſword but ſeldom forc'd his way;
For Plutus, more politely, turn'd the key.
Thus, in *the houſe*, when orators contend,
A place, or penſion, makes each patriot bend.
For gold, the father proſtitutes his ſon;*
And the pimp huſband ſees his ſpouſe undone.
For gold, the judge decides, the felon ſwings,
The parſon chatters, and the laureate ſings.

* See for example, the ſtory of Old Nightingale, in the novel of Tom Jones.

PECULIAR DISADVANTAGES

OF

A MODERN POET.

If a rash rhymer honestly intends
To rectify the follies of his friends,
Lamenting loudly, as each former bard,
For ninety generations has declar'd,
" That still, in spite of parsons and their rules,
" Nine-tenths of all mankind are knaves and fools;
" Nay, that the best of us, at times, are willing
" To let our father starve, and save a shilling;"
He finds his virtuous efforts are in vain,
" The Beast of Reason" hears him with disdain:
The vulgar gape, the learn'd, like Shakespeare's fool,
Profess themselves too old to go to school:
The clergy love no sermons but their own;
Each crabbed pedant pants to pull him down;
Each puppy curses the contemptuous dog;
And every swindler swears that he's a rogue.
  But, viewing matters on the other side,
What shall be gain'd by fawning upon pride?
On *panegyric*, if he turns his head,
The lowest of all beggars lies for bread;
And every body knows he wants a hire,
And every living mortal scorns a liar.
Sir Bob his bounty for his bawd reserves,
The lacquey fattens, but the laureate starves.
  Add, that the dull, the busy, and the great,
With boundless ridicule your labours treat;
For almost nobody has taste, or time,
To feel and cultivate the sweets of rhyme.
The doctor must trepan, dissect, and bleed;
The priest has work enough to prop his creed;
And, while our reason and our faith debate,
To paint a heretic's tremenduous fate.

The lawyer wrangles in defence of knaves;
For ſtallions, girls, and port, the Game Law Juſtice raves;
Merchants, if men of ſenſe, mind only trade;
Enſigns would always ſtrut on the parade:
And which of theſe d'ye think will condeſcend
To hear the fineſt verſe that e'er was penn'd?
Such rank ſtupidity we ſcarce need mourn,
Since every claſs are uſeful in their turn.
And who would reap the corn, or mend the roads,
Were all intent on Tragedies and Odes?
How rare the man an office who has fill'd,
At once in tactics and in metre ſkill'd:
Nay, of the learn'd themſelves, but very few
That lonely calm Elyſian path purſue.
In ancient days, when Science was confin'd,
Philoſophers had little elſe to mind;
Then, every ſwain the fall of Ilion ſung,
And Sappho flow'd from every ſchool-boy's tongue.
But now, the properties of putrid air,
Some pointers itch, the genius of a hare,*
A ruſty coin, a cockle-ſhell, a mite,
Provoke the ſage to wonder and to write.
While ſome with air balloons amuſe the mob,
Some ſail in ſearch of ruſhes round the globe,†
Compute both age, and tonnage of the earth,
What tadpole cholic gave your fœtus birth,
Teach cannoneers to level, and to load,
Obſerve a planet, or diſſect a toad;
Tell the velocities of ſound and light,
Or preach that fractur'd limbs are firm and *right;*
Or, ſtraining mental and material ſight,

* There is an eſſay on this ſubject in the Gentleman's Magazine.

† What rational purpoſe can be anſwered by a HORTUS SICCUS? The plan of Captain Bligh's voyage was ſuggeſted thirty years ago by Voltaire.

Defcry a fhip five hundred leagues from land, *
And prove the Day of Judgment juft at hand. †
Nay, what is worft of all, the very men
Who really feel the beauties of the pen,
Whofe tafte, in juftice, ought to be preferr'd,
Who foar in fentiments above the herd.
Who love your verfes better than your wine,
And read with more attention than they dine,
None, but the fool who trufts them, can believe
Of thefe, what numbers at his progrefs grieve?
And fhould fuccefs await upon your lays,
They dare not cenfure, but *they will not praife*;
With all an eunuch's melancholy fpite,
They growl at you, becaufe *they* cannot write:
A gloomy filence, envy's pang imparts,
Or fome cold hint betrays their canker'd hearts.
" A fellow wanting food fhould hufband time,
" His idlenefs is more than half a crime;
" Bards, in all ages, have been very poor,
" And fome now famous beg from door to door:
" The jingling tribe are juftly reckon'd fools,
" Who never will attend to Reafon's rules.
" And why fhould vagabonds in queft of bread,
" Attempt to rhyme, to reafon, or to read."
Such are the crumbs of comfort they beftow,
And fuch the kindnefs you to critics owe.
But one erroneous accent let them fpy,
Then exultation fparkles in each eye;
And if an *in* for *into* has been us'd,
Of downright fcorn of grammar you're accus'd.
Sailors, when ftarving, deal their beer and grog,
And rogues have dy'd to help a brother rogue:
A porter with diftrefs will fhare his pay,
And for the parifh poor, poor actors play:

* The honour of this difcovery, real or pretended, has been lately claimed by a Frenchman.

† Whifton " lived long enough to fee TWO completions of his " own Millenium." OBSERVER, No. 36.

These may, 'tis always possible, do good,
No *speculation* petrifies their blood.
But would a sixpence free you from the jail,
To hazard *that* makes *letter'd* friendship fail.
On every side difficulties conspire,
Be wise and throw your verses *in* the fire.

ON GOOD NATURE.

THAT man has learn'd the wisest way to live,
Who can with pleasure injuries forgive.
To plot for vengeance, brings incessant woe,
For each half-friend becomes a serious foe.
And since ourselves so frequently mistake;
Why wonder at those errors others make.
Such is the in-born baseness of mankind,
A grateful heart we seldom hope to find;
But for revenge, the passion is so strong,
Not one in fifty would forgive a wrong.
Chance but to stumble on his gouty toe,
With honour's champion to the field you go,
And should your fortune when "the heroes join,"
Bury a pistol bullet in his groin;
Then, while a tertian gives him time to cool,
He sees, but dares not own, he was a fool.
Endeavour, if you can, to be sedate;
And shun the mad extremes of love and hate:
Censure, or praise, be cautious to proclaim,
For *all the world are more than half the same:*
Scarce can their virtues your esteem engage,
Far less their vices vindicate your rage.
View them you may, no doubt, with honest scorn,
And wonder why such bedlamites were born.
But never of yourself, absurdly vaunt;
The weakest feel some excellence you want.
In no man's quarrel take an active part;
But hide, if wise, the venom of your heart.

For when the mighty buſtle has blown o'er,
Thoſe you defended, thank your zeal no more.
Like Paul and Peter, *quondam* friends may fight,
And the worſt foes, like North and Fox unite.
Let this grand maxim in your minds be fix'd,
All mortal characters are oddly mix'd;
The wiſeſt men have many a fooliſh thought,
The dulleſt dunce acts often as he ought:
Thus, Job himſelf was peeviſh for a time,
And Nero reign'd five years without a crime.
The honeſt Cato ſometimes drank too late,
And Cæſar ſhed one tear for Pompey's fate.
Since then the heart is ſeldom long the ſame,
'Tis but a phantom you can praiſe or blame.
Parolles ſwears your verſes are divine;
And all the Muſes melt in every line;
" Swift if alive, his fading fame would mourn,
" And bluſh for Gulliver, at every turn."
To-morrow, not one ſtanza can be read,
Parolles grins, and hums, and ſhakes his head;
Cants o'er ſome axiom every ſchool-boy knows,
And next commences critic on your clothes.
But in the ſtreet, while trifling thus you ſtand,
Should ſome ſuperior frankly ſqueeze your hand,
At once good humour glows in every vein,
And all he ſpurn'd is excellent again.
In this inſipid worthleſs thing you trace,
The *taſte* of almoſt all the human race;
Then let your calm diſdain in ſilence die,
Is ſerious vengeance vented on a fly?
Remark yon maſtiff bay'd at by a cur,
The generous brute diſdains but to demur;
Yet ſhould the hapleſs miſcreant ſnarl at you,
What ſcolding, kicking, yelping, would enſue.
Your dog, before you venture to deſpiſe,
Vain man! be half as worthy, and as wiſe.
If, e'er as author, you pretend to fame,
All private pique, be patient, and diſclaim;

Were men of rhyme above unhappy ſpite,
Perhaps Pope's Dunciad had not ſeen the light.

Thus, while a Sage his eloquence diſplay'd,
Rappee fell ſhort, his ſnuffbox was miſlaid;
Around the Club he caſt an eager eye,
But not one pupil could a pinch ſupply.
The preacher's face contracted in a gloom,
A hearty curſe reſounded through the room;
His ſpouſe on Patience claim'd *her* turn to plead,
And Seneca was hurled at her head.

JUPITER AND THE FROGS:

A TALE.

ÆSOP aſſures us, that of old the Frogs
Were ſo vain glorious of their bogs,
'Twas their opinion,
They could be happy with a prince alone,
A Hero from the tadpole throne,
To ſpread dominion.

Two orators the loyaliſts elected,
To make their plea by Jove reſpected,
Or heard at leaſt;
Both hopping up a turf eight inches high,
Levell'd their noſes at the ſky,
Jove ſmok'd the jeſt.

The thundering fornicator took a ſtool,
(He was with Juno's leave no fool)
And whirl'd it down;
The plenipoes preſum'd it was the devil—
It popt with ſuch a ſquaſh uncivil
On each bald crown.

That morning the Dutch nightingales lay quiet,
Till one, impatient for a riot,
Thruſt forth his ſnout,
Survey'd his Majeſty in all directions,
Made, like a Frog of ſenſe, reflections,
And rais'd the rout.

Their monarch now the hopeful tribe aſcends;
My readers know what nameleſs ends
A *ſtool* may ſerve.
But Jove, to pepper them, a Crane diſpatch'd,
Who dozens at a morſel ſnatch'd;
Through every nerve,

The croaking fugitives with terror ſhook;
Repentance burn'd in every look;
"Friends!" cry'd a Frog,
"Jove was, for ſuch a ſorry trick, our debtor,
"We might have all behav'd much better
"To poor King Log."

ALL's WELL THAT ENDS WELL.

Some ſage philoſophers of old
Were vain to undervalue gold,
Alleging, that the learned rules,
So loudly chatter'd in their ſchools,
Abundant pleaſure could ſupply,
And teach us how to live and die.
To die is nothing; Are you ſad?
A halter always may be had.
But the grand point at which we drive,
Is how to keep ourſelves *alive*,
When all the bitterneſs of ſcorn,
And cold, and hunger, muſt be borne.
And what are virtue, fame, and health,
Without the ſovereign aid of *wealth*?

Keen appetite avails but little,
Unlefs the purfe can purchafe "vittle*."
What fignifies a handfome form
If undefended from the ftorm?
And will a taylor now a days,
Rig out a rhymer for his lays?
He tires, alas! to hear us read,
And murmurs but to break a thread.
  Then mind not what the pedants fay,
But *act* with as much phlegm as they.
Nor pamper up the parifh poor,
But fweep the vermin from your door;
Nor borrow with a view to lend,
Nor pawn your breeches for a friend:
But if to pay your claim he lingers,
Wrench the laft farthing from his fingers:
And fhould that generous effort fail,
Be fure to fend the rogue to jail.
There let him rot, and ftarve to death,
Nor quit him till his dying breath:
And when his yelping fpoufe appears,
With all her tatter'd flock in tears,
To prove—"Were hell demolifh'd, now,
"Another muft be had for you;
"That Providence were falfely nam'd,
"If fuch a monfter is not damn'd;"
To this ungrateful, faucy ftyle,
Reply with a contemptuous fmile;
Nor let remorfe your bofom rack,
But plug your ears, and turn your back.
The boys will pelt the crazy jade,
Their mothers wonder why fhe's mad;
And fome fage active Juftice fend her
To Bridewell, as an old offender.

* SWIFT.

ON THE DEATH OF A FRIEND.

INSCRIBED TO A YOUNG LADY.

Whenever he, who ſince the world began,
Has felt for all the miſeries of man;
Who Folly's mean ſuſpicions to remove,
Requeſts us to remember HE IS LOVE;
Who guides all nature to a noble end,
By ways our weakneſs cannot comprehend;
When from the tireſome ſcene of trifling here,
He takes his fav'rites to a higher ſphere,
While the freed ſpirit leaves her load of clay,
And wonders we behind ſubmit to ſtay,
The feelings of falſe pity are obey'd,
And mortals mourn for thoſe they call the dead.
 How many Lectures have we heard in vain?
But truths neglected, muſt be told again:
Stupidity itſelf can ſcarce forget
That death is an inevitable debt;
That too much pleaſure muſt itſelf deſtroy;
That ſomething ſtill is wanting in our joy;
That modeſt Merit rarely meets her due;
That happineſs recedes as we purſue;
That Pride's poor play-things are not worth a ſigh;
That 'tis our higheſt privilege to die;
And all our grief muſt fairly be confeſt
But ſelfiſhneſs, or ignorance, at beſt.
 You, Madam, anſwer—" That our friend was young;
" That ſcandal never ſtain'd his faultleſs tongue;
" That his whole ſoul was free from ſordid art;
" That virtue never fir'd a nobler heart;
" How cruelly cut off before his time,
" His every joy juſt riſing in the prime!"
Let me, from ſad experience of the paſt,
Wiſh my firſt moment might have been my laſt;
And think, with fondneſs, of that happy ſhore
Where he who ſhar'd our ſorrows, mourns no more;

Where envy ſhall not interrupt our peace,
And human anguiſh finds a full releaſe.
The young when ruſhing on their quickſand ſtage,
Avoid, and pity, and deſpiſe old age;
With ſullen hatred hear it's frigid rules,
And fancy that their fathers have been fools;
That they the manners of the world will mend;
That every gay companion is a friend;
That native merit their ſucceſs inſures;
That ſhe they ſigh for has a heart like yours.
But ſoon, by life's calamities oppreſt,
Conviction, burſting on the tortur'd breaſt,
Their blaſted hopes the bitter truth reveal,
That men may talk of what they do not feel;
Nay, that the beſt ne'er practiſe as they know,
That words are all a wiſe man will beſtow:
Then venerable Miſery fails to move,
Suſpicion freezes every ſource of Love;
They feel no pleaſure, they forbear to pleaſe,
And who would ranſom life on terms like theſe?
Come let each thought in grateful rapture ſwell,
Since he, who lov'd us, hath eſcap'd ſo well;
Without one pang, from tenderneſs forgot,
With ſcarce one cauſe to murmur at his lot;
To all which goodneſs infinite can give,
'Twas in expiring he began to live.
From this low ſcene, when ſuch a ſoul retires,
What heart could cenſure, what the heart inſpires;
A parting tear to Nature muſt be paid,
Nature, in ſpite of us, will be obey'd;
And kindling, like his friend, at Beauty's charms,
While every honour'd paſſion's up in arms,
The coldeſt of all ſongſters muſt avow,
Life worth ambition, if enjoy'd with you.

A POETICAL PROSPECT.

If Nature to welcome the birth of your boy,
A vein of pure wit had allow'd,
Let him not, like a hero, twelve pounders employ,
In ſhedding of innocent blood:

Nor venture his purſe, and his neck to diſplay,
That he gallops as firm as his Grace;
Nor yet at a card-table ſhuffle away
The hours which are flying apace.

Let him not, like the lawyer, make juſtice a job,
Forget what a gouty limb feels;
Far leſs round the pulpit aſſemble a mob
Of women to rave at his heels.

But bid him retire to converſe with the dead,
And rifle the ſweets of the Muſe;
And each of the Bards, if devoutly he read,
A ſpark of their fire will infuſe.

His humour ſhall tempt the ſevereſt to ſmile,
His wiſdom enlighten the wiſe;
In grandeur, ſimplicity, ſweetneſs, his ſtyle
To the ſummit of excellence riſe:

Nor ſhall he ſend half written traſh to the preſs,
And boaſt that he ſcorn'd to take time;
That a ſhoal of ſubſcribers inſure his ſucceſs,
That he pities the drudges in rhyme;

That original talents are always undone,
By pauſing like dulneſs to read;
That Genius around him her mantle has thrown,
That ſcribblers may borrow who need.

Such impertinence ſhall not diſhonour his page,
Though rung in our ears every day;
Nor ſhall he, with critics, at random engage,
Nor growl at the young and the gay:

But truth and good nature ſhall aptly combine
With eloquence, freedom, and wit,
And thoſe who their follies forbear to reſign,
His candid politeneſs admit.

And when he hath chaunted full many a verſe,
Which duuces themſelves muſt admire;
He ſhall, while his rivals his talents aſperſe,
The great ſervile homage require;
And the all-worthy Public his glories rehearſe,
In a jail or a garret expire.

And, when they are certain the beggar's quite dead,
His friends to befriend him ſhall haſte;
And Weſtminſter Abbey, in marble ſhall plead
Their munificence, feeling, and taſte:

And how they were ſhock'd that a Genius ſhould ſtarve,
And have paid him a generous tear;
That lofty diſtinction, O fops! ye deſerve,
Shall finiſh, I truſt, your career:

And he who but ſuch baſtard bounty beſtows,
While Ketch and the Parſon attend,
And his laſt words are bellowed under his noſe,
From the top of a ladder deſcend.

THE VOLUNTEER.

WHEN fivepence a ſolid meal cannot ſupply,
To a jolly young man five feet ten inches high;
Who has jogg'd with his knapſack twelve leagues through the rain,
While his wench and three brats had each ancle to ſtrain;
The poor Volunteer to the halberts is tied,
For ſtealing two chick-eggs and getting them fried:
What carters and jockies ſhould ſuffer he feels,
And the blood guſhes down from his nape to his heels.
The Commander in chief, who is almoſt fifteen,
And a taylor's apprentice by right ſhould have been;
Now ſtruts round the circle, then turns on his heel,
To belabour the drummers *who don't make him feel*—
Swears England could ne'er have produc'd ſuch a rogue,
And diſcerns in his howling the true Iriſh brogue.
The Surgeon, whoſe ſympathy ſwells in each vein,
When a ſwoon interrupts the convulſions of pain,
Makes them flog till he ſtart to his ſenſes again.
Nay, Doctor and Drum for attendance are *paid*,
And his pockets are fleec'd while his ſhoulders are flay'd.
He's pack'd in a tranſport on every ſtate quarrel,
More tightly than biſcuit and beef in a barrel;
In torrents each ſummer ſhower ſtreams through his tent,
In barracks more diſmal, December is ſpent;
In damp rotten bedding, the moment he's laid,
To the rage of whole armies his rear is betray'd;
In health he infallibly more than half ſtarves,
In a tertian, he's us'd as a raſcal deſerves.
His Chloe, by hunger, compell'd to ſad pranks,
Is chas'd as a ſwindler in form through the ranks;
His children, when ſome baggage cart is o'erthrown
In a ditch, like blind puppies are ſuffer'd to drown.
And when for his king thirty years he has toil'd,
In Canada froſt-bit, in Africa broil'd;

Has been thrice a week handcuff'd for drinking his pay,
Got nine thouſand laſhes for running away;
Has oft like a hero been wounded *before*,
And clear'd with a cudgel each concubine's ſcore;
At laſt, with the Dons, point to point he engages,
For more than one fourth of a ſcavenger's wages;
Some merciful volley then ſhatters a leg,
And his crutches obtain him permiſſion to beg.

THE DIGNITY OF HUMAN NATURE:

OR,

A PANEGYRIC UPON THE WORLD.

" Pride was not made for man," ſome Preacher ſays;
Yet pride, alas! directs us all our days.
The happier brutes we venture to contemn,
And thank our ſtars we were not made like them;
Yet every fault the four-foot race have known,
From Adam, downward, centers in our own:
And ſince below the laſh they ſilent bend,
Let truth proceed their virtues to defend.
With what ſurpriſe, poſterity ſhall ſee
A *panegyric* penn'd without a fee!
What right have we to trample on the weak,
Or ſtab a lamb becauſe he cannot ſpeak?
The driver of a cart is proud to ſhow
His horſe obeys the better for a blow.
The generous, faithful dog, we dare deſpiſe,
For we alone were made to mount the ſkies;
And when his ſirloin to the board is borne,
Forget the honeſt ox once plow'd to raiſe our corn.
The Dutchman's model in an ant we ſee,
And China's wiſdom animates the bee.
The very fondeſt votaries of love
Can but at diſtance imitate the dove;
And where's the architect would plan ſo well
As beavers in the building of their cell?

As far in moral worth, as ſtrength and ſize,
See the ſage elephant beyond us riſe!
Our ſavage hunger deſolates the earth,
The miſeries we make afford us mirth.
For us below the ſurface of the pole,
Where no ray vibrates, and no billows roll,
The herring ſpawns; for us the camel toils,
The pheaſant fattens, and the lobſter boils:
Nor can his mail defend the turtle's ſize,
A worm is baited, and the dolphin dies.
To Kilda's cliff the gannet ſoars in vain;
The ſhark lies vanquiſh'd on his ſubject main;
From his dark den the rugged bear we chace;
The rapid buck falls breathleſs from the race;
The frog, the ſeal, the viper, and the boar,
The crocodile himſelf we dare devour;
From his profoundeſt deeps we drag the whale,
And forty blackbirds furniſh half a meal.
Thus, land and air, the foreſt and the flood,
Are all unpeopled to ſupply our food.
We ſtyle ourſelves the *maſters* of the globe.
Nay, boaſt a ſerious right to kill and rob;
Some folks obtain'd a charter to deſtroy,
And we, their heirs, that ſacred truſt enjoy.
The prieſt a ſanction to the knife imparts,
And ſolemn canting ſteels our ſtupid hearts,
Our fare, while ſlaughter every day ſupplies,
We ſtill humanity pretend to prize;
We brand the name of Nero with diſgrace,
And ſay his deeds reproach the human race;
Becauſe he burn'd that den of robbers, Rome,
And gave a female fiend her proper doom.
Voracious murd'rer! view yon deſert hive,
Where not one denizen is left alive!
All in black heaps, beneath thy rapine roll'd,
As Judah's Judges butcher'd young and old!
Nor had thoſe innocents offended thee,
Nor gave neceſſity an honeſt plea.

The prince of quadrupedes finds ample food,
Without the baleful art of ſhedding blood:
With all deteſted Nero ever ſpilt,
His utmoſt crimes can ſcarce approach thy guilt.
Vaunt as thou wilt about thy right divine,
The wolf may plead a better far than thine.
O might bold Juvenal my breaſt inſpire
With all his ſacred, his immortal fire;
To trace the progreſs ſince the world began,
Through all his freaks of that poor puppet—Man!
To ſhake his coward heart with conſcious fear,
And rend with hoſtile truth the tyrant's ear.
Compar'd to us, the peacock is not vain,
Compar'd to us, the tyger is humane.
No ſpaniel ever ſhook with ſo much fear,
As bankrupt farmers, when the term draws near;
And though the hogſtye ſeems an horrid ſcene,
Five hundred nations are not half ſo clean.
An ape might learn the ſcience of grimace
From ſome field preacher, bawling faith and grace;
But when embattled ſects through ages bleed,
To prop ſome trivial antiquated creed,
Sure this is madneſs to the brutes unknown,
And Hell muſt teſtify 'tis all our own.
Of all the victims of the preſent ſcene,*
Man feels the ſhorteſt joy, the ſharpeſt pain.
On yon poor aſs we turn contemptuous eyes,
And his calm patience pity and deſpiſe;
But yet he never ſwills the heady bowl,
Till every frantic paſſion tears his ſoul:
On thiſtles, graſs, and ſtraw, content he lives,
And each pure ſtream a welcome beverage gives.
For him no dappled dame has broke her heart;
No batter'd bawd refines each damning art;
No dark attorney whets the vulture quill;
No hungry quack rears up a monſtrous bill.
No pulpit mountebank o'erſets his brains;
No rooted pox ſhoots venom through his veins:

* A part of this paragraph is borrowed from Menander.

What ills afflict him, nature hath bestow'd,
He never madly multiplies the load.
If what the scriptures teach us were not true,
That virtue shall heareafter reap her due;
If Cato's worth is nothing but a name,
And good and bad are in the grave the same;
If Shakespeare's intellect be gone to dust,
And keen Voltaire survives but in his bust;
His envied wound if Hampden has forgot,
And Frederick sleeps, unconscious why he fought;
If Howard shall not from the silent grave,
Survey that happiness his bounty gave;
Nor Hawke review the glorious path he trode,
But moulder with a Swift or Sully's clod;
Vaunt as you please of Nature's gracious plan,
I'd rather be a pismire than a man.
This doubt so terrible to human pride,
Reason's dim rushlight never can decide:
The pious piercing eye of Faith alone,
Assures our rise to worlds beyond our own.

THE MAGPYE:

A TALE FOR THE CRITICS.

My reader may fancy the labour but light,
In penning by thousands the trifles I write;
Sit down, my dear sir, and your faculties try,
To excel these loose sketches your skill may defy.
A frivolous art is oft hardest to win,
Eighteen workmen are paid for completing a pin:
Or else for yourself manufacture your lays,
Or blush to repine at our pitiful praise.
On this head allow me your ears to regale,
With a short, but perhaps with a sensible tale.
The birds all complain'd that in building a nest,
The Magpye was wiser by far than the rest;

That ſhe with a roof, could her lodging encloſe,
And laugh from within at the rage of her foes;
While to raiſe half a houſe was the height of their power,
And when a cloud broke they were drench'd in the ſhower.
  Before a grand council the matter was laid,
And the Gooſe, Rook, and Mavis, ambaſſadors made,
By force or perſuaſion, to pump from the Pye,
In what might her ſecrets of maſonry lie.
  "Lay two ſticks," ſaid the feather'd Vitruvius, "acroſs,
"For that," cry'd the Rook, "I was ne'er at a loſs."
"Mix your mud with freſh ſtubble."—The Mavis replied,"
"In treading firm plaſter I ſpurn at a guide."
"If theſe," bawl'd the Gooſe, "be the beſt of your rules,
"I fear nobody, Madam, will mind you but fools."
"My very kind teachers," ſaid Mag, with a ſneer,
"If ſo wiſe, and alert, what the plague brought you here?
"Go thatch for yourſelves;" ſo ſhe hopped away,
And her neighbours have wanted a roof to this day.
  Our ſtory applies to the raſhneſs of thoſe
Who by Nature, confin'd to the region of proſe,
Reproach, without mercy, the maſters of rhyme,
For each petty fault as a perſonal crime;
With the cant of fine taſte, while each coffee-houſe rings,
'Tis the pedant who barks, not the poet who ſings.
The grave, learned gown-man, too jealous to love
The bard whom his penſion has plac'd him above,
Would do well to remember, that, but for our art,
He could not get vented the gall of his heart;
That learning to genius can be but a foil;
As dung does not *form* though it *fattens* the ſoil;
That talents untutor'd may ſoar to the ſky,
But a lame underſtanding no crutches ſupply.
  Then let each remarker malevolence drop,
And humbly remember this maxim of Pope:
"He ſhould judge of a painter, whoſe paintings excel,
"And cenſure bad verſes, who verſifies well."

ON THE LOSS OF ANCIENT LITERATURE.

The fathers of our church, 'tis widely known,
Damn'd every kind of learning but their own.
Did not Tertullian's worſe than brutal rage
Curſe and belie Menander's ſacred page?
And did not Gregory his power exert
To burn the nobleſt monuments of art?
Before her ſaints, Rome ſaw her Livy fall,
And Tully periſh'd to make way for Paul;
And Pindar's elegies, and Sappho's odes,
For ſome old monk's more pious palinodes.
Polybius, Plutarch, Salluſt, were deſtroy'd,
That Polycarp and *Co.* might fill the void.
Four-fiſths of Tacitus we ſeek in vain,
He, too, was dull, indecent, and profane;
Atteſted miracles which were not *true*,
And hated (who could wonder?) every Jew.
What indignation warms each ſcholar's breaſt,
When charm'd with half a page, we loſe the reſt.
This wreck was eaſy in a ſtupid age,
When prieſts and Vandals fill'd the human ſtage;
But did not all the world grow learn'd and wiſe,
When light once more deſcended from the ſkies!
When Calvin's pen the Deity defin'd,
And Luther's eye could pierce his Maker's mind!
That famous pair who led the pious horde,
Anew convuls'd the world with fire and ſword,
And, by the foggy truths for which they fought,
Repell'd the progreſs of pure manly thought.
When rampant Harry quarrell'd with the Pope,
And gave his Gothic conſcience all it's ſcope,
In the worſt terms a bagnio can afford,
When Knox revil'd his queen *to ſerve the Lord!*
At that all-glorious dawning of Reform
Ten thouſand volumes periſh'd in the ſtorm;

And lest some novice think me too severe,
In their own words their sacred logic hear.
"Horace! what need we more than David's metre,
"Or can Demosthenes compare with Peter?
"Let Euclid's magic in the bonefire roll,
"Do rhomboids and right angles save the soul?
"Be sure to pulverize the Book of James,
"Substantial virtue, that vile papist claims:
"Forgetting Paul, he spurns at faith alone,
"And bids our saintship by our lives be shown:
"All Cato's candour was not worth a pin,
"And Phocion's exit but a shining sin."
Such was the cant of those atrocious days,
On which weak bigots lavish all their praise;
Yet we on Omar's madness dare to lay,
That loss twelve Shakespeares hardly could repay:
With all their tricks our common sense to blind,
With all their holy frauds to cheat mankind,
The conclave never coin'd a viler lie,
And here plain Truth may challenge a reply.

HORACE, LIB. I. ODE I.

IMITATED.

FIELDING, and twenty others, tell us,
That long since an Olympic race,
There have been young light-headed fellows
Who did not think it a disgrace,
Though worth ten thousand pounds a year,
To play themselves the charioteer;
But then they had a glorious aim,
To rival some postilion's fame.

Suppose a pamphleteer be witty,
And tease the Minister with jokes,
The patriot sages of the city,
Present their freedom in in a box;

And if he takes uncommon ſcope,
Deſerving well to ſtretch a rope,
They never think it a reproach,
When harneſs'd in their hero's coach.

And he who fills the jockey's part,
  Or charms with petulance the crowd,
Is juſt as happy in his art,
  And fifty times at leaſt as proud
As the grave quarto-building ſage,
Who fancies that Apollo's page,
Will pay the vaſt arrear of fame,
And through all nations ſound his name.

The Cit who ne'er a ſous beſtows,
  Of all the guineas he has won;
Who, let himſelf get food and clothes,
  Cares not what orphans are undone;
More merit claims than he who's willing,
To ſhare with Want his only ſhilling;
Whoſe penury may patch his coat
But pays the taylor to a groat.

The ſailor who in ſearch of bread,
  Muſt broil below the torrid zone,
Prefers the life he's forc'd to lead,
  Scorns all profeſſions but his own;
Is happy round the world to roam,
And pities fools who lounge at home;
In Danger's lap he's lull'd aſleep,
Nor minds the terrors of the deep.

The ſoldier too enjoys his pride,
  And when the drum begins to rattle,
Forgets the drummer flay'd his hide,
  And thinks of nothing but the battle.
Through blood, and fire, and froſt, and ſnow,
To ſerve his betters let him go;

Returning with an oaken leg,
The man of war muſt ſtarve or beg.

The Chilian from his native height,
  Who hears below the rolling thunder,
Through the dark boſom of the night,
  Down ruſhes to revenge and plunder;
Like Pyrrhus in the ſack of Troy,
Nor fights to conquer but deſtroy.
Yet this barbarian ſeeks a name,
And bids the ſong atteſt his fame.

And thus, whatever be our ſtation,
  Our hearts in ſpite of us declare,
We feel peculiar conſolation,
  And taſte of happineſs a ſhare.
Your laureate's chearful, when at times
You condeſcend to hear his rhymes;
He plunges into verſe again,
And talks of hunger with diſdain.

Our ſtate with all our reach of thought,
  We were not born to comprehend;
But peace will come if wiſely ſought,
  And pleaſure if we gain a friend.
Then let us not our ſenſes drown,
Staring at ſhadows in the moon;
Gueſſing why Saturn's belt was given,
His ſatellites—if ſix or ſeven.

AN OCCASIONAL

PROLOGUE TO THE TRAGEDY OF DOUGLAS,

Spoken at Dumfries on the 14th June, 1780.

WHEREAS, it ſeems, this week to be the vogue,
To tag ſmart Plays, with a dull Epilogue;
Living but by the humour of the day,
Though very far to ſeek, for what to ſay,
We've got one, in your ears I'll try to cram it;
Critics, ye're welcome, if ye pleaſe, to damn it.
  The wag who on your ſervant caſts an eye,
Will, as we all have done, impatient cry,
"Shall every dunce ſquirt doggrel through his quill,
"More rugged than the rumbling of a mill;
"And does the fellow fancy he'll ſay more
"Than men of taſte have fully ſaid before,
"That ſenſe is no where ſacrific'd to ſound;
"That every ſcene is built on claſſic ground;
"That all muſt here acknowledge and admire,
"An Otway's ſweetneſs, and a Shakeſpeare's fire.
"No lines are overdaub'd, till they diſguſt,
"But every word is pleaſing, nat'ral, juſt;
"And every thought ſo happily diſplay'd,
"No more, no leſs, was proper to be ſaid."
  Thus ye give verdict—nor dare we deny
Our verſes humble, and our taſk too high.—
One ſentence let us ſay, as yet unſaid,
Our debts of thanks at leaſt ſhall all be paid;
That who like us *, North Britain's ſons may truſt,
Shall find their ſouls are generous, great, and juſt;
That on their friendly hoſpitable ſhore,
No Coxcombs hiſs—rakes pelt—or bullies roar.
  Oft has French pertneſs in our ſcribbling age,
Preſum'd to dictate precepts for the ſtage;
Chanted their prattling volumes up and down,
And told all Europe Shakeſpeare was a clown.

* The company were from England.

While from the chair by British genius hurl'd,
While Rodney drives them round the Western world,
While o'er Misfortune's precipice they haste
For genius, learning, eloquence and taste,
Athens whose name the friends of wit revere,
May one day meet, who knows? a rival here.

PROLOGUE,

On the falling of the Gallery of Dumfries Theatre on the 14th June, 1780.

His learn'd phiz with deep importance big,
Stern as your Sheriff in his three tail'd wig,
Some critic, when he sees me, with a sneer
Will cry; "what vengeance brings that spouter here."
Ye, as who would not, his decrees admit,
And an indignant growl runs through the pit.
Our friends above while fury fires each eye,
Apples, suck'd oranges, and oaths let fly.
The Ball-room echoes to poor Cuthell's * rout,
While terror petrifies the folks without,
For fifty wise old women tell the town,
That Providence once more has brought the gallery down!
 Then in a minute what a shoal arrives,
Aunts, mothers, daughters, sisters, sweethearts, wives.
For though they'll cry "the fellows can't enchant us,"
The dear good natur'd fools don't care to want us.
In tears they come to carry off the slain,
But when you tell them that their tears are vain,
Press'd to each panting heart their clamours stop,
And with a kiss wipe off the falling drop;
Their pious tongues the story book expound,
As how they've caught you on the Devil's ground; †
Louder than Whitefield will the Whetstones clack,
And clap a downright judgment on your back.

* The name of the manager.

† Tertullian was the father of this wild fable.

With grief, ſolicitude and ſhame oppreſs'd
We would not wiſh to break an ill-tim'd jeſt;
Our pride was, we muſt own, completely humbled,
When laſt week from yon roof our patrons tumbled;
But ſince 'tis certain that the danger's paſt,
Since the firſt accident ſhall be the laſt,
We truſt this tragic farce may form hereafter,
A ten days theme for merriment and laughter.

VERSES

WRITTEN IN A FINE SUMMER MORNING.

Though the whole univerſe be glad,
When Summer in his glory reigns,
Reflection makes my boſom ſad,
While vegetation ſwells the plains.

For if a girl your love hath won,
Should fate beſtow the darling prize,
One tender evening cannot drown
The ardour kindled by her eyes.

And in the height of paſſion's fever,
If dawning forces you to part,
From her embrace, perhaps for ever,
A ſigh will ſurely heave your heart.

So, when I ſmell the bluſhing roſe,
And hear the birds on every bough,
And think how ſoon December ſnows
Muſt bury all that's charming now;

When polar nakedneſs ſucceeds
The flow'ry tribes which deck the green,
No Mavis warbles in the meads,
And not a ſingle leaf is ſeen;

I feel this joyous Summer day,
With all its beauties dearly bought;
I cannot bid my ſoul be gay,
Nor bear the bitterneſs of thought.

PRICKLE:

A CHARACTER.

When Prickle kindly condeſcends,
By learning, eloquence, and wit.
To teach, or entertain his friends,
With ſilent awe the circle ſit.

He lectures, as Achilles fought,
One neither needs reſiſt nor fly;
So deep, ſo brilliant, every thought,
Conviction bluſhes to reply.

We wonder how a ſingle head
Was fit to ſtudy, or retain
The world of volumes he has read,
And planted in his fertile brain.

But, mark him burſting into rage
At barbers bawling to be paid;
Or with his trembling ſpouſe engage,
Becauſe his ſnuffbox was miſlaid;

Or, ſpouting bawdry with a punk,
Blaſpheming with an air ſo cool!
For human nature never ſunk,
As far in any former fool.

Or ſtagg'ring home at break of day,
Or gormandizing at a feaſt,
And then, in Prickle's words you'll ſay,
" Is man ſuperior to a beaſt?"

COMMON SENSE.

What ſignify the wealth of nations,
The wiſdom of a thouſand ſages,
Where the gout ſpreads its depredations,
Or through each nerve a tertian rages?

The bulk and diſtance of the ſun,
With ſad indifference I read,
When, to my knee, Love's pledges run,
And, bootleſs beg a piece of bread.

Plain men lack leiſure to lament
The wreck of Plautus and Menander:
When thoſe we owe their vengeance vent,
In ſearch of plagues we need not wander.

Though Tully from the ſhades aſcend
He cannot lend yon bankrupt aid;
Nor ſtern Demoſthenes defend
His honour, till his debts are paid.

Some doubt, while ſome deride, his grief;
Each honeſt pang reproaches double;
His friends, 'if he deſerves relief,
Convince him friendſhip is a bubble.

But let him bear a brazen front,
With impudence and cunning gifted,
The world ſhall ſmile as it was wont,
And ſcorn, to humbler guilt be ſhifted.

THE PRIMUM MOBILE.

No taylor will take up his needle,
  No cobler patch a pair of ſhoes,
No lawyer with a jury wheedle,
  When diſappointed of his dues.

No ſurgeon will extract a tooth,
  No ſtrumpet exerciſe her trade,
No parſon preach eternal truth,
  Where not a ſixpence can be made.

Unbaptiz'd, bare-tail'd you muſt wander,
  The loſs of every lawſuit fee,
Nay, want in this chaſte age, a pander,
  Unleſs you can preſent a fee.

That artiſt only toils for nought,
  Who, in adulatory verſes,
While greatneſs ſpurns him as it ought,
  A great man's moral worth rehearſes.

ON THE DIVERSITIES OF LIFE.

The human race, a thouſand various ways,
Purſue the road to happineſs and praiſe;
Fancies ſo ſingular inſpire each ſoul,
Scarce would you think one artiſt made the whole.
The flatteſt dunce ſome humour cannot hide,
Which marks him out from all mankind beſide;
For in the mind, as plainly as the face,
Features peculiar to itſelf we trace.
Though all in many points, reſemblance claim,
No ſingle pair are perfectly the ſame;

So every grain of ſand, the learn'd atteſt,
Varies in ſize and figure from the reſt.
  The band term'd heroes, launch a privateer,
In queſt of ſpoil through every clime they ſteer;
Thirſt, famine, quickſands, and the ſcurvy ſcorn,
By three inch planks ſcarce through the tempeſt borne;
On every danger, every inſtant led,
Not one in ten among them dies a-bed.
  Another claſs prefer a quiet farm,
No martial ardour bids their ſpirits warm;
They never ſee the deeps beneath them roll,
Fry at the line, or ſhiver at the pole;
Their rough but ſolid ſenſe, nor ſeeks the main,
Nor ſcales the ramparts for a guilty gain.
Their pride is but to pay their landlord's rent,
And through inceſſant toil they drudge content.
  The merchant, by his debtors, daily wrong'd,
Of wares which never to himſelf belong'd,
Submits with patience to the will of Fate,
And, ſince he muſt be cheated, learns to cheat;
Hears with a ſmile each female and each fop,
And ſpins out life in ſtalking round his ſhop:
But recommend the compaſs or the plow,
Contempt and terror darken on his brow.
With pudding, beef, and porter, fully fed,
And every morn, to ſnore till breakfaſt, bred,
How ſhould he with the ruſtic riſe to work,
Or combat famine with corrupted pork;
Or rouſe to rage the ſhark's terrific form,
Or mount the main-maſt in a midnight ſtorm;
Or when the burning deck beneath him rends,
And death in every horrid ſhape deſcends;
When through each craſhing port the grapeſhot ſweep,
And the torn yards roll headlong to the deep;
Each burſting ſeam ſucks in the heavy flood,
And the grim boatſwain almoſt wades in blood;
Shall this poltroon behind the counter bred,
Who ſhudders but to ſee a ſick man bled,

While half the ſhip is into ſplinters blown,
Snatch the laſt ſecond as her hull goes down?
Survey the victor with a markſman's eye,
And give one parting broadſide ere he die.
The vintner, but a ſycophant at beſt,
Muſt bow the knee to every ſotted gueſt;
And ſtill the more you're mad enough to ſpend,
The more Iſcariot calls himſelf your friend.
To pleaſe the company his brains he'll drown,
Nor dares affirm his ſoul itſelf his own.
Whate'er you ſay, whatever be your ſtile,
He ſeconds your aſſertion with a ſmile;
Train'd to debauch, and flattery, and fraud,
He's hardly ten degrees above the bawd.—
Here equity proteſts that nine in ten,
Are not one iota worſe than common men;
Nay, half a dozen moſt of us have ſeen,
Whoſe hearts were upright and whoſe hands were clean;
And ſhould but one prove honeſt in a ſcore,
For what profeſſion can you promiſe more?
The doctor, the attorney, and the prieſt,
Have furniſh'd merry bards with many a jeſt;
One cloud of ſages pore upon the ſky,
Others engrave the features of a fly;
While mad to know what never can be known,
In metaphyſics ſome their ſenſes drown.
The chemiſt feels a juſt and curious paſſion,
But botanizing now ſeems moſt in faſhion;
And yet it's votaries make wond'rous din,
On many topics dearly worth a pin.
For though the oak our juſt attention claim,
Does every pigmy plant deſerve the ſame?
To ſquander pages on ſome uſeleſs weed,
Is but a very ſilly taſk indeed;
Their language too, at which all mankind ſtares,
No mortal tongue articulates but theirs*.

* A very intelligent writer once aſſured the Editor, that Botany was the moſt trifling ſtudy in the world; and that Linnæus

The ſon of grammar on all theſe looks down,
He conjugates a verb, declines a noun,
And could he but correct one claſſic page,
His name deſcends to every future age.
With him obſcenity becomes divine,
If Horace chanc'd to pen the precious line.
Supreme dictator in ſome pariſh ſchool,
He dreams, perhaps, that Shakeſpeare was a fool;
That Tully muſt be ſtudied ere we ſpeak,
That all true wit is borrow'd from the Greek*;
That melody is only to be found,
Where dactyls gallop, and ſpondees drawl round.
'Tis poſſible the reader may inquire,
To what diſtinction I myſelf aſpire,
Let ſongſters of ſuperior notes to mine,
Sing Rodney ruſhing through the Gallic line,

himſelf was more than half a fool. This perſon was at that very time compiling a Syſtem of Botany, which every body has ſeen. Such is often the harmony between an author's converſation and his works.

* "To *attempt to underſtand poetry*, without having diligent-"ly digeſted this treatiſe," (Ariſtotle's Poeticks) "would be as "*abſurd* and *impoſſible*, as to pretend to a ſkill in geometry, with-"out having ſtudied Euclid," *Warton's Eſſay on Pope*, Vol. I. p. 170. By this remark, we learn, that Homer did not "underſtand "poetry;" for as he died many centuries before Ariſtotle was born, he could not have peruſed the ſaid treatiſe. It is to be fear-ed, that Shakeſpeare knew as little of Ariſtotle; ſince, in one of his moſt correct plays, he introduces *Hector* quoting him. Now, as it is needleſs to read any author who does not *underſtand* his ſubject, the admirers of Mr. Warton may perhaps think it ad-viſeable to commit theſe two poets to the flames.

In the ſame work, Vol. I. p. 196, we are told, that "he that "has well *digeſted* theſe four ſhort Cantos, (Boileau's Eſſay) can-"not be ſaid to be ignorant of any *important rule of poetry!*" It is not requiſite to add, that theſe two paſſages are in the direct-eſt contradiction to each other, as well as to common ſenſe.

In p. 229, of the ſame volume, a few very trifling lines in Pope's Rape of the Lock, are ſaid to have "excelled any thing "in Shakeſpeare, or in any other author."

Or Elliot earning the great Pruſſian's praiſe,
While Calpe's ſky deſcended in a blaze;
A ſcene compar'd to which, fam'd Ilion's fall
Bore but the ſemblance of a ſchool-boy's brawl.
To pomp or pathos I make no pretence,
But range in the broad path of common ſenſe,
Nor ever burrow in the *dark ſublime*,
Nor cramp a thought by ſcantineſs of rhyme;
And if by turns contemptuous and ſevere,
Candour muſt own the verſes are ſincere;
Nor at a fool's command politely grieve,
Nor vindicate a ſyſtem none believe*;
Nor whet a pimp, nor ſerve a tyrant's end,
Nor gain their ſire a farthing or a friend.

TO THE MALE VIRGINS.

No caſe excites ſuch tender pity
In men of feeling hearts like me,
As when a girl, kind, handſome, witty,
Remains a maid at twenty-three.

While ſuch a croud of love-ſick laſſes
Around the world ſo wanton walk,

The reſt of this work, and eſpecially the dedication, is wrote in the ſame ſtyle. The author is, in particular, very angry that the world ſhould have miſtaken Dean Swift for a poet; a miſtake in which we are likely to continue. His publication conſiſts of a ſeries of digreſſions, and is only an abrupt diſcharge of all he knows upon all ſubjects. His quotations from the Greek, in an eſſay deſigned for the million, betray the true ſpirit of quackery. He is one of the moſt popular critics of the preſent age; and his volumes have been ſo generally circulated, that a man of ſenſe muſt find it difficult to kick them out of his way.

* Such as Popery in "the Hind and Panther," or Optimiſm in "an Eſſay on Man." The preceding line of this couplet refers to the dedication of Dryden's *Eleonora*.

Our ſex are ſomething worſe than aſſes,
  To let them wither on the ſtalk.

To multiply the human race
  Is man's ſublime and ſacred duty,
Shall we the glorious truſt diſgrace,
  And fly a warm though baſhful beauty?

Let ſaints in monkiſh precepts read,
  Confirm their continence by pray'r,
But ſince the cloth is fairly ſpread,
  'Twere folly to refuſe a ſhare:

Yet ſhun a well frequented coaſt,
  Nor level at a mark that's common;
Nor let it be your ſavage boaſt
  To wrong each ſilly helpleſs woman.

Provide ſome jolly bouncing ſpouſe
  That's qualify'd to cool your flame,
And ſhould ſhe fortify your brows,
  A Dutcheſs might have done the ſame.

ON POETICAL FAME.

'Tis weak in any man to laviſh pains,
And rifle and confound his brains,
  In ſearch of rhyme;
For though he ſhould acquire the loudeſt fame,
That ever buzz'd about a name,
  A glimpſe of time

Shall ſee his reputation melt away,
Some new blown bubble of the day
  Supplies his place,
With freſher topics entertains the world;
And early in its turn is hurl'd
  To like diſgrace.

Thus far-fam'd Churchill was not five years dead,
When nobody alive could read
Quite through his pages;
Yet ſome, who have not half his ſenſe and wit,
Preſume their precious works are fit,
For diſtant ages.

The bays of Dryden almoſt fade with years;
No mortal now with patience hears
The Panther's ſtory;
His *Dedications* are ſuch fulſome ſtuff,
His *Plays*—but what could be enough
To drown his glory.

Shakeſpeare himſelf ſhall one day be forgot,
And each dull critic ceaſe to blot
And damn the reſt; *
For, ſoon or late, our language muſt expire,
And graceleſs cookmaids light the fire
With Falſtaff's jeſt.

AN INDEX TO FEMALE VIRTUE.

Sweet are the ſex, but one eternal blot,
Too ſhocking to be pardon'd or forgot,
Till death adheres to them like a diſeaſe,
Yet old and young may quit it when they pleaſe.
The fault I mean is—fondneſs to reveal
Thoſe errors of the ſex they ſhould conceal.
On other points, with patience, we beſtow
Whole hours to hear their "lively nonſenſe" flow;

* Fielding, in his Journey from this World to the Next, has introduced Shakeſpeare ſaying, "Where a paſſage in my works "admits of two meanings, neither of them can be worth a far- "thing." The commentators on this writer have, in truth, become a ſort of nuiſance.

On teas and laces let them ſtill diſpute,
But on *themſelves* we beg them to be mute.
When envy fluſhes o'er a beauty's bloom,
Stark indignation drives us from the room.
The girl whoſe mere good-nature grants a child,
By all the herd is hooted and revil'd;
Nay, hags, who play'd that very prank before,
With matchleſs impudence her guilt abhor.
'Tis farcical with what a whining face
They fly to ſound the trumpet of diſgrace;
Belch out the fumes of Preſbyterian rage,
And mourn the madneſs of the riſing age!
Yet females, who poſſeſs the faireſt fame,
Perhaps at bottom, are the very ſame,
Train'd to the ſport and "daughters of the game."
Men of true feeling take Misfortune's part,
Nor tantaliſe, but ſoothe a bleeding heart.
The soureſt Methodiſt may chance to fail,
Like Æſop's fox entangled by the tail.
Though modeſt wives are ſurely to be ſought,
Their brittle boaſted worth is often dearly bought.
If private ſcandal half her time employs,
If night and day you're deafen'd with her noiſe,
How dares that viper hope to be careſs'd,
Who gives you ſuch a ſample of her breaſt?
How bleſt the man! from ſuch a monſter free,
Her ruffian virtue has no charms for me;
I grant you, decency her name adorns,
But rather would embrace a buſh of thorns.
Let hen-peck'd ſlaves their tame forbearance boaſt,
What Chriſtian phlegm inſpires them when they're croſs'd;
And while their hack is bawling o'er amours,
Forbear to kick the baggage out of doors.
Till my laſt ſpark of underſtanding ceaſe,
No pamper'd vixen ſhall invade my peace;
No concubine ſhall curb, no canting wife,
Claim a church-warrant to confound my life.

Her pipe, when pious indignation rears,
And ſcare-crow texts are thunder'd in your ears,
A cat-o'-nine-tails, and a whipping poſt,
Would richly pay whatever they may coſt.
We know the *charmers* honeſtly intend
By ſuch a tune themſelves to recommend,
To prove their feelings infinitely nice,
And teſtify, like Paul, their rage at vice;
But every man who has not ſhut his eyes,
Deciphers at a glance their thin diſguiſe.
The very graveſt virgins wiſh to wed,
Like us they ſlight a ſolitary bed;
And when our aunts at roving wenches rail,
We always know for certain what they ail;
Juſt as a tradeſman feels his courage drop,
When good old cuſtomers go by his ſhop.
Indulgence for their ſpite may be allow'd,
Since females, like ourſelves, are fleſh and blood.
Ladies!—the beſt among you are but frail,
And may be ruin'd by ſome traitor's tale:
The coldeſt girl, complete experience proves,
Denies no favour, where ſhe really loves:
The moſt demure ſtarch'd maiden of you all,
If worth a firm aſſault, may likely fall.
Suppoſing, then, the caſe became your own,
And ye the ten days tattle of the town,
What bitter curſes would ye pour on thoſe
Who took ſuch pains your folly to expoſe.
If Pity's voice your *virtue* ſcorns to hear,
Prudence, at leaſt, forbids to be ſevere;
For can the beſt of parents, pray, be ſure
Their daughters wont be wreck'd each paſſing hour?
The pureſt lives expos'd to cenſure lie,
And dare we beg that pardon we deny?
A ſiſter's faults in ſilence let us mourn,
Then we may claim her ſilence in our turn.

ALL FOR THE BEST.

THE ways of Providence are dark,
 We cannot trace their plan,
To level at ſo high a mark
 Is inſolence in man.

A pious bard preſumes to ſay
 That every thing is right,
Let pedants in their own dull way
 Through metaphyſics fight:

For if you bluntly bid them read
 The *Candide* of Voltaire,*

* " The novels of Voltaire are not pictures of life, or of man- " ners, and the perſons which figure in them, are pure crea- " tures of the imagination, fictitious beings, who have *nothing* " of nature in their compoſition, and who neither act nor rea- " ſon, like the ordinary race of men. Voltaire, then, with " a great deal of wit, ſeems to have had *no* talent for humour- " ous compoſition." *Eſſay on the Principles of Tranſlation*, printed in 1791, p. 240. To a liberal mind nothing can be leſs pleaſing, than that diſreſpect with which ordinary men ſome-times treat works of genius, to the production, or even compre-henſion of which, their underſtandings are utterly unequal. To attack the novels of Voltaire, is to attack, in by far its ſtrongeſt quarter, a character which, in ſpite of many faults, has for half a century obtained the attention of Europe. We laugh at Pan-gloſs; we ſympathize with Candidus; we feel a cordial eſteem for Martin and Cacambo; and he muſt have ſeen but little, who has not obſerved correſpondent characters in real life. Pococu-rante is a natural, juſt, and admirable picture of a philoſophical voluptuary. Even the ſullen bigotry of Samuel Johnſon was mol-lified into approbation by the beauties of this charming volume. His other novels poſſeſs, for the moſt part, uncommon merit. At the death of Miſs St. Ives, we may exclaim with the firſt of mo-dern poets.—" If you have tears, prepare to ſhed them now."

In the midſt of our offence at the paſſage above quoted, it is amuſing to reflect that Voltaire himſelf has decided with equal candour and judgment on the genius of Shakeſpeare.

Senſe cannot enter ſuch a head,
Nor has it buſineſs there.

A gouty toe, a rotten tooth,
Refute his flimſy ſong,
And ratify the mournful truth,
That many things are wrong.

THE PROGRESS OF MORAL SENSIBILITY.

Though a young rogue impatient to be great,
May ſtudy all he can to play the cheat,
Contemn the frankneſs of a generous friend,
Nor ſpare one ſmile but for ſome ſelfiſh end;
Without remorſe, a train of falſehoods tell,
And with ſeduction the black progreſs ſwell;
Though fraud pervades the eſſence of his ſoul,
Something is wanting yet to crown the whole;
The harveſt of corruption is not ripe,
The human wolf ſhall often quit his gripe:
His milky heart compells him now and then
To melt and ſympathiſe like better men.
The parſon's bawling, or the widow's tear,
May warm with pity, or may chill with fear;
Revolting nature fluſhes in his face,
For callow guilt can feel its own diſgrace.
But when our hero turns of thirty-five,
And dreams no truly honeſt man will thrive;
Sees that by candour little can be gain'd,
That talents without money are diſdain'd;
That he, and he alone is courted moſt,
Who can the plenty of his table boaſt;
That a fine lodging and expenſive clothes,
Are the beſt proofs of worth the public knows;
That ſhould a beggar rival Dryden's rhyme,
Genius in him is but a kind of crime;

A petty treafon, giving deep offence
To men of rank, who feel their want of fenfe;
His own misfortunes make his heart fo hard,
That human mifery meets with no regard.
He fancies fellow-men mere beafts of prey,
And if lefs fierce, yet falfer far than they.
His friends, no doubt, will many a promife crack,
In their own coin he pays the traitors back.
He fadly wonders why the world was made,
That fuch a motely fcene might be difplay'd:
Where virtue finks, where fuperftition rules,
Where almoft none are fair but arrant fools;*
Nor cares though the whole fpecies were deftroy'd,
Might he, like Japhet's father, fill the void.
Such is the progrefs (if I don't miftake)
That age in morals feldom fails to make;
The underftanding is improv'd of courfe,
But oft experience makes your feelings worfe;
A thoufand various accidents controul,
Or crufh the nobler feelings of the foul.
Have you a fpoufe whofe humour is to chide!
You hate fincerely the whole fex befide;
Or, elfe with fome kind concubine you moor,
While female *worth* againft her bolts each door.
In either cafe, nor vow the maxim wrong,
Morals, moft likely, are not wond'rous ftrong.
Perhaps you marry fome enchanting maid,
By whom your love is perfectly repaid;
Who never teafes with too pert advice,
Nor would defert your arms for Paradife;
Who owns that women are a woeful charge,
Nor on affum'd importance dares enlarge;
Nor never triumphs o'er a fifter's fin,
Nor quarrels with her girl about a pin,
Nor like a ftrumpet ftrolls around the ftreet,
To ftare on every coxcomb fhe fhall meet;

* "Children and fools tell truth," fays the proverb.

Nor waves a feather fabric eight feet high,
For fear ſhe ſhould not catch the vulgar eye;
Nor prates aloud that paſſengers may hear,
Nor hints her wiſhes by a wanton leer.
Her bloom is ſacred from coſmetic dirt,
She knows when wanted, how to waſh a ſhirt;
She, when you lead her to an evening walk,
Can talk of trifles, yet amuſe by talk.
If ſuch a miracle you hap'ly find,
Though ſtill but the fag-end of human kind;
No more with wide benevolence you burn,
On her alone your tender tranſports turn.
Your tavern friendſhips moulder and decay,
As Venus ſinks before the blaze of day:
In love alone felicity you place,
And while encircled by her fond embrace,
Your obligations to us all forget,
Till twelve months hence your dear is drown'd in debt;
Diſeaſe invades the features once ſo fair,
And *infant anguiſh racks you with deſpair;*
While noiſe annihilates your midnight reſt,
The quack's predictions harrow up your breaſt;
And twenty pounds are nothing to his ſcore,
Which half a crown *per annum* clear'd before.
Then once again your ſentiments are chang'd,
And every dream of happineſs derang'd;
Then you'd, perhaps, if fairly left to chooſe,
Prefer the hangman's to the huſband's nooſe.

ODE TO INNOCENCE.

FROM THE LATIN OF SECUNDUS.

O INNOCENCE! be thou my guide
  Through the tempeſtuous path of life;
Teach me in thee to place my pride,
  And fly the miſeries of ſtrife:

Nor crush the early-opening flower,
Exterminate the toilsome bee;
Nor, in the wantonness of power,
Enslave the lark so dear to thee:

Nor from the goldfinch force her young,
Nor bid the blackbird's bosom swell,
While anguish animates her tongue
To pour a parent's fond farewell:

Nor butcher the mild helpless hare,
Nor, on the barb the worm suspend;
But make it my incessant care
To act the universal friend.

For me no maid shall mourn her vow,
No sire reproach his ruin'd son;
Nor tortur'd conscience tinge my brow,
For what my yesterday hath done.

By thy pure sentiments inspir'd,
My conduct virtue shall revere;
And Vice, to emulation fir'd,
Shall drop a penitential tear.

ODE TO SLEEP.

FROM THE SAME.

O SLEEP! to thy seductive charms
My clay with gladness I resign;
Let madmen court the din of arms,
The rapture of repose be mine;

Let others watch the midnight sky,
The cavern's horrid gulf descend,
Above the clouds on smoke-bags fly,
Or to the pole their passage rend.

For me, 'tis juſt enough to read
The terrors of the frozen ſea;
No burſting wave ſhall drench my head,
No ſtarting plank ſhall baniſh thee.

No burning deſart ſhall I range,
No Nabob rack in queſt of gold.
Can Peace admit a fair exchange?
Are thy embraces to be ſold?

When Thou, with Innocence, art gone,
How ſad, how terrible to live!
Domeſtic happineſs alone
A pure tranquillity can give.

'Tis night; our cares are thrown aſide,
Our liſping prattlers lull'd to reſt;
Through every vein I feel thee glide,
And preſs my Julia to my breaſt.

FROM THE SAME.

Though thou, my charming boy, wert born
Before the church a licence ſold,
Thou ſhalt not, helpleſs and forlorn,
Thine arms around an hireling fold.

Since what a thoughtleſs girl could loſe,
Thy mother forfeited for me,
Dare I, to ſtab her laſt repoſe,
Rend her young doating heart from thee?

Or, would a vulgar hackney'd nurſe
To all thy little wants attend;
Ten thouſand times my ſlender purſe
Muſt fail to buy thee ſuch a friend.

Though thy juſt claims thou canſt not plead,
I own the honeſt warmth of Nature,
And what I was, reflected read,
In each fond artleſs infant feature.

Deteſting haughty, harſh reſerve,
Thy tender titles I avow,
Thy father feels through every nerve
A joy he never felt till now.

THE PULPIT ORATOR.

All mankind ſcorn the man whoſe narrow mind,
To panegyrick never is inclin'd;
Who, when you bid him juſt applauſe allow,
Feels a cold ſweat come ruſhing down his brow;
Damns every fault in a triumphant ſtyle,
And feaſts on cenſure with a ſavage ſmile.
To ſuch a wit, a due reward is made,
For envy by contempt is conſtantly repaid.
The wiſe retire with pity, and with pain,
The dull may halt but hear him with diſdain.
Yet to ſuch vipers though we cannot truſt,
Weak admiration gives alike diſguſt.
And this misfortune happens every day,
The mob have little new to think or ſay,
But follow where ſome pedant points the way;
The maddeſt nonſenſe cheerfully goes down,
If he who fills the chair has got a gown.
How far beyond all paſt, this century ſhines,
For ardent active orthodox divines!
Our picus Iſle alone, were paſtors wanting,
Could ſpare enow Great Tartary for planting.
Yet ſuch a happy ſurplus ſwarm at home,
That all would wonder whence the colony had come.
Our parſons ſpeak, with ſo much force and ſpirit,
That Tully might have marvell'd at their merit.

They never teaſe us with abſurd advice,
Nor ever chaunt the ſame dull ſtory twice;
Nor ſtun our ſenſes with a drawling ſound,
Where noiſe and jargon only can be found;
Nor veer about with each diſcordant text,
Preach peace this day, and turbulence the next.
No. They are all ſuch bright, ſuch matchleſs men,
Their praiſes would exhauſt a Shakeſpeare's pen;
One recent burſt of oratorial ſkill,
Compell'd this humble homage of my quill.
Sagacious Snuffle! what haſt thou to ſay,
More than old women chatter every day?
" That not in human ſtrength the wiſe will truſt,
" For ſtrength and beauty moulder into duſt;
" That all are ſinners born, that all muſt die,
" And all in fire and brimſtone ought to fry;
" But that kind Providence, if we believe,
" Perhaps will pardon us the guilt of Eve;"
Shreds of divinity ſo trite and ſtale,
That faith itſelf nods o'er the taſteleſs tale.
One time thou bid'ſt us propagate our race,
Then talk'ſt of wedlock with wiſe Paul's wry face.
Some lighter penance if juſt heaven require,
Nor for an apple plunge a world in fire,
Let graceleſs hereticks from hell ſet free;
Eke out " eternal death" in hearing thee.

DECEMBER: A PANEGYRICK.

When ſhall this rude weather grow ſoft and ſerene,
And ſmile with the ſweetneſs of May?
For winter is ſurely a terrible ſcene,
Compar'd with a calm ſummer's day.

And yet if a ſick man ſhould venture to cry
" The natives of Chili are bleſt,"
A thouſand ſage patriots will fiercely reply,
Our climate is ſurely the beſt;

That lungs-rending froſt will refine the foul air,
  That ſnow fertilizes the duſt,
That were not fine weather ſo conſtantly rare,
  Fine weather itſelf would diſguſt.

Let weak ſuperſtition admire if ſhe will,
  That vengeance which damns half our year;
But ſhall reaſon be thankful for evident ill,
  Or welcome what coſts us ſo dear.

From the comfortleſs field when the cattle retire,
  When the ſparrow falls dead on the wing,
When creation herſelf ſeems about to expire,
  Can gratitude tempt us to ſing?

Dares a bard out of bedlam pretend to be glad,
  For a long dark tempeſtuous night,
Or preſume when all nature around him is ſad,
  His fantaſtical verſes are right.

As if this peſtiferous Iſland of ours,
  Could rival Miſſiſſipi's plains;
Where the heav'ns never burſt in ſuch horrible ſhowers
  But ſummer eternally reigns.

Yet ſuch is the cant we perpetually hear,
  From the moment we enter the ſchools,
And this age and nation affect to revere
  Such flow'ry nonſenſical fools.

If your fancy be really enamour'd of ice,
  If ſnow hath ſuch charms for your ſoul,
You cannot with honour reject my advice,
  Of attempting a trip to the Pole.

And I prophecy frankly, if e'er you return,
  That your keenneſs for cold will be loſt;
For the lapſe of December no more ſhall you mourn,
  Nor rejoice in the fetters of froſt.

VERSES

Inſcribed to John Hamilton, Archbiſhop of St. Andrew's.
From the Latin of Buchanan.

Born of a ſtrumpet, in a common ſtew,
No wonder nobody thy father knew.
At length a rich old dotard was beguil'd,
Vain to be fancied fit to plant a child;
But though he ſuffer'd this domeſtic ſhame,
Thy morals mark the ſchool from whence they came.
Falſe, cunning, fierce, rapacious, ever proud
With proſtitutes to ſoak the price of guiltleſs blood.
How pure a prieſt! He neither faſts nor prays,
But in a bagnio ſpends his leaſt atrocious days.
O Hamilton! with talents thus ſublime,
Commit for once a meritorious crime;
Thy dagger's point let mankind ceaſe to fear,
And in a halter cloſe thy black career.

AN EPITAPH.

Mute here a merry Poet lies;
He only made pretence
To ſimple, limping, laughing lines,
Which never gave offence.

Himſelf was peaceful, like his Muſe,
The worſt which we can ſay
Is, that he ſold his apples dear,
And on the Sabbath day.

More happy far he was than wits
In higher ſcenes who mov'd;
But who, nor liv'd, nor dy'd like him,
Lamented and belov'd.

No Patron flatter'd and betray'd;
  No Bookſeller oppreſt:
His meal was light, his ſleep was ſound,
  His verſes were his jeſt.

Nor, treading on the old man's turf,
  Can he who writes forbear
To pay departed Innocence
  An undiſſembling tear.

Critic, forgive the *firſt* eſſay
  Of one whoſe thoughts, are plain,
Whoſe heart is full, who never means
  To ſteal your time again.

TO THE PRINTER OF THE BATH CHRONICLE.

SIR,

IT is one character, and I think the privilege of old age, to hate the preſent times, and to complain of degeneracy; in this character I preſent myſelf to you, and I hope that you will ſo far indulge my foible, as to allow a ſmall corner in your Miſcellany for my complaint.

It is now above fifty years ſince I firſt began to frequent the Bath waters, and enjoy the ſalutary pleaſures of this famous place. I have drunk with Quin, chatted with Naſh, and played whiſt with Cheſterfield; I now find wonderful changes, not wholly for the better. I ſhall confine my complaint, at preſent, to one article. I have always been a warm admirer of our beſt dramatic entertainments, and my acquaintances have eſteemed me as a critic of ſome note in that line. I entertain a fixed opinion, that, in England true dramatick genius moſtly, *exiſted* and *expired* in one age; I mean in the age of Shakeſpeare, Johnſon, Beaumont, and Fletcher; this was a prevailing opinion ſince the Rehearſal checked the miſerable courſe of falſe taſte, till of late years, when that excellent ſatire ſeems forgotten, and falſe taſte again triumphs among our writers and our auditors. In our tragedies, fuſtian paſſes for the ſublime; and in our comedies, a ſtrange ſort of quaintneſs for wit and humour. Our plots are improbable, our characters are not drawn from life, but from plays or romances, and our ſongs have no ſenſe at all. Shakeſpeare's cenſure of bad dramatick writings in his time, is applicable to our modern drama:

"Extremely ſtrain'd and conn'd with cruel pain."

Our writers compoſe *invita Minerva*, and the character given of bad plays in the Rehearſal, is ſtill more applicable in our time, that they are "dull and fantaſti-"cal;" a ſtrange compoſition! The "old plain way of "wit" is now no longer in vogue, yet every ſeaſon produces new tragedies, comedies, and numberleſs comic operas, which are recommended by critics, and acted with aſtoniſhing applauſe. For my part, and I know I am not altogethet ſingular, I damn them all, with a very few exceptions.

I now come to my ſpecial matter of complaint; I have reſided in Bath for two months paſt, yet I have not ſeen one of the old plays announced for performance; in former times, we had no comic operas, excepting Milton's Comus, (undeformed by Garrick's alterations) and the Beggar's Opera, exquiſite entertainments. The old plays (alſo unadulterated by our vile modern alterations) were frequently exhibited and well acted.

I am, Sir, your very humble ſervant,

BATH, *May* 8, 1789. AN OLD CUSTOMER.

P. S. I muſt fairly confeſs, that I do include under my cenſure, the favoured comedies of two illuſtrious Generals; and I admit of no proper exceptions but the Douglas in tragedy, and in comedy a few of Foote's careleſs imperfect pieces, and the writings of Mr. Sheridan.

TO THE PRINTER.

SIR,

I THIS morning read over that incomparable comedy, the Merchant of Venice. Had the author compoſed only that play, he would have deſerved a place in the firſt rank of dramatic writers.—A groupe of the fineſt moral characters are all admirably ſupported.—Anthonio, Baſſanio, and Portia, are each in the higheſt ſtyle of Shakeſpeare's excellence. When Portia, with a noble ſimplicity, ſays,

"I never did repent of doing good,
"And ſhall not now,"

we feel an irreſiſtible impreſſion, that the poet himſelf muſt have been a worthy honeſt man. I ſhall quote one of thoſe paſſages that ſtruck me as remarkably pathetic. When Solarino is about to mention the ruin of Anthonio, affection and ſorrow almoſt ſtifle his utterance.

"It is true, without any ſlips of prolixity, or croſſing "the plain high-way of talk, that the good Anthonio, "the honeſt Anthonio—*O that I had a title good enough* "*to keep his name company!*"

Gratiano is likewiſe a character of exquiſite entertainment. His reply to Baſſanio, who had exhorted him to caution, is in that ſort of ſolemn ludicrous ſtyle, almoſt entirely peculiar to Shakeſpeare.

"Signior Baſſanio, hear me;
"If I do not put on a ſober habit,
"Talk with reſpect, *and ſwear but now and then,*" &c.

In his addreſs to Shylock, however, in the beginning of the fourth act, he kindles into the moſt generous and eloquent indignation.—We ſee, with much ſatisfaction, that good humour does not merely play on the ſurface of his mind, but is ingrafted on a manly feeling heart.—During the trial that follows, he preſerves a ſtrict and becoming ſilence: But the moment that his friend is out of danger, the poet, ever attentive to chaſtity of character and to nature, repreſents him relapſing into the moſt tumultuous exultation.—There is a whimſical portrait of this charming phantom drawn by Baſſanio, which I beg leave to recommend to James Boſwell, Eſquire, as a motto for the title page of his Life of Dr. Samuel Johnſon, if print and paper ſhall ever be ſquandered on a ſecond edition.

"Gratiano ſpeaks an infinite deal of nothing, more "than any man in all Venice: his reaſons are as two "grains of wheat hid in two buſhels of chaff! You ſhall "ſeek all day e'er you find them; and when you have "them, they are not worth the ſearch."

The learned and facetious Lord Monboddo was converſing ſome years ago on this laſt topic: "I have lived," ſaid his Lordſhip, "to ſee my country humbled in arts, "and humbled in arms; but I never expected to have "ſeen England humbled to the admiration of *Dr. Samuel* "*Johnſon.*"

T. T.

TO THE PRINTER.

Sir,

In a late paper you informed us, on official authority, that previous to the 18th of March 1791, two thouſand and twenty-nine convicts have been ſhipped from England for New South Wales. We alſo learned, that prior to the 9th of February in the ſame year, the expences of this eſtabliſhment amounted to three hundred and ſeventy-four thouſand pounds. Beſides this ſum we are told of contingencies, "that cannot as yet be ſtated." It was for the miniſter's credit to make his project appear as frugal as poſſible, and to ſuppreſs a part of this enormous expenditure to ſerve the temporary purpoſes of debate. We may ſafely affirm, that the contingencies referred to, make no trifling ſum. Ten additional months fall now alſo to be added to the account; and it is not unreaſonable to compute the total expence, up to this date, at ſix hundred thousand pounds. These exiles have not, upon an average, been more than three years in New South Wales. During that short period we see that each of them has cost this country three hundred pounds. As the climate is much more healthy than our own, they may be expected to survive transportation for twenty years to come. By that time, the additional expence of each convict will amount to, perhaps, six hnndred pounds. It may indeed be alleged, that before that time, the country will be reduced to a state of cultivation. But a circumstance mentioned by the governor sufficiently shows the great distance and uncertainty of such a prospect. It cost him and a party five days to penetrate thirty miles into the desart; and the fatigues they underwent during this journey were excessive. In the same paper you tell us, that eighteen hundred and thirty additional convicts were then under orders for shipping. It is impossible to estimate, with any degree of certainty, what may be the annual expence of this colony before the end of the eighteenth century. By a very moderate estimation we may suppose, that before ten years elapse, the colony will receive at least ten thousand additional convicts; and it is but fair to compute, that of the whole number by that time transported, ten thousand will then be alive, and maintained at the expence of Government. Now, if each of these gentry shall cost us only thirty pounds a year, the whole annual expence will amount to three hundred thousand pounds. At the end of twenty years it may rise to double that sum. To this we must add the charming item, of fifty or an hundred pounds Sterling per head for the expence of their voyage. Will the British nation, with its eyes open, walk into such a gulf? Had each of these criminals been discharged from the bar, it is very unlikely that he would have committed one tenth part of the mischief by abusing his liberty at home, which he entails on us by enduring slavery abroad.

These premises are unanswerable, and we must infer that the Botany-bay scheme is the most absurd, prodigal, and impracticable vision that ever intoxicated the mind of man. A poor fellow ſteals a watch, or a horſe worth five or ten pounds. The loſs is paltry, but mark the conſequences. His trial, in Scotland at leaſt, coſts the public, between expence and perſonal trouble to individuals, perhaps, four times that ſum; and then his tranſportation, the devil knows where, and the devil knows why, perpetuates a burden upon his country to the amount of ten times the loſs incurred by the robbery and trial put together. In the modern ſtate of matters a criminal when convicted does not deſerve that title for breaking a ſhop, or a ſtable; but, becauſe, if he eſcapes the gallows he plunders the public treaſury of three, or five, or perhaps fifteen hundred pounds. Tranſportation to North America was, in compariſon, but a ride before breakfaſt. New South Wales is at the diſtance of ſix or eight thouſand leagues, if we include the windings and turnings neceſſary on the paſſage. In the former country, the price of a felon, when landed, was ſufficient to pay the expence of his voyage. But in the latter, a footpad, the moment we ſet him on ſhore, is enrolled with many other *right honourable* gentlemen in the reſpectable and uſeful band of *national penſioners.*

There is not an old woman in the three kingdoms who could not have ſuggeſted a better reſource. A bridewell in each county, on the plan of the *Panopticon* *, and under a few obvious regulations, would effectually diſpoſe of convicts; and inſtead of coſting the nation an enormous annual expence, would produce a large annual revenue. Mr. Pitt has, however, pledged his character and abilities in ſupport of this project, and he will, no doubt, adhere to it with his uſual *firmneſs*, till the period of his reſignation. If he ſhall continue in office for ten years longer, every fool in this country will ſee what every man of ſenſe ſees already. By that time this chimera will be treated with univerſal execration, as a millſtone hanging at the

† This is a priſon on a new and improved plan, by which priſoners can be kept entirely ſolitary, without a poſſibility of corrupting each other.

neck of public credit; and the new miniſter, as a ſpecimen of his importance, will inſtantly abandon the ſettlement. But indeed this ineſtimable deſcription of Britiſh ſubjects may very poſſibly ſave him that trouble, by cutting the throats of their taſkmaſters, and embarking on board the ſhipping in the bay. Could this *revolution* be accompliſhed without bloodſhed, it is in itſelf an event extremely deſireable.

Edin. Dec. 16, 1791. TUMBLEDOWN.

TO THE PRINTER.

SIR,

FOR about five years paſt, we have been amuſed by the bookſellers with an inceſſant chorus of verſes in the Scottiſh dialect. Every county in Scotland has a number of words and phraſes peculiar and intelligible to itſelf only, and it is uſual for the bard to borrow, without ſelection, the provincial vulgariſms to which he has been accuſtomed. Before an author can pleaſe, he muſt make himſelf underſtood. To a native of Annandale the dialects of Aberdeenſhire and of Somerſet are equally diſcordant. The fame of ſuch poetry can hardly be extenſive or laſting. But beſides, theſe writers commonly deform their pages with every antiquated phraſe which perverted induſtry can diſcover; and it would not be difficult, though indeed invidious and uſeleſs, to point out paſſages where vulgarity itſelf is evidently miſunderſtood and miſapplied.

When a man of ſenſe intends to publiſh in rhyme, he will firſt make himſelf familiar with at leaſt a few of the beſt and moſt popular Engliſh poets. By an attentive compariſon of their works with his own, he will either learn the art of elegant compoſition, or the propriety of ſilence. When a perſon diſcharges upon the public a volume of dull and tireſome verſes, it is charitable to believe he is unacquainted with Swift and Dryden. In knowledge of books, the claſs of poets I mention are ſome times deficient; and thus between artificial groſſneſs and actual ignorance, there is no wonder that they often fall ſhort of perfection. It is indeed a principal argument with their admirers, that a poet of true genius does not require the help of learning. The author of a quaint eſſay on original compoſition ſeems inclined to ſanctify this chimera. But Horace more properly ſays, "I neither ſee what learning can accompliſh without genius, or genius without learning."

The advocates of ignorance have adduced Shakeſpeare as an example of uncultivated excellence; but thoſe critics talk at random who aſſert him to have been illiterate. He underſtood both French and Latin, though perhaps imperfectly. His extenſive acquaintance with ancient and modern hiſtory, and the completeneſs of his ideas on every ſubject, atteſt, with a force far beyond the parade of citations, that he muſt have been a very diligent reader. When he repreſents Bohemia as a maritime country *, and an Illyrian as referring to "the bells of St. Bennet †," we can only ſuppoſe that he was ſporting with his audience. His ſtyle alſo, wherever he chuſes to exert himſelf, is more various, more nervous, and more elegant, than that of any Engliſh writer of the ſixteenth century.

Of poets in the Scottiſh dialect, the beſt and greateſt, beyond all compariſon, is Allan Ramſay. He appears to have ſtudied Dryden's works with much attention, ſince his verſes flow with the moſt pleaſing volubility. His provincial phraſes are few, when compared with thoſe of ſome of his imitators; and at leaſt in the Gentle Shepherd, he has ſelected them with ſuch dexterity that they are almoſt equally familiar in every part of the kingdom. But this is only a ſecondary part of its merit. A vein of ſolid good ſenſe, a nice diſcrimnation of character, a nervous elegance, and a pathetic ſimplicity of expreſſion; in a word, the genuine language of nature, of paſſion, and of poetry, place this paſtoral comedy almoſt beyond our praiſe. From the chemiſt and aſtronomer, to the girl at

* Winter's Tale. † Twelfth Night.

her ſpinning-wheel, the poet's eloquence kindles every heart, and irreſiſtibly commands our tears. It is true that we have here no bawdry, no jealous alderman cuckolded, no amorous ſuicide, no wire-drawn ſoliloquy, no pedantic ill-jointed epithet, no raving deſpot, ſuch as never exiſted but in the frenzy of a modern play wright. But the Gentle Shepherd does nor reſt its reputation on the caprice of a theatrical audience. Were all the copies of Ramſay's comedy annihilated, the grateful memories of his countrymen would eagerly ſupply the loſs. Many of his readers have almoſt the whole poem by heart; and what other Scottiſh author can pretend to ſuch indelible admiration?

It has been ſaid, that Ramſay did not write this play; and when that ſtory was no longer tenable, it has been loudly affirmed, that at leaſt a great part of it was written by ſomebody elſe; and the whole corrected by gentlemen who were the author's patrons. The word *patron* is pronounced, by men of ſenſe, with a tone of contemptuous pity. If theſe critics ſuggeſted any proper alterations, this ſeems to have been the only act of benevolence which they beſtowed on the author; for, in the proper ſtyle of *patronage*, they ſuffered him to live poor, and die bankrupt*.

In Scotland, the firſt circulating library was kept by Allan Ramſay. His original profeſſion is often mentioned by himſelf; and to thoſe who are weak enough to deſpiſe it, we may reply that Ramſay "was not a man who "could mean by a mean employment."

T. T.

* His debts were afterwards paid by his ſon, the famous painter.

THE LAW SUIT.

A TALE.

FROM BUCHANAN, LIB. I. EPIG. I.

Calenus, when his purſe was light,
  Got twenty guineas as a loan,
Swearing he would repair his plight,
  And pay me e'er a week was gone.

A year went off, the lawyer Aulus
  Perſuades me to commence a ſuit,
Crying, " the raſcal ſhan't cajole us,
  " His bond, Sir, cannot bear diſpute !"

But lo ! this paper war has laſted
  Longer than Homer's ſiege of Troy;
Ten times my debt has Aulus waſted,
  And ten times more would fain deſtroy.

Now, ſince I'm not ſo rich as Clive,
  Nor yet for Neſtor's age deſign'd,
I'll quit the combat while alive,
  Nor force my heir to purchaſe wind.

Calenus, at the triple tree,
  Ought ſurely his ſucceſs to tell;
But Aulus, no ſufficient fee
  Can hope for till he reaches hell.

Wherever ſuch attornies trudge,
  Who mountains on a wart have thrown,
By all that's juſt ! my lord the judge,
  Muſt dive a ſtory farther down.

ON THE CHARACTER OF A WIFE.

A WIFE, you ſay is an expenſive toy,
But, wanting coſt, we cannot purchaſe joy;
The richeſt miſer muſt remain in rags,
Unleſs he condeſcend to looſe his bags;
The thread-bare bard, a coach who cannot hire,
Is fain to ſtraddle through December's mire;
And he, whoſe income won't extend to port,
To the more frugal ale-houſe muſt reſort.
Before a doctor takes the pains to kill,
His patient's purſe muſt pay for every pill:
A Britiſh Premier too muſt bribe the *houſe*,
Before they'll vote his Majeſty a ſous.
At church, you know, as well as at the play,
We cannot have a ſeat unleſs we pay;
And you and I, till ſome few pence are given,
Muſt like two ſpaniels from the pew be driven;
Nor gain one glimpſe of glory, or of grace,
Ere firſt we buy the *freedom of the place.*
For all commodities a price is paid,
Why, then, refuſe your money for a maid?
  A wife, you ſay, deſtroys domeſtic eaſe,
You cannot then do juſt whate'er you pleaſe.
But tell me truly, when a fool is drunk,
And all his ſenſes in the liquor ſunk,
Shall he be ſuffer'd to diſturb the ſtreets,
And bruiſe with every vagabond he meets?
Embrace infection, founder in the mire,
Or, reeling homeward ſet his houſe on fire?
Far better fate attends the happy man
Who weds a mate as early as he can:
His faithful ſpouſe his every want attends
(One ſpouſe is worth ten thouſand bottle-friends);
She flatters, ſtrips, and rolls him into bed,
Then binds a fillet round his aching head;

She covers, carefully, each wearied limb,
For all her wiſhes centre but in him;
And, while coherently to curſe he tries,
The briny ſhower comes burſting from her eyes.
In humble tone ſhe ventures to complain,
He ſwore laſt night he ne'er would ſoak again;
Reminds him that he plays a thoughtleſs part,
And hints what agonies have wrung her heart.
Then which all other mortals would deſpiſe,
Beſide her hopeful huſband down ſhe lies.
But leſt his horrid breath may do her harm,
She clings behind, to keep his ſhoulders warm.
A wife, beſides, will bring you girls and boys;
And though the monkies make inceſſant noiſe,
Though other children's din you cannot bear,
Yet theirs, believe me, wont annoy your ear.
None but an actual father ever knows
With what fond joy a father's heart o'erflows,
To ſee all Lilliput friſk up and down,
When every look reminds him of his own,
Or her's, who, in the ſummer days of youth,
Taught him the charms of tenderneſs and truth.
And are you ſick? 'Tis then her actions prove
(No words can paint) the frenzy of her love:
'Tis then the grandeur of her ſoul ſhines forth,
Then firſt you learn the vaſtneſs of her worth.
Your kindeſt comrades in attendance fail,
For all muſt weary of a ſick man's tale;
But, night and day, ſhe ſtill is at your ſide,
More ſoft, more charming far, than when a bride;
For though corroding cares her bloom deſtroy,
Her generous love excites ſuperior joy.
She watches every motion of your eye,
Your every want impatient to ſupply.
Affected ſmiles conceal her inward care,
Hopeleſs herſelf, yet checking your deſpair:
While oft, in ſpite of all her female art,
A ſigh eſcaping, cuts you to the heart.

How cold mere Friendſhip, when compar'd to this;
Without ſuch women, what were human bliſs.
 And ſhould, as it may happen, Fortune frown,
And from the height of greatneſs hurl you down,
When every friend, as uſual, turns his back,
And your ſoul lingers on the mental rack;
When every inſult muſt be cooly borne,
The pedant's pity, and the rival's ſcorn;
When thoſe you truſted, their connections change,
And thoſe who hate you, give reſentment range;
When every look, where e'er you ſhew your head,
Is ſure to make you feel "your kingdom's fled;"
When ſordid Prudence ſtiffens every face,
And every tongue exults in your diſgrace; *
At ſuch a time, does female friendſhip fail?
No; ſhe herſelf attends you to the jail.
Such friendſhip cheaply with a world were bought;
Her boſom juſt admits one ſingle thought.
Your peace of mind ſhe breathes but to purſue,
Nor dreads a dungeon to be ſhar'd with you.
 She, too, when death arrives to your relief,
Shall watch its progreſs with the pureſt grief;
Perform each duty that diſtreſs can crave,
And, with fond tears bedew her huſband's grave;
And ſtill, with you, her tender mem'ry teems,
Still your lov'd image haunts her broken dreams,
And blaſts each phantom of returning peace,
Till Heav'n, in pity, gives her own releaſe.
 Such are the ſex we modeſtly deſpiſe,
And ſuch the fools whom every fool decries.
 To this you anſwer with a ſcornful ſmile,
That common ſenſe adopts a colder ſtyle;
That many a wife turns out ſo very bad,
As ſoon to drive the tameſt partner mad.
The ſcrub, who bargains for a maſs of gold,
May catch, no doubt, a ſlattern or a ſcold.

* No paſſage, in any writer, can be more inſtructive or interesting, than the fall of the Duke of Sully, as deſcribed by himſelf.

The brute whofe paffion is but rank defire,
May feel ten days exhauft his carnal fire.
The fool who marries for the fake of wit,
Is fure to find himfelf feverely bit;
And he who feeks a fpoufe of noble blood,
Muft bear with patience, lectures long and loud.
But men of fenfe, with reafon, hope to find
A graceful perfon, with a modeft mind;
Whofe various charms we ever muft admire,
At once the choice of wifdom and defire;
And for mere merit, if you fearch around,
Believe me, that is always to be found.
The fureft rules for chufing fuch a mate,
Would furnifh topics for a fine debate;
But, left the fpirit of the verfe expire,
Your preacher, for the prefent, fhall retire.

ON

READING MEMOIRS OF FREDERICK III.

BY JOSEPH TOWERS, L. L. D.

A CLOUD of books o'erwhelms the prefent days,
Worthlefs alike of cenfure and of praife;
Where not a fingle fentence in the whole
Exifts, but what the wretched Grub hath ftole:
Or home-bred nonefenfe fhould he rafhly fquirt,
The pilfer'd diamond fparkles through his dirt.
What indignation muft each fcholar feel,
When Plutarch's limbs are broke upon the wheel;
When fweet Herodotus our ears hath tir'd,
And nervous Salluft is no more admir'd;
Sublime Thucydides his murther mourns,
And fage Polybius to a dotard turns,

The heart, when Xenophon forbears to win,
And lively Juſtin ſlumbers in Rollin. *
While theſe reflections had begun to riſe,
A freſh delinquent ruſh'd upon our eyes;
Twelve hundred pages pouring from the preſs,
Revile the benefactor kingdoms bleſs.
On martial worth, if Slander muſt await.
What future monarch ſhall contend with Fate?
Had Frederick's heroes gain'd no higher fame,
Than this poor pamphleteer has right to claim,
Poland as yet had unpartition'd been,
Sileſia ſtill obey'd her bigot Queen;
Nor Prague's wide boſom blaz'd with Pruſſian fire,
Nor Daun from Torgan haſted to retire.
His portrait had not mock'd each dauber's hand,
Nor o'er theſe heavy volumes, Patience yawn'd.†

* Robertſon's Hiſtory of Greece may be quoted as a pleaſing exception to this general cenſure.

† When this Prince ſucceeded to his father, the Pruſſian dominions did not contain two millions and a half of inhabitants. At his death, after a reign of forty-ſix years, the number exceeded four millions; beſides above two millions in the provinces of Sileſia and Pomerellia. And ſo much at eaſe do the peaſantry feel themſelves, that the annual number of births ſurpaſſes that of burials, by upwards of fifty thouſand. Baron Trenck is an unſuſpected witneſs to the rapid increaſe in every ſort of improvement, as well as population. He informs us, that after the ſeven years war, the King rebuilt every farm houſe in Eaſtern Pruſſia, which had been burnt by the enemy, except that of the Baron's ſiſter. When we have reflected that he had, at this time, but juſt ended a third bloody war in which his armies had fought nineteen battles; that his capital had been plundered with every circumſtance of barbarous rapacity; that almoſt every pariſh in his provinces had been a ſcene of carnage and devaſtation; that he had not added a ſingle impoſt, nor borrowed a ſingle ſhilling; we may then, with what grace we can, condemn him as a hateful tyrant.

The juſtice of his title to Sileſia has been diſputed; but the Proteſtant inhabitants of that oppreſſed province received him as a

ON NOTHING.

I HARDLY now with patience hear
  The metaphyfics of the fchools,
For mankind I fincerely fear,
  Are frequently fuch knaves or fools,
Their talents are not worth attaining,
Far lefs their paffions worth explaining.

A joint of juicy roafted beef,
  A dozen of October ale,
Give us more fenfible relief,
  Than reveries fo vague and ftale,
About the origin or nature,
Of fuch a fhallow fordid creature.

Try, Sir, to make us honeft men,
  In fpite of all the devil's doing;

deliverer. And is there now any Briton who wifhes to fee it revert to the houfe of Auftria? In Pomerellia, he began his career, by erecting one hundred and eighty fchools, as he himfelf tells us in a letter to D'Alembert; and the only object of regret with men of fenfe is, that he did not acquire poffeffion of the whole kingdom.

That he had fome faults, we know; but has the reader feen or heard of a character WITHOUT FAULTS?

"Before fuch merit, all objections fly,
"Pritchard's genteel, and Garrick fix foot high."

That he was the firft general and ftatefman of his age, is a trite truth. That he was a patron of literature, is not the leaft honourable part of his praife. In the latter part of his reign, when prefent at the performance of a French tragedy, "I would not," he cried, "exchange the glory of writing ZARA for all my "victories."

Convince impoſtors by your pen,
  That roguery muſt end in ruin:
But never take a random flight,
To prove that every thing is right.

THE WINTER DAY;

OR,

A PROSPECT OF LIFE.

The top of tall Arthur* ſtands cover'd with ſnow,
  The verdure lies hid in the vale,
Her wood-notes no more from the linnet ſhall flow,
  And the goldfinch forgets his fond tale.

The ſun ſeems afraid from his ſky to look forth,
  "Elder night" now revolts from his ſway;
All the hail hoarded up in the terrible north,
  Pours down in a tempeſt to-day. †

How many poor ſhepherds expire with their ſheep;
  O! how ſhall December be borne,
Let us think of the ſtorms which convulſed the deep,
  When Anſon ſurrounded Cape Horn. ‡

See the Wolſey of Ruſſia projected from power,
  At Zembla to wander and die; §
He receives in his boſom the rage of the ſhower,
  While ambition yet lours in his eye.

* An eminence near Edinburgh. † Dec. 31, 1783.

‡ Mr. Thomas Paſcoe, a teacher of mathematicks on board of the Centurion, printed an account of this voyage. It contains many very curious particulars omitted by Mr. Walter; they ought to be extracted, and ſubjoined to the next edition of his narrative. As the book is extremely ſcarce, this improvement may in a few years be impracticable.

§ "The Czar baniſhes you to a town under the Pole, and his "ſublime generoſity allows you twopence a-day."

VOLTAIRE's Hiſtory of Ruſſia.

The ſavage of Greenland now ſhrinks in his cave,
From the froſt of his long winter night;
For a dungeon more horrible far than the grave,
He muſt loſe all the bleſſings of light.

Then cold as it is, we'll be thankful for home,
To the ſocial fire ſide we'll reſort,
And defy all the cares that to-morrow may come,
With a catch and a bumper of port.

We'll forget for one evening that mankind are knaves,
The ſordid adorers of pelf;
That our friend *with whatever grimace he behaves*,
Is only concern'd for himſelf;

That the beggar we feed, from our ſorrows will fly,
Exulting they are not his own;
But we'll never forget, that ere long we muſt die,
And anſwer for all we have done.

Our life is at beſt but a long winter day,
Hope at morn blows the bloſſom of joy,
But the blaſt of Misfortune ſoon ſweeps it away,
Or poſſeſſion compells us to cloy.

'Tis thus the poor maid whoſe too ſenſible heart
Diſſolves in the frenzy of love,
Will ſcorn to be told her adorer has art,
And the worſt of all tyrants may prove.

The fond aged father, who lives but to form
The mind of his favourite heir,
Sees the demon Ingratitude treble the ſtorm,
And tear down his laſt fence from deſpair.

The hard hearted landlord who racks every ſcheme,
His unhappy dependents to fleece,

Will find with confuſion, he plays the wrong game,
  For guilt is a ſtranger to peace.

Infallible Johnſon whoſe laws we now hear,
  With the reverence due to his name,
At his trade had ſpent many a comfortleſs year,
  Ere he crawl'd to the ſummit of fame.

And though, when for want of a ſhilling diſtreſs'd,
  They would ſcarce let him enter their door;
The patrons of verſe are now forward to feaſt
  The bard they neglected before.

Poor Chatterton taught by each eloquent muſe,
  With pity to moiſten the eye,
Preſum'd his admirers would bluſh to refuſe
  Unfortunate worth ſome ſupply.

But a ſage moral author deny'd with diſdain,
  The requeſt of the marvellous boy;
For petrified pedants are proud to explain,
  The pleaſures they dare not enjoy.

Had the *forger* been born to five thouſand a-year,
  Peeviſh Walpole had echo'd his name;
And ſummon'd all England with raptures to hear,
  This victim of hunger and fame.*

* Mr. Walpole's apology for his conduct, has been coldly received by the public; but, the proper apology is, that not one perſon in fifty would have behaved better. The ſtory may be ſhortly ſtated thus. The ſon of a poor widow under indentures to an attorney, employs his leiſure time in literary purſuits. Feeling within himſelf the germ of genius, and perhaps of generoſity, he forms a plauſible ſcheme of applying for that protection ſo eſſential to ſucceſs, to a quarter where a young man unacquainted with the world would have been moſt likely to expect it. Mr. Walpole, himſelf, an admirable writer, and a judge of taſte above exception, reads over the verſes; and in the paper referred

But he who wants money will always want ſenſe,
  In the grovelling eſteem of the croud,
And he who is amply provided with pence,
  Of happineſs needs not be proud:

Since all ranks and ages alike muſt prepare,
  For a courſe in Adverſity's ſchool;
And that giddy novice who never was there,
  Till then muſt continue a fool.

The full flowing bowl may inſpire us to brave
  Rude winter's peſtiferous breath,
But when ſhall bright morning ariſe in the grave,
  And burſt the dark priſon of death.

The ſnow will ſoon melt and the ſummer return,
  And the lambkins will baſk in the fold;
But when ſhall each breaſt with benevolence burn,
  And Charity bluſh to be cold?

Yet the man who enjoying a generous tear
  Neglects not his partner in woe,
Shall be amply repaid for his tend[illegible]eſs here,
  With all which kind Heaven can beſtow.

And who can imagine what Infinite Love
  Has reſerv'd in the world for to come,
No Columbus returns from the regions above,
  And Shakeſpeare lies mute in his tomb.

to, pronounces Chatterton to have poſſeſſed abilities of an aſtoniſhing magnitude. But, what anſwer does he give to the poor widow's ſon? " I can do nothiug to ſerve you." Such is the reception that dependent merit may always expect to meet with, till chance, or perhaps impudence, has buoyed it into notice, and then the great patronize from vanity.

BUCHANAN, LIB. III. EPIG. I.

IMITATED.

For heavy crops the farmer prays,
  The tradeſman but for *cent. per cent.*
The bard would rival Shakeſpeare's lays,
  The gambler gain the ſums he's ſpent.

The bed-rid victim begs but eaſe;
  A place repels the patriot's whim;
The parſon thunders for his fees;
  The ſurgeon ſcents a fractur'd limb.

With me the utmoſt fate can give,
  The greateſt bliſs I dare conjecture,
Is only—"Long may **** live,
  "Merit's munificent protector."

HORACE, LIB. III. ODE XXVI.

IMITATED.

Once a buck of high renown,
The art of love was all my own;
My locks were always *a-la-mode*,
My paſſion preſſed in an ode.
I led the fair to balls and plays,
And waſted time a thouſand ways;
But now the ſpring of life is o'er,
And all ſuch folly fits no more.
  Nay, worſe, I'm moſt completely tir'd
Of all the books I moſt admir'd.
I laugh at *Eloiſe Nouvelle*,
And hate to hear of *Marmontel*;

No time on *Telemaque* I waſte:
Such is the progreſs of my taſte.]
 Nor needs the fatal change ſurpriſe,
Since wedlock every want ſupplies,
Confounds me with a million more
I never heard about before,
Sucks all the vigour from my veins,
And purſe and perſon duly drains.

AN ELEGY.

From the Latin of Politian.

IF, when they quit the preſent ſcene,
 Our ſouls are conſcious to the paſt,
And, through the ſhades which intervene,
 A look of fond remembrance caſt,

My deareſt boy! ſupport me now;
 Wipe off this vain rebellious tear;
Replace compoſure on my brow;
 Teach me this piercing ſtroke to bear.

While ſilent midnight ſhrouds the ſky,
 When oft as beauty's bards have ſaid,
Gleams on the pale ſeducer's eye,
 The form of her his vows betray'd;

Ah! leave the regions of the bleſt;
 Reviſit this devoted earth;
Aid me in ſoothing into reſt
 That injur'd girl who gave thee birth.

Though, ſince Affliction's helpleſs heir,
 Her treſpaſs holy ſpite reprov'd,

She once, I bluſh not to declare,
  Like thee, was lovely and belov'd.

Let pedants, whoſe unſocial nerves
  Nature's firſt impulſe ne'er could fire,
Whoſe frigid virtue never ſwerves
  From what Diſcretion's rules require:

From every vulgar failing free,
  Let them deteſt me, if they can;
I neither ſeek, nor wiſh to ſee
  A mortal more, or leſs than man.

Whate'er a father's pride could aſk
  Was center'd in thy infant charms;
Each dream reſtores my pleaſing taſk,
  And fancy feels thy claſping arms.

Again to view thy features riſe,
  Again thy prattle lulls my ear,
While prompt imagination eyes
  The childiſh laugh, the childiſh tear.

A guſh of joy o'erwhelms my breaſt;
  Starting, to preſs me cloſe to thine,
I wake—let him deſcribe the reſt,
  Who knows an agony like mine.

To parents death diſtracts not yet,
  Whoſe hearts have ne'er like ours been wrung,
Whiſper that pity ſhould forget
  What paſſion forces from my tongue.

When ſhe, whoſe tortures ſhock my ſoul,
  Is to her early grave conſign'd,
My victim's tender cares controul,
  Tell her, I dread to ſtay behind.

A HINT FOR COUNTRY GENTLEMEN.

A MAN ambitious to do ill,
Who hath at once the power and will,
Can always find a fair pretence
In juſtice, law, and common ſenſe,
To grind the faces of the poor,
And turn his tenants to the door;
To ſtop the ſtarving orphan's plough,
And kill, for rent, the widow's cow.
For all ſuch gentlemen as theſe
(They may depend on't, if they pleaſe,)
A ſpacious elegant *Chateau*,
Hath long been fitted up below;
The landlord there, will ſcorn to fleece,
Or ſtrip his lodgers of their leaſe.

HORACE, LIB. I. ODE I.

IMITATED.

To lively Horace we allow,
The human heart was known;
And each of us, he ſays, purſue
Some caprice of our own.

One never thinks a horſe too dear,
Whatever ſum he coſt;
And ſcorns to halt in his career
Till every farthing's loſt.

Another on his gallant cocks
Will venture an eſtate,
While a third cully cogs the box,
And dice decide his fate.

The parrot of the ſtage aſpires
  To entertain the pit;
The punſter in a huff retires
  When you decline his wit.

But all the bullion of Peru,
  Would hardly make him fly
Through fire and blood, with Rodney's crew,
  To vanquiſh or to die.

The ſmuggler when a tempeſt blows,
  Is happy to retreat;
Commends a farmer's life, and goes
  To view his country ſeat.

But when the hurricane is o'er,
  Repairs his ſhatter'd ſhip;
Can ruſt in idleneſs no more,
  And ruſhes on the deep.

Another with ferocious joy,
  The din of battle hears;
And flies impatient to deſtroy,
  Nor minds his mother's tears.

Monſieur, we notice in his look,
  Would always dance and caper;
The parſon, for the paſtry cook
  Prints mountains of waſte paper.

And each of theſe good folks deſpiſe
  The foibles of the reſt,
Preſume themſelves ſupremely wiſe,
  Their neighbours but a jeſt.

Thus, in the Parliament you bawl,
  Which is but loſing time;
And wonder I pretend to ſcrawl
  Such quantities of rhyme.

HORACE, LIB. I. ODE II.

IMITATED.

WRITTEN IN JANUARY 1784.

Such dreadful ſhowers of hail and ſnow
  Have uſher'd in the preſent year,
Such ſtorms above, and floods below,
  That pious folks began to fear
    All Nature would have gone to wrack,
    And Noah's days were coming back.

It muſt have been an awful ſight
  To ſee another ark begun,
The clumſy oſtrich take her flight,
  And elephants from India run
    To Calais; and, from thence to Dover,
    With the firſt ferry-boat fly over;

And then how queer to ſee them all
  Parading on the banks of Thames;
The rat, rhinoceros, jackall,
  So ready when they heard their names;
    The ſtag and panther ſkipping near,
    And ſheep, no wolf attempts to tear.

And now, ſuppoſe the deluge come,
  The ſcaly monſters leave the ſea,
Along our verdant meadows roam,
  The ſhark entangled in a tree;
    And, where a Chatham fir'd the ſoul,
    Their ſlimy bulk the dolphins roll.

Where a plump alderman of old,
  His turtle and roaſt beef took in,

The hippopotamus makes bold,
  For provender to give a grin;
    In ſearch of herrings while the whale
    A premier's levee room ſhall ſcale.

And, ſure, if any former nation
  Has ever met with ſuch a doom,
Well may the preſent generation
  Be looking for a wat'ry tomb:
    Methuſalem's, though woeful times,
    Were ignorant of half our crimes.

Our bankrupt ſons will hear, with ſhame,
  The bitter tale of Engliſh glory,
And, while our *debts* enſure our fame,
  Sincerely curſe both Whig and Tory;
    And pity and deſpiſe the quarrels,
    Which coſt ſo dear for North and Charles.

But what expedient ſhall we try
  To tear us from the jaws of ruin?
Alas! what patriot can deny,
  His zeal promoted our undoing?
    One party made all mankind foes,
    The other triumph'd in our woes.

Let Pitt remove each rotten borough,
  And lay the land-tax fairly on,
Raiſe Bengal from her preſent ſorrow,
  For Ireland's injuries atone;
    And then all Europe ſhall exclaim,
    " This youth tranſcends his father's fame!"

HORACE, LIB. I. ODE III.

IMITATED.

O SHIP, thou bearer of my better part,
The man whoſe friendſhip long has fix'd my heart,

Hear, if thou can'ſt, his abſence how I mourn,
And grant my friend a fortunate return.
And may kind Fate protect and ſhelter thee,
From all the perils of the raging ſea;
Where winds and waves inceſſant ſtorm and roar,
And thouſands hourly ſink to riſe no more.
And ſure his heart was ſheath'd in threefold braſs,
Who firſt preſum'd the frowning deep to paſs;
Who puſh'd his leaky pinnace from the ſtrand,
Forc'd his faint crew to quit the ſight of land,
And, on his keel, acroſs the billows fly,
While their blue boſom hid the bending ſky;
Each trembling plank ſcarce ſtemm'd the ſtream beneath,
And every blaſt beſpoke deſcending death.
What form of danger needs his ſoul affright,
Who reſts his honeſt pride on acting right?
He knows that life, at beſt, is but a ſtorm,
That ſome foul ſqualls the fineſt day deform;
He knows a generous Judge ſurveys him here,
Who tries his fav'rites by a fate ſevere.
In vain the tempeſt howls, the waves are broke,
Collected in himſelf he meets the ſhock;
Secure alike below the burning zone,
And where grim Winter graſps a world his own;
Where ancient Night extends her ſtill domain,
And blaſted vegetation buds in vain.
With what a ſhock the froſt-bound ocean rends,
When through the arctic night the long loſt ſun aſcends;
The bleak hills hear the diſtant echo riſe,
The veſſels ſhatter, and the ſeamen's cries;
The cloud topt fragments cleave the foaming flood,
The ruins craſh, the ſeals are bath'd in blood;
How loud, how terrible the ſurges ſweep,
While the huge whales plunge trembling down the deep.
Not all this hoard of dangers, can reſtrain,
Raſh man from roving o'er the riſted main;
The barriers fix'd by Fate we dare defy,
And court the vengeance of that horrid ſky.

As if wide ocean gave too little room,
We proudly try to pierce the polar gloom,
To bathe it's bulky monſters in their blood,
And from its wretched ſons to force their wretched food.*
In vain Almighty Goodneſs had deſign'd
The ſea to check the quarrels of mankind;
The broad Atlantic ſtops our arms no more,
And guiltleſs blood now ſtreams on every ſhore.
Columbus firſt, and Gama led the way,
And waſted empires all their toil repay;
Who has not heard what more than wonted crimes
Have damn'd our conqueſts in the weſtern climes.
Let bluſhing hiſtory with tears atteſt,
That Cuba's ſons were once completely bleſt;
Unknown to care, they danc'd their time away,
And every wiſh was innocent and gay.
But when our pirates on their coaſt appear'd,
And Murther's cry the helpleſs victims heard,
Then welcome death allow'd a quick releaſe,
The new made wilderneſs was huſh'd to peace,
The proud oppreſſor ſheath'd his reeking blade,
And Rapine mourn'd the waſte herſelf had made.
Nor let old England with abſurd diſdain,
For deeds like theſe inſult atrocious Spain;
Since, in the taſk of ſcourging human kind,
Calm Truth can hardly rank us far behind.
Our monks like theirs have lighted many a fire,
Where holy fools were eager to expire:
Like them we trembled at a tyrant's frown,
Till daring Hampden tore the puppet down.
See! every tie of faith and mercy broke,
Ill-fated Bengal bleed beneath our yoke.

* The number of the poor inhabitants of Greenland is daily diminiſhing, in conſequence of the deſtruction of their marine animals, by adventurers from happier climates. See Goldſmith's Natural Hiſtory, Vol. IV. p. 182.

Its ample ſpoils impell'd us to renew
The dreadful ſcenes once acted in Peru. *
Whatever baſeneſs can degrade mankind,
Whatever Cade or Cataline deſign'd,
Whatever outrage Rome's red ſtreets deform'd,
When Sylla rul'd her, or when Bourbon ſtorm'd,
Whatever Timur did to win a throne,
Or faith-defending Harry would have done,
All ſeems but nothing in our poliſh'd times,
Nor can our ſons eclipſe our preſent crimes.
But ſoon the hapleſs Indian ſaw repaid
The wrongs of thoſe who chas'd him from his ſhade;
A new diſeaſe invades the fount of joy,
And ſcorching ſuns the tyrant race deſtroy.
With all the riches Potoſi can boaſt,
How few return from that polluted coaſt?
The planter ſhrivels in the prime of life,
The injur'd negroe thruſts his deadly knife;
Here, while a tertian deſolates around,
And Pain's laſt pangs, poor human pride confound,
Lo there contending elements conſpire,
Each black cloud burſting in a ſheet of fire;
And earth and ocean as diſſolving rend,
While guilty cities down the gulf deſcend.
And ſure ſince heaven is juſt, the weſtern ſkies
Shall ſee, ere long, ſome Spartacus ariſe,
To bid our ſlaves the Chriſtian yoke diſown,
And ſeize the land they labour as their own;
Behold the hero burſt Oppreſſion's bands,
The blood of ruffians reeking on his hands;
Hark how he echoes Freedom's honour'd name,
And boaſts how vict'ry vindicates his claim.

* Colonel Alexander Dow, an author of uncommon merit, affirms, that between the years 1765 and 1771, the province of Bengal alone had loſt five or ſix millions of inhabitants.

See round their chief the jetty nation throngs;
What horrid vengeance anſwers all their wrongs.
Extermination ſteeps the trembling ſhore;
Europa's robbers lift the laſh no more.
Vindictive Juſtice ſweeps the race away;
Our toil of ages periſh'd in a day.
  Nothing ſo wild which man will fear to try;
From pole to pole in ſearch of gold we fly;
Nor even contented to ſurround the globe,
Remoteſt ocean of her ſpoils we rob. *
Fearleſs we range below her gloomy deeps,
Where the keen ſhark through purple ſlaughter ſweeps;
And leaving eagles in their flight behind,
We ſoar above them on the ſwelling wind.
We teach reſiſtleſs lightning where to fly,
Nor dread to drown the thunders of the ſky;
We tell cold Saturn's diſtance from the Sun,
We count what orbs around his center run;
We meaſure all the ſkies, ſome air baloon
One day, who knows, may land us in the moon.
We long ſince ventur'd with indecent ſkill,
To trace the height of every lunar hill.
Our daring crimes the Deity offend,
Well might his thunder on our heads deſcend;
Our folly yet inclines him to forgive,
The Judge of Nature pities and we live.

THE MONITOR.

With Spartan patience you can bear
  The progreſs of another's pain,
Repel my head-ach with a ſneer,
  And count my fractures with diſdain.

* The Diving Bell and other late diſcoveries are pointed at, which, as they are familiar to every body, it would be needleſs to recite.

But when the caſe becomes your own,
You feel 'tis quite a harder ſtory;
The Hero, by a ball o'erthrown,
To heal his limbs would loſe his glory.

When I am ſick, you ſagely wonder
My heart ſhould turn at ſlops and pills;
My ſon expires—you bawl like thunder,
That death is but the leaſt of ills.

When Beauty bids my boſom ſigh,
You preach that Beauty is but duſt;
Some Hector's courage when I try,
You tell me where, and how, to thruſt.

The quack may ſmile to give injections,
Poltroons inform us how to fight,
On death your Vicar eke reflections,
A balmy kiſs the Book-worm ſlight.

To lecture, carp, and criticiſe,
Is fine amuſement for a fool:
But though the weakeſt may adviſe,
No wiſe man always walks by rule.

ON SHAKESPEARE.

WHOE'ER attempts like Shakeſpeare to compoſe,
Shall certainly his time and labour loſe;
Like thoſe unwary fops who once, we know,
Eſſay'd to bend their abſent Monarch's bow.*
This mighty poet every key can hit,
Riſe in the hero, rally in the wit;
Each various particle of man has read,
From the proud palace to the peaceful ſhed;

* Vid. Homer.

And ſtill the paſſing ſcene ſupports ſo well,
You think 'tis *there* his talent muſt excel.
When the wrong'd Moore invokes his murder'd wife;
When doughty Falſtaff runs to ſave his life;
When honeſt Brutus pleads the cauſe of Rome,
And midnight hags foretel Macbeth his doom;
When lively Benedict at marriage ſneers,
And poor Ophelia fills your eye with tears;
When ſimple Timon finds himſelf too fond,
And Shylock claims the forfeit of his bond;
When moralizing Jacques ſends forth a ſigh,
And gay Mercutio lets his ſallies fly;
Deſdemona recites her virgin vows,
And arch Petruchio tames his rampant ſpouſe;
When bloody Richard trembles at his dreams,
And Wolſey reads the wreck of all his ſchemes;
When John would hint what Hubert ſhould perform,
And houſeleſs Lear raves amidſt the ſtorm;
In what a blaze of eloquence he ſhines!
How reaſon opens, how the heart refines!
When Anthony, with more than magic ſkill,
Compells the mob to weep o'er Cæſar's will;
When the proud Welchman, by his ally croſt,
Of ſpells and prodigies pretends to boaſt;
The ſword of Douglas vindicates his name,
And dying Warwick points the path to fame.
In every page, we never fail to find
Inimitable pictures of mankind.
When Quickly's rambling tongue attempts to ſay,
How falſe Sir John had fix'd their wedding-day;
When the old Ruffian, in a ſtrumpet's arms,
On Vice and Folly ſquanders all his charms;
When Poins and Harry are compell'd to hear
What puppies, in his judgment, they appear;
When Hall's attack the bold diſſembler turns,
And virtuous Tearſheet her plump pigeon ſpurns;
Parolles braves the laſh of public ſcorn,
And frantic Ford holds up the fancy'd horn;

From Hotſpur, Troilus, Hamlet, Romeo, down
To the dull Juſtice and the gibing Clown;
From the ſtern victor at the Volſcian gate,
To Grumio's antics, and Malvolio's prate;
What vary'd features does his pencil yield?
Puns in the bagnio, thunders o'er the field;
What brilliant tints of character combine!
How loudly Nature ſpeaks in every line!
When Ajax murmurs, Therſites reviles;
Grave Henry lectures, frank Menenius ſmiles;
When Iſabella kneels, pert Lucio lies,
And ſad Conſtantia for her Arthur cries;
When Bottom ſpouts,* and Buckingham diſplays
Th' uſurper's birth-right in a peal of praiſe,
The blunt abruptneſs of the hardy Greek,
The ſhrewd poltroon with blows compell'd to ſpeak,
The Monarch chearful till *his reign began*;
The forward, gay, facetious good old man,
The modeſt, eloquent, unhappy maid,
The pleaſing coxcomb by his chat betray'd,
The blockhead's ignoranee, the mother's pangs,
The monk's chill comfort, the ſtate-quack's harangues,
All in ſucceſſive viſion ſeem to riſe,
Each chaſte original arreſts our eyes:
A burſt ſo ſplendid dazzles human thought,
And in his phantoms, Shakeſpeare is forgot.
Down Fancy's torrent vanquiſh'd Reaſon glides,
Grief melts our boſoms, Laughter aches our ſides;
While pathos, truth, propriety, and art,
Strike blank amazement through the coldeſt heart.
What centuries of rhyming ſhall have roll'd,
What crouds of Rowes and Congreves fate unfold,
A ſecond Shakeſpeare ere the world behold.

* The plan of the Rehearſal is borrowed from Shakeſpeare, a circumſtance which ſeems to have eſcaped all his Commentators.

VERSES ON FRIENDSHIP.

INSCRIBED TO A*** B***, ESQUIRE.

KIND Sir, you once desir'd to see
A specimen of verse from me;
And though I rather might have chose
To give my sentiments in prose;
Yet since, with many more in town,
Your tender goodness I must own;
Which neither length of time can tire,
Nor all the favours fools require,
From wit, that like a rush-light shines,
Accept these humble hobbling lines.
The Muse would rather mount her hearse,
Than strut, like Thompson, through blank verse;
For, if she may your taste oppose,
'Tis sometimes neither verse nor prose;
Nor dares she in Pindaric lays,
To publish her preceptor's praise.
She knows you pity and despise
Bombast adulatory lies:
And conscious that you hear with pain
Poor pension'd Warton's woeful strain;
That not a couplet will go down,
But naked sterling truth alone;
That not a hint will be allow'd
Of all the talents Fate bestow'd;
In short, that, should I loose my heart,
Malice might say, "'tis all but art;"
I'm forc'd to whisper *inter nos*,
Melpomene is at a loss.
She dares not tell e'en what is true,
Or give your virtues half their due;
And, if she has not room to play,
What can your luckless Laureate say.

We'll venture, as the ſafeſt ſhift,
To imitate immortal Swift;
Put on the plainneſs of his ſtyle,
And try, perhaps, to raiſe a ſmile;
And ſince his Worſhip was by nature
Leſs plentiful of praiſe than ſatire,
And made it his unvaried courſe
To ſcourge the world without remorſe,
We'll in the progreſs of our ditty.
Expoſe that wretch to ſcorn and pity,
Who would not give a groat's deduction
To ſave his debtor from deſtruction.
But of yourſelf we'll ſay no more
Than all the world have ſaid before,
And coldly, as it were in jeſt,
Some happier pen ſhall tell the reſt.
Deſcend great ſhade! and Oh! inſpire
My boſom with thy matchleſs fire,
Thy wit ſevere, thy fancy ſtrong,
Thy common ſenſe to point my ſong;
And with thee bring the Ladies nine,
To poliſh each majeſtic line.
Let "proper words in proper places"*
Supply the want of higher graces.
Our invocation thus perform'd,
The outworks of Parnaſſus ſtorm'd;
Apollo's poney climbs it's height,
And mounts, like Maſon, out of ſight.
Ye planets pauſe! Ye ſyſtems bend!
While we above your ſpheres aſcend:
Soon ſhall ye hear ſo ſweet a ſong,
Your orbits will not hold you long;
Your vaineſt bigot need not ſmile
To hear me talk in ſuch a ſtyle;
Ye cannot have forgot when Young
On Friendſhip, and Philander ſung;

* Dr Swift gave this definition of a correct ſtyle.

Your Seraphs liſten'd with amaze,
And fairly yielded up the bays.*
The learned Philoſophic Sages,
Who wrote and ſtarv'd in ancient ages,
Were wond'rous proud to ſay and ſing,
What pleaſures from true Friendſhip ſpring;
That they alone of all mankind,
The road to happineſs could find;
That he who plays a generous part,
And wins one ſympathizing heart,
O'er all the world ſupremely bleſt,
In calm felicity may reſt:
This doctrine all our bards avow,
And 'tis adopted, Sir, by you.
The man who never ow'd a ſhilling,
May truſt theſe viſions, if he's willing;
And fancy thoſe who toaſt the glaſs,
To her they think his fav'rite laſs,
Who echo every word he ſays,
And ſweat him with inſipid praiſe;
Who fly to hail him in the ſtreet,
And bow profoundly when they meet;

* The Editor has received from a correſpondent the following note, which is inſerted verbatim.

" Your panegyric on Dr. Young, may admit of much abate-" ment. From the works of this ſingle author only, materials " might be furniſhed for a ſecond Rehearſal. The following " paſſage, for example, is perhaps the moſt nonſenſical in the " Engliſh language. Alonzo addreſſing Leonora, cries out

" Thoſe eyes which tell us what the ſun is made of!
" Thoſe lips whoſe touch is to be bought with life!
" Thoſe heaps of driven ſnow which ſeen are felt!

" I have been preſent more than once in a London theatre, du-" ring the performance of the Revenge, and I have heard this " horrid jargon, when embelliſhed by a proper accent and ac-" tion, receive the moſt unbounded applauſe from every corner " of the houſe."

That ſuch alone, of all the croud,
Would ſpill for him their deareſt blood;
His page with treble raptures read,
And ſell their ſhirts to buy him bread.
Yes! were he humbled in the duſt,
His friends to merit would be juſt,
Rejoice with him to ſhare a throne,
Nor think their empire leſs their own.
He never knew the power of pelf,
He deems them ſerious like himſelf;
He cannot gueſs (good honeſt man!)
Each ſycophant's perfidious plan.
To-day, the one a ſum would borrow;
The next expects a place to-morrow;
"And if, kind Sir, you'll ſend a letter,
"His Lordſhip is, we know, your debtor;
"And would not for a thouſand pounds
"Tempt you to advertiſe his grounds;
"Or ſell that ſplendid houſe in town,
"It's owner cannot call his own."
And thus it is the matter goes;
Each ſuitor leads him by the noſe.
A club, to ſerve their dirty ends,
Preſume to call themſelves his friends;
Though well ſupplied with ſenſe and learning,
Candour prevents him from diſcerning
Each little, mean, inſidious art,
That ſaps the fortreſs of his heart;
But when the darling point is gain'd,
'Tis like his viſits are diſdain'd;
And thoſe eternal friends, alack!
Find ſome pretence to turn their back;
For men who have moſt meanly bended
Are always worſt, when once aſcended.
Another ſet ſucceed to theſe,
And ſtudy every trick to pleaſe;
But ſtill ſome accident attends,
To ſcatter or fatigue his friends;

And ere the prime of life be paſt,
He ſees that all are knaves at laſt;
His finer feelings are exhauſted,
And his good heart is qûite diſguſted;
He ſmiles at Friendſhip as abſurd,
And bluſhes at the very word.
Forgive your Bard this boyiſh crime
Of telling all his thoughts in rhyme,
Proteſting the reſemblance true,
And owning, he remember'd you.
Not all the candour you poſſeſs,
Not all that fond deſire to bleſs,
That zeal to publiſh worth unknown,
And blaze all merit but your own,
Should Fortune ſnatch her gifts away,
Could ſave you many a diſmal day;
The warmeſt friend would ſoon grow cold,
The wiſeſt wiſh to ſave his gold,
And all the poor dependent croud,
Lament they could not do you good;
With ſerious anguiſh hear you mourn,
And leave you, never to return.
Authors would ſeldom croſs your gate,
They leave Misfortune to her fate.
We read the labours of the pen,
And think them more than common men;
But ſad Experience bids us ſay,
They're only form'd of vulgar clay.
Whate'er a pedant may pretend,
Iſcariot prov'd a better friend;
His frozen heart is hard as ſteel,
'Tis quite a vulgar thing to feel.
The cant of "theſe degenerate days,"
Is but a poor unmeaning phraſe;
For knaves at preſent do no more
Than what their fathers did before.
A man whoſe mind is amply fraught
With all which Greece and Rome have taught,

Muſt know what Socrates deſerv'd,
And how his ſhoulders would have ſtarv'd,
Had not the poor Profeſſor ſpoke,
And begg'd his pupils for a cloak.
And can you ſtill ſuppoſe your friends
Superior to all little ends?
The ſhrewdeſt man Apollo knew
Could only find a ſcoundrel crew;
And can we in the living race
Sublimer, ſofter, feelings trace;
The preſent age are juſt the ſame,
True to the ſtock from which they came.
The vulgar, timid, ſelfiſh mind,
Forms the great herd of human kind;
The reſt are only beaſts of prey,
More ſavage and more vile than they.
And thus, my unſuſpecting friend,
You ſee where common friendſhips end;
Caprice and accident conſpire
To light up an eternal fire;
The farthing-candle burns, no doubt,
Till pride or int'reſt puffs it out;
And then each friend begins to wonder
How he committed ſuch a blunder;
Perceives how little love he had,
And ſees his neighbour juſt as bad.
'Twould take a Lapland ſummer's day,
To ſum up all that each can ſay;
Such unions nothing will produce,
But envy, malice, and abuſe.
The novice, eager to impart
His wiſhes to ſome ſocial heart,
An hundred chances runs to one
Of having all his ſecrets blown.
Cant then of Friendſhip as they will,
Mortals are only mortals ſtill;
A motley maſs of contradictions,
Their friendſhips merely traps and fictions;

For, in a thouſand, ſeldom one
Is built on love and truth alone.
This, Solomon himſelf hath ſaid,
Who, no doubt, very dearly paid
For all the ſterling force of thought
That ſparkles through each line he wrote.
Oh! Friendſhip thy unfading charms
Awake my ſoul to ſweet alarms;
The loudeſt racket Folly raiſes,
Is all too frigid for thy praiſes.
At four-and-twenty, I believe
What leſſer fools at ten perceive;
That every wiſe man thinks and cares
For nothing but his own affairs,
And fancies it moſt fooliſh labour
To ſave from want a ſinking neighbour;
Unleſs he can, without delay,
With twice its worth his aid repay.
This rule, admitting no exceptions,
Includes all ranks and all deſcriptions;
Though, once in ninety thouſand years,
A G**** or a Quin appears.
Did my experience but atteſt
That all theſe murmurs were a jeſt;
That every heart was fond and true,
That every friend reſembled you;
Then ſhould I, in the Laureate's phraſe,
Fill every line with fulſome praiſe,
And ſing up ſcribblers to the ſkies,
For all thoſe virtues they deſpiſe.
May heav'n forbid, you e'er depend
Upon the promiſe of a friend;
For if you do not need his aid,
Or, if he's certain he'll be paid,
At half a nod, behold him fly,
For you he lives, for you he'll die!
But ſhould you drop the word *Subſiſtence*,
A ſurly, cold, forbidding diſtance

Announces you muſt lick his ſpittle ;
That he is great, and you are little :
And then you ſee, too late, indeed,
His Friendſhip juſt a broken reed !
A thouſand times you muſt have known
A caſe like this, though not your own :
Then how can one forbear to laſh
Theſe mean, deteſted ſordid traſh.
I am not talking of the mob
Whom want impells to ſteal and rob ;
No ! I am ſpeaking of their betters,
Of men of taſte, and men of letters ;
Of men who honour their high ſtations,
Whoſe works extend the fame of nations,
Who Virgil's verſes would admire,
And let him in a jail expire ;
(As fifty Bards have done before),
And then his woeful end deplore.
And if, perhaps, my credit fail,
Turn over the laborious Bayle ;
Remark what monſters croud his pages,
All Claſſics of enlighten'd ages !
The beſt of us have many a fault,
And act but ſeldom as we ought :
Yet, if our planet be poſſeſs'd
Of one ſublimely generous breaſt,
A friend who really feels your grief,
Who, when he can, will lend relief ;
A friend, who, like immortal Quin,
Will free you from the turnkey's gin,
And ſtrictly charge you not to tell
That he (good ſoul !) has acted well ;
In ranging forty ſyſtems round,
If ſuch a wonder ſhall be found,
The conſcious Muſe could gueſs his name,
But modeſt worth deſpiſes fame.

ON DAVID HUME, ESQUIRE.

What better way, to ſpend a day,
Than turning over thoughtful Hume;
For though on prieſts he broke his jeſts,
He fairly rivals Greece and Rome.

He did, 'tis true, deny their due
To Bacon, Shakeſpeare*, Hampden, Brutus;
But ſtill we know he did not ſhow
A mean ſervility to Plutus.

He took his pen, like other men,
Becauſe he wanted food and fame;
But then he wrote whate'er he thought,
Nor courted praiſe, nor feared blame:

And ſince we know he roaſts *below*
For what he ſaid upon the Bible,
It would be wrong to make our ſong,
Like Beattie's bitter book †, a Libel.

ON THE VANITY OF AMBITION.

The horſe, when well ſupply'd with corn and hay,
With patience bears the labours of the day;
At his hard lot he never once repines,
Nor pants to know what Providence deſigns;

* His character of this Poet is invidious and abſurd, and ought, for the honour of Literature, to be expunged from every future editon of his hiſtory.

† In attempting to peruſe this work, we find the author unintelligible, unleſs in a few paſſages where he is remarkably ſcurrilous. We have all heard of the Eſſay as an admirable defence of Chriſtianity, which ought not, one ſhould think, at this time of day, to ſtand in need of a defence. After wading through one hundredand ſeventy pages of the firſt part of his performance, the Reader will be ſurpriſed to find *nothing at all about Religion.*

And, after all the wise pretend to see,
Perhaps our nags know just as well as we.
The dog is happy when his paunch is full,
No phantoms of ambition plague his skull;
To serve his owner, modestly content,
He reaps the raptures of a life well spent.
Puss, killing mice, exults through every vein,
Nor lets the longitude derange her brain.
The mouse entrenching in a rotten cheese,
No higher happiness or seeks or sees.
In short, all animals but restless man,
Are pretty well content with Nature's plan;
And though with ills they stand incessant strife,
Yet never in contempt relinquish life.
And we, inheriting a soul *divine!*
Above blind Instinct surely ought to shine;
But *Reason* only maks us greater fools,
We're constantly at war with Reason's rules;
Ten thousand idle wants we madly make,
And for each phantom cast our all to stake.
  This frantic wish, for instance, fires the breast;
Each mortal would rejoice to rule the rest.
Had haughty Cæsar been content to keep
In Alpine solitudes, a herd of sheep,
More happy had he liv'd a humble swain,
Than when at Munda he reconquer'd Spain;
Where Courage to Despair began to yield,
And Chance bestow'd the honours of the field.
Or, was he blest when senates round him bow'd,
And foes to his contempt their safety ow'd;
When Tully's tongue was panting to obey,
And Egypt's Syren mark'd him for her prey?
  Let all such heirs of Glory, if they will,
Determine either to be kill'd or kill.
That mode of madness shall not crack my head,
My grand ambition is to die a-bed.
I care not what the Russians are about,
Nor whether France and Germany fall out,

What tawny tyrant keeps the Moors in awe,
What Tartar chief fucceeds to Nadir Shaw;
By Japan when the Pope fhall be obey'd,
Or all Amboyna on the Dutch repaid.
England, for me, fhall never rule the main,
I would not break one limb ten cat-fkin marts to gain;
Nor quit the comforts of my kitchen fire,
That gaping mobs my courage may admire;
That fome vile Statefman, of his blood-hounds vain,
May fpread deftruction through a frefh campaign,
And bankrupt nations add an endlefs fcore,
To what both Indies could not pay before.

HORACE, LIB. I. ODE. IV.

IMITATED.

THE furly winter now has fled,
And fmiling fpring fupplies his ftead;
The fky diffolves in gentle fhowers,
And April paints the mead with flowers;
No hoar-froft in the dawn is feen,
But lambs are leaping o'er the green.
The farmer feels the cold retire,
And quits, in hafte, his kitchen fire;
Turns out his oxen from the ftalls,
And to the plow his fervants calls;
How beautiful the budding grove,
All nature melting into love.
The linnet lines her little neft,
With feathers from her tender breaft,
The wealthy bee is on the wing,
To rifle all the rofy fpring;
While vegetation burfts around,
And daifes deck the teeming ground.
At this fweet feafon, when I fee
My friend beneath fome fhady tree,

Perusing Dryden's classic page,
Or tracing man through Shakespeare's stage;
When gen'rous Brutus acts his part,
Or fond Ophelia pours her heart;
While music swells along the sky,
And rapture trembles in his eye,
'Tis then I bless my humble fate,
And pity all the pompous great;
When can they eatch an hour serene,
To taste the joy of such a scene.
But ah! his virtues will not save
My Lucius from the silent grave;
Impartial Death one message brings,
To rich, and poor, to slaves and kings.
Life lends but very narrow scope,
To the fond reveries of Hope:
And when committed to the shroud,
No modern mortal is allow'd,
Though weeping worlds his absence mourn,
Like Hamlet's father to return.

HORACE, LIB. I. ODE V.

IMITATED.

Ah! tell me, dear Pyrrha, what beautiful boy,
This evening shall rifle these charms;
Some jessamine arbour the scene of your joy,
And Paradise all in your arms!

For whom are you combing your long jetty hair,
So gracefully artless you dress;
So tender a look! so bewitching an air!
Admiration swells into distress.

Your simple young fav'rite, will fondly suppose,
That he is the lord of your heart;

I ij

But, when the ſeas frown, and the hurricane blows,
With how much amaze ſhall he ſtart!

How happy the lovers who calmly deſy
The fair one they cannot eſteem;
But yet in the midſt of your ſcorn let me die,
Ere I live to be frigid like them.

ON READING THE BEAUX STRATAGEM.

Farquhar's looſe ſcenes let every good man ſhun,
Where all our morals to perdition run.
A crew like theſe the world ne'er knew before;
A rake each huſband, and each wife a whore;
How vile a pimp to every human vice!
What wretched fools who read his pages twice!
When ſhall a Britiſh ſtage be ſwept quite clean,
Nor actors need to bluſh for what they mean.
Lay Shakeſpeare, and a ſelect few aſide,
And that ſweet paſtoral Edina's pride,
Where honeſt nature ſoars above ſtage art,
And each pure thought flows warmly from the heart;
And then remark what hateful traſh remains;
Traſh, taſte abhors, and common ſenſe diſdains.

HORACE, LIB. I. ODE VI.

IMITATED.

Dear Harry you affect to wonder
I never echo Rodney's name,
And ſwell my ſong with blood and thunder,
Since Horace would have done the ſame.

The ſweet immortal Bard of Rome
  To ſing his heroes had a right;
But never ſhall a wren preſume
  To emulate an eagle's flight.

What muſe could elevate a verſe,
  To tell how Keppel chac'd our foes?
Homer had trembled to rehearſe
  The rival valour of the Howes!

And never, ſince the world began,
  Did ſo much wiſdom rule a ſtate;
How deep and ſteady in each plan,
  How calm and decent in debate?

What generous pity we diſplay'd
  When Rumbold was to be defended!
When North and Fox the ſceptre ſway'd,
  How wide our glory was extended!

'Tis true, their reign was very ſhort,
  For which poſterity will mourn;
But 'tis a faſhion at the Court
  That every party riſe in turn!

And every patriot of them all
  Hath ſuch a fund of public ſpirit;
Bards to eternity might bawl,
  And ſcarce do juſtice to their merit.

Then how can you ſuppoſe that I
  Should venture on ſo vaſt a theme;
For ſome young doxy let me ſigh,
  And pen a ballad to her fame.

ON THE POWER OF WEALTH.

Fire and the Sun the Perſians once ador'd,
And pious Egypt her dead bull deplor'd;
The ſons of Brama venerate a Cow,
And Rome to relicks condeſcends to bow;
The Moon when full, the Hottentots admire,
And China's idols fervent faith inſpire;
The Turk to Mahomet for pardon prays,
The Jew from Moſes, hopes for better days;
And each of theſe in turn contemns the reſt,
While Engliſh wiſdom ſees them all a jeſt;
Admires what nonſenſe mankind ſwallow down,
And finds no creed conſiſtent but her own.
Yet though no ſect admits a rival right,
All parties in one point of faith unite;
From Japan to Peru, from Pole to Pole,
The luſt of gold enſlaves the human ſoul.
Beggars themſelves ſincerely ſcorn the poor,
And ruſh enraptur'd to the rich man's door;
The blaze of grandeur fills your houſe with friends,
To ſerve his own, each ſerves your meaneſt ends.
See them! like moths around the candle dance,
Even pride herſelf, will pay the firſt advance.
For you the lawyer's tongue perverts the laws,
The Judge, we daily mark it, nods applauſe.
Your heir himſelf is anxious for your health,
And rates your virtues far above your wealth;
Nay Sunday's Orator muſt now be fee'd,
And ſcorns, like honeſt Paul, to work for bread;
Though beſt or worſt have nothing new to ſay,
But trudge the ſame trite circle every day.
One muſt be nimble, ſhould he chance to meet,
Our Vicar's carriage ruſhing down the ſtreet;
The wildeſt fanaticks will ne'er neglect,
To treat a monied man with due reſpect;

But by their ſilent reverence ſeem to ſay,
He's as much wiſer as more rich than they.
And ſhould ſome portly Dean their price allow;
Quakers themſelves alas! begin to bow.
Thus every ſect purſues one common end,
And riches are the Baal to whom they bend.

HORACE, LIB. I. ODE VII.

IMITATED.

Horace, in his enchanting lays,
  Old Tiber's praiſe proclaims;
And Denham happily diſplays
  The grandeur of his Thames.

A thouſand ancient Bards have ſung
  The lovely Banks of Tweed;
And winding Leven lately rung
  With Random's tuneful reed.

And yet, methinks, my native ſtream
  Is far above the reſt;
Its diſtant beauties, like a dream,
  Are ruſhing on my breaſt.

But why ſweet * * * ſo fondly praiſe,
  Or why it's abſence mourn?
Alas! our childhood's happy days
  Are never to return.

When Camoens, who, for hunger died,
  From India took his way;
Thus, while their veſſel cut the tide,
  The Poet pour'd his lay.

" Though Fate allow me once again
  " To ſee my native ſhore;

" 'Tis like the long-lamented ſcene
" Shall know my name no more.

" The rich will very wiſely ſhun
" A man ſo very poor;
" Nor will the croud with raptures run
" His friendſhip to ſecure.

" In ſullen ſilence all agree,
" Or coldly condeſcend,
" To hint they once admitted me
" Their equal and their friend.

" Then muſt I feel this humbling truth
" Strike heavy on my breaſt;
" The fond attachments of our youth
" Are nothing but a jeſt.

" Nor would old Homer, if alive,
" A kinder welcome meet;
" But all his ſunſhine friends ſurvive
" To periſh in the ſtreet.

" And yet, perhaps, a future age
" My miſeries may hear;
" And drop, while they peruſe my page,
" A fond though fruitleſs tear."

ON FRUGALITY.

Few ills occur more frequently in life,
Than ruin from the folly of a wife;
The wiſeſt of the ſex are rather vain,
And ſolitude, and ſilence, give them pain;
They cannot read, nor think, nor ſtay at home,
In ſearch of ſcandal, ſilks, and tea, they roam.
Their friends to viſit them in courſe return,
And then the candle at both ends muſt burn;

To pleaſe the company what haſte is made,
What noiſe, expence, and flutter, and parade.
The viſitors are always very free,
In finding faults with every thing they ſee;
They ſhew their envy, though they call it taſte,
And teach your ſpouſe new leſſons how to waſte.
'Tis ſtrange, that any man of common ſenſe,
Permits his wife to drown him with expence;
And when, like moſt of us, he ſcarce can live,
More than his own for idle toys to give;
Why truſt his helm to ſuch a feeble hand?
Why not enjoy the pleaſures of command?
Why thus reſign his native right to rule?
Or, who ſhould ſympathize with ſuch a fool.
The coward who can bear this ſhameful plan,
Deſerves to loſe the title of a man;
The worſt effect muſt very ſeldom fail,
Debt, and diſgrace, and hunger, and a jail;
Nay, oft the victim hath reſolv'd to die,
And cut the knot, he never could untie.
Without frugality, we try in vain
The dignity of riches to attain;
It is not what we win, but what we ſave,
That fits us future accidents to brave;
And happy, ſo far, muſt that mortal be,
Who feels himſelf from duns and debtors free;
Who every bill can at an inſtant pay;
Nor needs indulgence for a ſingle day.
If 'tis the gentle reader's glorious fate,
To find himſelf ſo ſingularly great;
His friends will flock around him in the ſtreet,
Nay fawn upon his children when they meet:
His faithful kin though forty times remov'd,
Will let him hear how tenderly he's lov'd;
Silence when he harangues will ne'er be broke
But every tongue repeat his pooreſt joke.
Treat none, let prodigals and bankrupts treat,
For *fools make feaſts that wiſer men may eat.*

And when you ſeem ſo frugal and ſo wiſe,
Your credit with the world will daily riſe;
And though you ſhould not wear ſo fine a coat
As ſome vain coxcomb, hardly worth a groat,
The public will have ſenſe enough to know,
From what ſage thrift theſe marks of meanneſs flow.
For wealth in tatters forces full reſpect,
When gaudy Indigence excites neglect.
My lord may live on a more ſplendid plan,
But you who lend him caſh, are much the greater man.
To you the petulant will ſmooth their ſtyle,
Pedants be frank, and pride ſubmit to ſmile;
The prieſt to pleaſe you will relax his creed,
The ſanguine ſurgeon own he ſhould not bleed.
And though your ſon your health at bottom curſe,
And feel a juſt impatience for your purſe,
As each young ſquire turns ſick by twenty-five
If the old dog, his father, lags alive;
Unleſs you fairly ſtrip yourſelf like Lear,
One ſerious frown ſhall freeze his ſoul with fear;
The want of money keep his temper mild,
And kings, with envy view the ſire of ſuch a child.
Good ſenſe muſt make him think what he's about,
Nor ſpurn your orders till your breath is out.

HORACE, LIB. I. ODE VIII.

IMITATED.

DEAR Madam, you ruin your ſon
  By loving the youth to exceſs,
For Billy of late hath begun
  To think upon nothing but dreſs.

Laſt year he was learning at ſchool
  To gallop, to fence, and to ſwim;
But a ſword, and a horſe, and a pool,
  Have loſt their attractions for him.

Laſt year he was hardy and bold,
Now alter'd ſo far and ſo ſoon;
In December he ſhivers with cold,
And droops in the ſunſhine of June.

No longer to rein the raſh ſteed,
To plunge in the boſom of Thames,
With Rodney to conquer and bleed,
The pupil of Luxury claims.

The Ladies are all his delight,
The ſequel you certainly know;
His courage will ſoon take its flight,
And the ſoldier be ſunk in the beau.

Like you, tender Thetis of old
Debas'd her invincible boy;
And petticoats, long, as we're told,
Retarded the ruin of Troy.

ON POPERY.

How can a Catholic of common ſenſe
Believe ſalvation ſhall be bought with pence?
As if the Lord of Nature, like himſelf,
Could feel a pleaſure in collecting pelf.
The blindeſt eye may ſee the whole a jeſt,
Contriv'd to glut the rapine of the prieſt;
And the vaſt code, invented in their ſchools,
A vulgar trap to catch the caſh of fools.
'Tis not, my Friend, by burning bulls and goats,
By ſhaving heads, and cutting human throats,
By kneeling at an altar, thrice a-day,
Collecting ancient maids to hear him pray,
By flaying of his back, rehearſing creeds,
Refuſing roaſted beef, or counting beads;
'Tis not by ſwearing that he'll want a wife,
Clean beds and decent linen all his life;

'Tis not by building dungeons to immure
Young girls, and make them twenty deaths endure;
Nor yet by kiſſing an old wooden poſt,
The Pope's indulgence, or the wafer-hoſt;
That he who wrongs the poor ſhall purchaſe reſt,
When conſcious guilt is throbbing in his breaſt.
Let Tillotſon eke folios, ſince he will,
To prove that wafers are but wafers ſtill;
Preachers on ſuch a point who rack their brain,
Are ſcarce above the bigots they diſdain;
How vile the Sophiſts then who condeſcend,
Such rank and fatal folly to defend.
We hope the riſing age may live to ſee
That glorious day when Parſons ſhall agree;
When Truth ſhall force one ſacrifice from Pride,
By burning all the traſh on either ſide;
When every Nun ſhall burſt her priſon door,
And Popery's laſt relick be no more.*
But though the Conclave may have led us wrong,
And kept the world in ignorance ſo long,
Let us purſue the *only* path that's given,
By which poor mortals may pretend to Heaven.
That man who will not tread his neighbours down,
Becauſe their faith is diff'rent from his own;
Who ſacred keeps his promiſe to a maid,
And inly bluſhes till his debts are paid;
Who, though a lawyer, ſcruples at a lie,
And, though a ſurgeon, feels the patient's ſigh;
Who, if a ſoldier, ſcorns to draw his blade
When ſmugglers quarrel, for ſome lawleſs trade;
But, ſhould Oppreſſion trample on the laws,
Is proud to periſh in a Hampden's cauſe;
Suppoſe there be ſome blunders in his creed,
His fate, nor here, nor elſewhere, ſhall he dread,
Though Hecla's baſis burſt upon his head.

* This article was written about eight years ago; ſince that time it is pleaſing to obſerve how far the French nation, and the Emperor Joſeph, *diſcordia ſemina rerum*, have agreed in advancing this event.

HORACE, LIB. I. ODE. XI.

IMITATED.

It is not fit that you or I
Should know the period when we'll die;
But then your Ladyſhip, it ſeems,
Expects to learn it by your dreams.
All men of common ſenſe diſdain
Theſe idle viſions of the brain;
Much better the complaint endure
Than crack your head with ſuch a cure.
'Tis little odds to me or you,
(As all our ſound Divines allow)
How many winters intervene,
Or if this preſent cloſe the ſcene;
Since He whoſe goodneſs guides the whole
Will find new quarters for the ſoul,
And who would wiſh to linger here,
Where every day demands a tear?
Pretend no longer, if you're wiſe,
To pierce the ſecrets of the ſkies;
At fleeting years no more repine,
But fill your Bard a bowl of wine:
For while we talk, invidious Age,
Advances o'er Life's little ſtage:
Come, let us catch the current hour,
To-morrow is not in our power.

HORACE, LIB. I. ODE XVI.

IMITATED.

I beg you, dear Fanny, to do what you pleaſe,
With that raſh unlucky lampoon;
Let it riſe in the chimney or ſink in the ſeas,
Your implacable vengeance to crown.

Some others, I feel it, are handſome and fair,
  But your charms even the coldeſt avow;
And, Oh! let me ſay, that in ſpite of deſpair,
  My wiſhes muſt center in you.

Forbid the effects of implacable rage
  From rending that delicate breaſt;
You have ſeen raſh Othello expire on the ſtage,
  And wiſdom will tell you the reſt.

When David, the Jew, rifled Rabbah of old,
  What feats did his fury perform!
To the choſen themſelves the ſame meaſure was told,
  When Zion was enter'd by ſtorm.

From all theſe examples, too ſenſible maid,
  The danger of paſſion you ſee,
Then be not alas! by juſt anger betray'd,
  To rejoice in the ruin of me.

When Adam was moulded, the devil they ſay,
  Inſerted a ſpice in the plan;
And we, his deſcendants, proceed to this day,
  As that ſorry being began.

Then why, my dear Fanny, continue to charge
  The tricks of the devil on me?
Or is there one lover, take mankind at large,
  From fits of impertinence free?

By thoſe fooliſh verſes I try'd to conceal,
  An ambition I bluſh'd to avow,
Nor did I, at that time, ſo terribly feel
  My exiſtence depended on you.

But ſince every quarrel is ended at laſt,
  Your heart let humanity move;
Let us both, like fond Joſeph, forget what is paſt,
  And plunge in the torrent of love.

HORACE, LIB. I. EPIST. IV.

IMITATED.

WHILE you, the kind corrector of my lays,
Remote from London paſs the ſummer days,
How ſhall I tell the world you ſpend your time
Still quite enamour'd with the ſweets of rhyme?
What! can a youth, ſo modeſt, really hope
With Dryden's rapid eloquence to cope!
Harmonious proſe demands no maſter art,
But who like Dryden, overwhelms the heart?
So ſweetly voluble his verſes run,
The line ſeems ended ere 'tis well begun.
Perhaps you ſaunter through ſome ſhady grove,
While your chaſte boſom glows with rural love;
Her charms the parſon's daughter has impreſt,
Or ſome kind milk-maid captivates your breaſt,
Sacred from paſte, and painting, and perfume,
And all her features freſh with Nature's bloom;
No barber's Babel nodding on her head,
Nor with town-ſcandal fit to talk you dead:
Or, ſhall I ſay, that, with the truly wiſe,
Your contemplations ſoar above the ſkies;
That 'tis eternity commands your care,
And all your ſage ambition centers there?
For, though a man of faſhion and eſtate,
With you religion is not out of date:
And let a friend applaud, without offence,
Mankind acknowledge your ſuperior ſenſe.
Your handſome perſon cannot fail to pleaſe,
And caſh, in plenty, ſets your ſoul at eaſe,
And you what Fortune proffers can enjoy,
Yet neither dignity nor health deſtroy:
You ne'er at midnight in a tavern roar,
Nor pledge your honour for a bagnio ſcore;

Nor at Newmarket bet with dirty rogues,
Nor ſtarve a pariſh to ſupport your dogs;
Nor with backgammon embarraſs your brain,
But cards and cockpits equally diſdain.
What farther could his doating nurſe requeſt,
For the young bantling ſmiling at her breaſt,
Than a clear, lively, comprehenſive mind,
A feeling heart, an eloquence refin'd,
A graceful form, an ample ſtock of health,
An happy temper, and ſome ſhare of wealth.
Since Nature then has every gift ſupply'd,
And Fate propitious rolls her richeſt tide;
Embrace the pleaſures of the preſent day,
But blend betimes the ſerious with the gay;
No tempeſt overclouds your morning ſkies,
But who can tell how ſoon the ſtorm may riſe?
Pardon, dear Sir, the preſent fit of rhyme,
To ſcribble nonſenſe is no deadly crime;
And did not conſcience whiſper what they coſt,
I'd ſend you ſuch epiſtles every poſt.

ON JULIUS CÆSAR. *

The firſt of the Cæſars to finiſh his praiſe,
Deſerv'd and demanded a ſprig of the bays;
And though as alert in proſcribing the rich,
As ſchool boys at pelting the frogs in a ditch,
As cool as a Taylor extirpating fleas,
While the blood of his countrymen iſſued in ſeas,
As anxious his foes on the head piece to knock,
As a Parſon with tithe-ſuits to torture his flock,
As unprincipled, blood thriſty, ſavage, impetuous,
As Jefferies, or Laud, or the judge of Servetus,
Or the very worſt king, or the very worſt prieſt,
That ever made all human feelings a jeſt,

* The barbarous manners of his age muſt be admitted as a very conſiderable apology for the blemiſhes of this eminent character.

He forgave, nay, he courted Catullus forſooth!
Who painted his crimes in the language of truth.
Yet no Laureate now a-days ventures to ſmile,
Left his Lilliput patron ſhould quarrel his ſtyle;
And diminiſh his Judas Iſcariot's bow,
To glance of diſtruſt and a cold "how d'ye do."
How manly the old Roman manner of thinking;
From what have we ſunk, or to what are we ſinking?

THE PROGRESS OF LIBERTY.

In times of old when Julius Cæſar,
Britannic laurels gain'd at leiſure;
Our cuckold anceſtors * were ſkill'd in
No art, and leaſt of all, in building.
Yet when they built a man was free,
To bore his roof to let him ſee,
Nor trembled for a Gauger's frown
Though ſmoke went up and light came down.
His cote when ſunſhine had forſook,
A bonfire ſhew'd him every nook;
He thought himſelf no more benighted,
Than if ten tapers had been lighted;
When like ourſelves of water tir'd,
His palate barley-corn requir'd,
No ſupervifor watch'd his ale,
Or thruſt an ell-wand in the pail.
But now, behold how Fate diſtracts us,
With window, barley, tallow taxes!
A draught of ale, a draught of air, †
A pinch of ſnuff will ſoon be rare.

* Caeſar tells us, that among the ancient Britons, ten or twelve huſbands enjoyed as many wives in common.

† In conſequence of the ruinous duty on window lights, a great number of windows were built up in the city of Carliſle, as well as in the reſt of the kingdom, in the year 1781. the

A fine, his Majesty must handle,
Ere you dare dip a farthing candle;
In dust no scavenger is laid,
Till three-pence to your prince be paid;
Another three-pence must be given,
A sort of entry-fee for heaven,
Before your pious heir begins
To wash away that world of sins
Contracted, if the church be right,
Long ages ere he saw the light.
No barber can retail pomatum,
But lo! the Chancellor is at him.
'Tis not enough to tax your crown,
His inquiries go farther down;
The Doctor when he vends a purge,
Must have a licence first from ******.
And since we buy the back-door scouring,
Why not excise all British urine;
'Twould have a twofold operation,
In working out this realm's salvation;
By forcing prodigals to think,
Better ere they begin to drink.

want of *free air* produced a putrid fever, which, before the beginning of February 1782, had attacked six hundred of the inhabitants; of these fifty-five died. See a pamphlet printed by Mr. Cadell in February 1782. The heavy tax on Peruvian bark, and upon other necessary drugs, is a tax on the health of the British nation; yet, as if the rest of Europe were inhabited only by slaves and poltroons, our political writers are incessantly chattering about the supreme excellence of the British constitution; and the Minister of the day, at the head of his disciplined phalanx, has the modesty to assure us that we are a free people. Britain has been justly compared to an apple in a cyder press, and the Premier to the man at the screw. No peculiar censure is here intended on Mr. Pitt. We can hardly suppose that his antagonists would, in his situation, have acted better.

ON DRYDEN.

HERE DRYDEN lies, and all his cries
  Of want and hunger are forgot;
And the whole croud, to whom he bow'd
  Are like himſelf, condemn'd to rot.

Had ſuch a man purſu'd a plan
  For gaining fair immortal fame,
No claſſic piece of Rome, or Greece,
  Had ſoar'd above his deathleſs name:

But when a Bard has no regard
  To Virtue, Decency, or Senſe,
We may admire his glorious fire,
  But ſhall we ſpeak in his defence?

Had Dryden ſcorn'd to be ſuborn'd
  To publiſh vile religious rhymes,
And had his Muſe dar'd to refuſe
  To vindicate a tyrant's crimes.

Each future age had read his page
  With endleſs wonder and delight;
The Poet's ſong can ſcarce be wrong
  Providing Truth direct his flight.

THE WISE MAN.

JESSE's fam'd grandſon ap'd his ſire,
Whoſe cut-throat reign we all admire;
He plunder'd every kingdom round,
Where handſome wenches could be found.
Like geldings from a fair he led,
Each wanton beauty to his bed;

But could not anſwer every call,
And act his duty to them all.
Great Cæſar's ſelf had ne'er ſupply'd,
The warm demands of every bride;
And then his royal wiſdom raged,
To catch them at the game engaged.
He plainly felt the ſprouting horn,
He felt it was not to be borne;
And in a fit of paſſion ſaid,
That every girl her faith betray'd.
His capons to be ſure would crack
Their whips on many a charming back;
And ſince they could not pleaſe, invent
Ten thouſand methods to torment.
But had the wiſeſt of all kings
Conſider'd well the ſtate of things,
He might with half an eye have ſeen,
That the bare title of a Queen
Would ne'er ſilence the ſimpleſt maid,
They know what tribute ſhould be paid;
And rogues, who rob them of their due,
Shall ſoon or late find time to rue.
Had he then manag'd as he ought,
And truth in one fond boſom ſought,
'Tis certain the ſagacious rake,
Had ſeen that moment his miſtake;
At the whole ſex he had not rail'd,
Nor had for once his wiſdom fail'd.*

*** What would be the ſituation of ſeven hundred, or a thouſand huſbands, reſtricted to a ſingle wife?**

REMARKS

ON

ENGLISH PLAYS.

THE HYPOCRITE:

A Comedy.

THIS plagiary mode of forming plays, has, in our servile age, become necessary from the want of original genius. The scenes borrowed from Cibber, are generally good. The translations, from Moliere, fall materially short of the sense, humour, and propriety of the original. The compiler's additions are very distinguishable from the rest. There is certainly an impropriety and ill judgment in transferring the characters of Tartuffo and Wolf, the opulent priests of established superstition, to the person of a poor enthusiastic fanatic preacher. The same author has exhausted the original spirit of the *Plain Dealer*, and metamorphosed it into a very insipid comedy, in the true taste of modern alteration.

A TRUE WIDOW:

A Comedy, by Shadwell.

THE scenes in this play are loose and unconnected. Some of the characters are outre, and there is hardly any plot, yet the language is easy and natural. We find in it true unaffected wit, and materials which would make a great figure in modern comedy.

THE SQUIRE OF ALSATIA:

A Comedy, by Shadwell.

THERE is a great variety of amusing adventure in this play; with some good scenes and natural characters; yet it falls off remarkably, after the first act, which is a piece of true comedy. Sir Edward is as pleasant and just a character of a ſenſible worthy gentleman, as can be found in the drama, or in real life; and the moral of this play is liberal and good, in various views. I value this play the more, as I was much prepoſſeſſed againſt the author, by Dryden's admirable ſatire in the Mackflecknoe; but great wits have commonly great pride and malice. Pope, with genius much inferior to Dryden, diſcovers a ſimilar pride and malevolence, by his illiberal abuſe of Colley Cibber, in his Dunciad, a ſatire, in which the malice is very natural, and the wit very artificial. On the whole, the play, though not altogether of a piece with the firſt act, merits the character as expreſſed in the dedication by its patron of "a true and diverting comedy."

THE BEAUX STRATAGEM:

A Comedy, by Farquhar.

This is a pleaſant comedy, has great variety of character and humour and is very entertaining, when well performed on the ſtage. There is leſs of the affected ſtudied wit, and more of natural converſation and humour, than is to be found in moſt of our later comedies. In this age, dramatic genius exiſts not; and

"Nature flies us like enchanted ground."*

Farquhar, however, neither in this, nor any of his plays, is able altogether to avoid ſome touches of low and indelicate humour.

POLLY:

An Opera, by Gay.

The introduction, by way of prologue, is perfectly in the happy ſtyle and taſte of the prologue to the Beggar's Opera. Every ſentence conveys, in eaſy, proper, and ſignificant language, ſtrokes of ſatire on the vices of the times, with peculiar force and pleaſantry. There is here no ſtudied affectation, and quaintneſs, which generally infeſt our modern wit, and gratify a prevailing ill taſte.

* Dryden.

A laboured ſingularity of expreſſion, and pompous language, diſguiſe the defects of ſenſe and true genius, from the days of ancient Seneca, down to a very modern and popular hiſtorian of the Roman empire.* Gay and Swift are, I think, the only unaffected Engliſh wits. I except the old poets, Shakeſpeare, Johnſon and Fletcher, and the ſingular wit and ſatire of the Rehearſal.

RULE A WIFE AND HAVE A WIFE:

A Comedy.

THIS is an admirable comedy. The characters are natural, and the converſation eaſy. The adventures are wrought up in an agreeable entertaining manner. The humour is unaffected, highly entertaining, and perfectly in character. All is in the old, plain, and happy ſtyle of poetry, which enlivens without conſtraining the author's compoſition. The BANEFUL RESTORATION introduced many and laſting evils to Britain; and, among the reſt, a falſe corrupted taſte in dramatic entertainments. From that period, our comedy has been infeſted with plots immoral and improbable, with affected ſimilies and ſtudied wit, which, like the prologue of Bayes, may ſerve equally for any character or any play. Garrick has altered this comedy, and, as uſual, for the worſe.

EPICŒNE; OR, THE SILENT WOMAN:

A Comedy, by Ben Johnſon.

ALL the characters of excellent comedy are to be found in this play. It is equally admirable in language, compo-

* Lord Mansfield being aſked his opinion of the ſtyle of this celebrated writer, replied, "It is abominable." Perhaps the reader may not be diſpleaſed with a ſhort anecdote of Mr. G. A friend having aſked him how, in caſe one ſhould happen to be d—d, it would be poſſible to ſupport the eternity of hell-torments; "I do "not know," replied the hiſtorian, "but of this I am certain that "none of our divines has yet been able to contrive a TOLERABLE "Paradiſe." The converſation was in French, but the tranſlation is literal.

ſition, wit, and judgment. Dryden beſtows high encomiums upon it, and prefers it to all the Engliſh comedies in his time; and I believe it is ſtill entitled to the ſame pre-eminence.

THE MOCK DOCTOR; OR, THE DUMB LADY CURED:

A Comedy.

THIS is a tolerable tranſlation from Moliere. The pleaſant naviete of the original is not fully preſerved, and in ſome paſſages a low indecent humour is introduced, to ſuit the taſte of a London audience. The ſongs are wretchedly in the modern London taſte; and not a tranſlation.

THE MISER:

A Comedy, by Fielding.

THIS is alſo a tranſlation from Moliere, and executed in a better taſte, and in more conformity to the original than the former. But the affected Coquette, the pert Chambermaid, and the Footman, are partly moulded into characters of modern Engliſh comedy, and ſuit ill with the maſterly ſimplicity of the reſt, though they ſerve to make the play more current and entertaining on a London theatre.

THE TWIN RIVALS:

A Comedy, by Farquhar.

POPE ſays juſtly,

"What pert low dialogue has Farquhar writ."

Though his humour is often low, and what is much worſe, often indecent, yet he had talents for writing comedy. He copies well from low life. His characters are natural, maintained with uniformity, and well diſtinguiſhed. But his higher characters are affected. His plots are amuſing, but commonly deficient in judgment and regularity; and upon the whole, his plays will always be entertaining on the ſtage, though they will not ſtand without cenſure, a trial of taſte and juſt criticiſm in the cloſet.

THE PROVOKED HUSBAND:

A Comedy, by Vanburgh, and Cibber.

I THINK this is the very beſt of our modern comedies. * The characters, both high and low, are formed from real life, finely diſtinguiſhed, and exactly maintained. The ſerious converſations are elegant, yet natural. The comical part is, in a high degree, entertaining, without indecency. The plot is intereſting, and the cataſtrophe is juſt, for merit and virtue are encouraged and rewarded; vice and folly are chaſtiſed, and expoſed to contempt.

THE RECRUITING OFFICER:

A Comedy, by Farquhar.

[*Vide* Remark on The Twin Rivals.]

THE WAY OF THE WORLD:

A Comedy.

CONGREVE writes with the greateſt purity of language, and all the charms of wit. But we muſt be told, in the courſe of the dialogue, who are intended for wits, and who for fools, otherwiſe we could hardly diſtinguiſh them, they all ſpeak ſo wittily. Indeed, the author utters his own wit and language in every character, with little diſtinction. His plots and cataſtrophies are generally perplexed and improbable. Though the language is pure and proper, yet I cannot help thinking, that it is often too ſtudied, and even affected, either for natural converſation, "Such as men do uſe," † or for the true dramatic dialogue. The characters are, however, well diſtinguiſhed, for the moſt part properly maintained, and the true ſpirit of comedy prevails in many of his ſcenes.

* The word MODERN is here applied to comedies written ſince the Reſtoration. This explanation appears neceſſary to make the preſent article conſiſtent with the encomium beſtowed on "The Silent Woman."

† BEN JOHNSON.

THE GENTLE SHEPHERD:

A Scots Paſtoral Comedy, by Allan Ramſay.

THIS excellent piece does honour to North Britain. There is no paſtoral, in the Engliſh language, comparable to it, and I believe there is none in any language ſuperior to it.

THE FAIR PENITENT:

A Tragedy by Rowe.

THIS author has the merit of ſentiment, delicacy, and powers, to touch the unthinking tender paſſions; but Shakeſpeare is my model of dramatic excellence, and the compariſon diminiſhes Rowe. He is toó romantic in his plots. There is a flowing ſameneſs of language in all his characters, and he pours out a profuſion of poetical words, without any meaſure of Shakeſpeare's nervous ſtrength, and ſententious meaning. I do not think this play, either bad, or good enough, ſor particular criticiſm.

THE PLAIN DEALER:

A Comedy by Wycherly.

THIS play, has a good deal of pleaſant wit, and ſevere ſatire. The characters are well diſtinguiſhed and preſerved, and the plot is leſs perplexed than in the bulk of modern comedies. A wretched attempt was lately made to alter this play, that is to mar it in the faſhionable way, to adapt it to the preſent taſte. Perhaps it ſucceded, and had a run at London; I am not informed, but I think it probable, as it vulgarized a play of uncommon ſpirit ſo very remarkably.

ROMEO AND JULIET:

A Tragedy.

THE fancy, delicacy, and love, in this play, the inimitable production of Shakeſpeare's genius, are, in my opinion, bloted by the alterations and additions. I can allow the propriety of retrenching ſome of his ſcenes, but I do not think it poſſible to add, or alter, in the productions of ſo ſingular and ſuperior a genius, without apparent incongruity, and abſurdity, though a London audience cannot perceive it. The very attitude of the prints ſhews a prevailing ill taſte; they are theatrical and affected, unlike Shakeſpeare and Nature. The original concluſion of this play might be retrenched; but as it ſtands, will be eſteemed by true judges, as infinitely ſuperior in poetry, judgment, and force, to the modern alteration. It ends with a melancholy, yet pleaſing reconcilement of the two familes: and with theſe two ſimple, natural, and tender lines,

" For never was a ſtory of more woe,
" Than this of Juliet and her Romeo."

which the reader of taſte may compare to the ſtiff unmeaning modern ones.

" Well may you mourn, my Lords, now wiſe too late;
" Theſe tragic iſſues of your mutual hate.
" From private feuds, what dire misfortunes flow;
" Whate'er the cauſe, the ſure effect is WOE.

CORIOLANUS:

A Tragedy, by Shakeſpeare.

JUDICIOUS readers will find much more of Shakeſpeare's merit, and peculiar genius in this piece, than our critics allow. On the whole, I think the managers and critics diſcover a remarkable defect of true taſte and judgment in the modelling of this play; which, from Shakeſpeare's precious materials, might eaſily be formed into one of the moſt pleaſing and perfect entertainments on the Britiſh ſtage. I muſt often repeat, that in modelling Shakeſpeare's plays for acting, judicious retrenchment, and ſometimes an alteration in the arrangement of ſcenes, may be allowed, but not a word to be altered or added. I have an opinion, almoſt to devotion, of his peculiar and extraordinary genius, and can hardly forbear application of a ſcriptural anathema to ſuch innovators.* The conduct of Coriolanus, rightly judged, was neither baſe nor treacherous. It was noble. Though induced by the entreaties, and indeed by the irreſiſtible perſuaſions of his excellent mother, he ſaved the ungrateful Romans, yet he made a prudent and advantageous peace for the Volſcians. Conſcious of innocence, he deſerted not their ſervice, but returned with their army, and in open ſenate, with his uſual magnanimity, maintained his defence, and was ſacrificed, not to the juſtice of the ſtate, but to the jealouſy of his ambitious rival. Shakeſpeare has moſt forcibly and judiciouſly introduced his juſtification, in his mother's admirable ſpeech, which apparently convinced Aufidius himſelf. She ſays,

" Thou know'ſt, great ſon, the end of war's uncertain.
" If it were ſo that our requeſt did tend
" To ſave the Romans, thereby to deſtroy
" The Volſcians, whom you ſerve, you might condemn us,
" As poiſoners of your honour; no, our ſuit,
" Is, that you reconcile them; that each, on either ſide,
" Give all hail unto thee, and cry be *bleſt*
" For *making up the peace.*"

In this fair view, the Coriolanus of hiſtory, and of Shakeſpeare, is a great ancient character, miſunderſtood by our puny modern critics.

KING HENRY VIII.

A Tragedy, by Shakeſpeare.

The critical introduction to this play is proper, juſt, and ſufficient; a ſingular caſe! There is a curious and excellent original prologue to this play, which, with other

* For I teſtify unto every man that heareth the words of the prophecy of this book, If any man ſhall add unto theſe things, God ſhall add unto him the plagues that are written in this book. And if any man ſhall take away from the words of the book of this prophecy, God ſhall take away his part out of the book of life, and out of the holy city, and from the things which are written in this book, Rev. xxii. 18. 19.

invaluable parts of Shakeſpeare, is in danger of being loſt, by the fault of modern editors and emendators, who have moſt abominably ſuppreſſed and altered his works. I wiſh that his juſt admirers, who will certainly join with me in condemning the bulk of his critics, and all his emendators, would alſo concur with me in obtaining a new publication of the oldeſt edition, without any criticiſm or commentary whatever; otherwiſe there is a ſerious danger that great part of the original may be totally loſt, and the reſt confounded and corrupted by modern alterations and additions. Among other fooliſh topics agitated by ſome of Shakeſpeare's critics, they make a queſtion if he was a Proteſtant. There are many proofs that he was; and one line of the Biſhop's admirable prophetic ſpeech, in this play, is deciſive on the point, viz.

" God ſhall be truly known, &c. *

THE FIRST PART OF HENRY IV.

SHAKESPEARE's genius tramples upon and tranſcends at once, all the rules of criticiſm, and the dull ſolemnity of

* After all, it ſeems extremely doubtful, whether Shakeſpeare was a Proteſtant, or any thing elſe; for the ghoſt in Hamlet is a zealous Roman Catholic. The following ſentence, in the Twelfth Night, may help to explain his ſentiments on religion. " If you " defy † the ſpleen, and will laugh yourſelves into ſtitches, fol- " low me; yond gull Malvolio is turned Heathen, a very rene- " gado; *for there is no Chriſtian, that means to be ſav'd by believ-* " *ing rightly, can ever believe ſuch impoſſible paſſages of groſſneſs.*" On another part, in the ſame play, Dr Johnſon obſerves, that, " It were much to be wiſhed, that Shakeſpeare, in this, and " ſome other paſſages, had not ventured ſo near profaneneſs." In the concluſion of the following extract, the author ſeems to hint his doubts on the nature of a future ſtate.

" Ay, but to die, and go we know not where;
" To lie in cold obſtruction, and to rot;
" This ſenſible warm motion to become
" A kneaded clod.

† Our Critic has here, for once, ventured to correct Shakeſpeare, and with evident propriety. *Deſire* is the common reading.—Note by the Editor.

critics, in this admirable play. Too much of the original is suppreſſed. But this commendation is due to our ſtage-reformers, that none of them have dared to alter a word, or to add a word, in the parts of the Henrys and Falſtaff. What Dryden, playing on the word, ſays, of the Church of England, may be applied here,

"And leſs deform'd, becauſe *re*form'd the leaſt."

THE DRUMMER:

A Comedy, by Addiſon.

I INTEND to have this piece taken into a volume of bad plays by good authors, in which Sir Richard Steele's Tender Huſband ſhould have a place, if I can find it.

THE SECOND PART OF HENRY IV.

THE capital characters are preſerved with amazing ſpirit and uniformity in this Second Part, though it pleaſes not the critics, and the million, ſo well as the Firſt.

The ſtage managers have taken monſtrous liberties with this play, and have ſuppreſſed whole ſcenes, ſome of them in the higheſt ſtyle of Shakeſpeare's excellence. For this infamous depredation, the lovers of Shakeſpeare can only be indemnified, by reſorting to the original. For one example, the firſt ſcene may be ranked with the higheſt and beſt of Shakeſpeare's writings, yet is totally ſuppreſſed in this play, though it has been almoſt wholly introduced by Colley Cibber, into different places of what he called his Richard the Third.

THE TEMPEST:

A Comedy.

THIS play is one of the wonders of Shakeſpeare's genius. He flies into the regions of romance, and imagination, and yet forms characters and ſcenes that ſeem natural and credible.

THE ALCHYMIST:

A Comedy, by Ben Johnson.

The alterations and additions in this play, were framed by Garrick, to make his London audience laugh, and so are good for nothing.

THE CHANCES:

A Comedy.

This is the only old play which has been altered to advantage; because it is the only one altered by a man of true taste and genius. This was Buckingham. I hardly know a more amusing play for the stage, or the closet. Here is no constrained improbable plot, no modern studied language and affected wit; but comical adventure, easy conversation, natural humour, and true character, such as comedy ought to be, and rarely is.

THE SPANISH FRIAR:

A Tragi-Comedy, by Dryden.

Dryden had many excellencies, and many faults. His dramatic pieces are generally bombast in the poetry, and absurd in the plots, and were justly the main butt of Buckingham's wit in his excellent play, The Rehearsal. Of his numerous pieces, the present is the only one which can be produced as a proper entertainment on the stage. His other works entitle him to a high rank among our poets. His prose writings have merit, though his dedications are fulsome and servile.

EVERY MAN IN HIS HUMOUR:

A Comedy, by Ben Johnson.

This is an admirable comedy, though it is rather defective in plot. The scenes are highly entertaining, and the characters are drawn and maintained with the finest strokes of nature, humour, and sense. Garrick's prologue is very good, but I cannot commend his alterations in the play. They are miserably distinguishable from the original, but good enough to please the bulk of his audience.

No word of Johnſon or Shakeſpeare can be changed, but for a worſe.

I doubt if ever Garrick wrote any thing ſo well as the prologue to this play, which indeed is admirable.

KING HENRY V.

A Tragedy, by Aaron Hill.

With what a diſgraceful motely of nonſenſe and abſurdity has the modern poet confounded the beauties of Shakeſpeare in this play.

As a ſpecimen of modern emendation, it may be worth while to compare the ancient and modern prologues.

PROLOGUE

BY SHAKESPEARE.

O FOR a muſe of fire that would aſcend
The brighteſt heaven of invention!
A kingdom for a ſtage, princes to act;
And monarchs to behold the ſwelling ſcene!
Then ſhould the warlike Harry, like himſelf,
Aſſume the port of Mars; and at his heels,
Leaſht in, like hounds, ſhould famine, ſword, and fire
Crouch for employment. But pardon, Gentles all,
The flat unraiſed ſpirit that hath dar'd,
On this unworthy ſcaffold, to bring forth
So great an object. Can this cock-pit hold
The vaſty field of France? or may we cram,
Within this wooden O, the very caſkes
That did affright the air at Agincourt?
O, pardon; ſince a crooked figure may
Atteſt, in little ſpace a million;
And let us cyphers to this great accompt,
On your imaginary forces work.
Suppoſe within the girdle of theſe walls
Are, now confin'd two mighty monarchies,
Whoſe high up-reared and abutting fronts

The perilous narrow ocean parts asunder.
Piece out our imperfection with your thoughts,
Into a thousand parts divide one man,
And make imaginary puisance.
Think when we talk of horses, that you see them
Printing their proud hoofs i' th' receiving earth:
For 'tis your thoughts that now must deck our Kings,
Carry them here and there, jumping o'er times,
Turning the accomplishments of many years
Into an hour-glass; for the which supply,
Admit me Chorus to this history;
Who, prologue-like, your humble patience pray,
Gently to hear, kindly to judge, our play.

PROLOGUE

BY AARON HILL.

FROM wit's old ruins, *shadow'd o'er with bays*,
We draw some rich remains of Shakespeare's praise.
Shakespeare!—the sound bids charm'd attention wake:
And our aw'd scenes, with conscious rev'rence, *shake!*
Arduous the task, to mix with Shakespeare's Muse!
Rash game! where all, who play, are sure to lose.
Yet—what our author cou'd, he dar'd to try,
And kept the fiery pillar in his eye.
Led by such light, as wou'd not *let* him *stray*,
He pick'd out *stars*, from Shakespeare's *milky way*.
Hid, in the cloud of battle, Shakespeare's care,
Blind with the dust of war o'er look'd the fair:
Fond of their fame, we shew their influence, here,
And place 'em *twinkling* through war's smoaky sphere.
Without their aid, we lose love's quick'ning charms;
And sullen virtue *mopes*, in *steril arms*.
Now, rightly mix'd, the enliven'd passions move,
Love softens war,—and war invig'rates love.
Oh!—cry'd that towr'ing genius of the stage,
When, first, his Henry charm'd a former age,
" Oh! for a Muse of fire, *our cause to friend*,
" That might invention's brightest heav'n ascend!

"That, for a ſtage, a *kingdom might be ſeen!*
"Princes, to act, *grac'd with their native mein:*
"And monarchs, to behold the ſwelling ſcene!
"Then, like himſelf, ſhou'd warlike Harry riſe:
"And, *fir'd with all his fame, blaze in your eyes!*
"Crouch'd, at his heels, and like fierce hounds, leaſh'd in,
"Sword, fire, and famine, *with impatient grin!*
"Shou'd, fawning dreadful! but for orders, ſtay,
"And, at his nod,—*ſtart horrible! away.*"
No barren tale t' amuſe, our ſcene imparts,
But points example at your kindling hearts.
Mark in their Dauphin, to our King oppos'd,
The diff'rent genius of the realms diſclos'd:
There, the French levity,—vain,—boaſtful,—loud,
Dancing, in death,—gay,—wanton,—fierce,—and proud.
Here, with a ſilent fire, a temper'd heat!
Calmly reſolv'd, our Engliſh boſoms beat.
Art is too poor, to raiſe the dead 'tis true,
But nature does it, by their worth, in you!
Your blood, that warm'd their veins, ſtill flows, the ſame,
Still feels your valour and ſupports their fame.

Oh! let it waſte no more, in civil jar:
But flow, for glorious ſame, in foreign war.

MEASURE FOR MEASURE.

There are ſome very high ſtrokes of genius in this play, which, upon the whole, is admirable, and bears all the uſual marks of the writer's ſuperiority over our other dramatic poets.

The additional lines, ſo much approved of by our critics, are truly modern, and ſufficiently diſtinguiſh themſelves from the original text. To intimate the Duke's kind purpoſe to Iſabella, Shakeſpeare ſaid juſt enough in one ſignificant line, which is only ſpun out, in the five finical modern ones, for no other reaſon but that the fag end of the act may have a rhyme to jingle at it, to pleaſe a London audience. The conduct of the cataſtrophe, in ſpite of our moſt wretched critic's cenſure, is admirably judicious, intereſting, and entertaining.

THE INDIAN EMPEROR:

A Tragedy, by Dryden.

[*From what is called a Select Collection of Plays, in three volumes, by Mr Donaldſon, Bookſeller, Edinburgh.*]

As bookſellers, are in general, the dulleſt of mankind, there can be no wonder that their Select Collections are very ill choſen. One of our poets gives a pleaſant enough reaſon for this character of bookſellers—

" Unlearned men, of books aſſume the care,
" As eunuchs are the guardians of the fair.

The ill taſte of London has been gratified with great variety; it is hard to ſay when it was at the worſt. Heroic plays, as they were called, were long in vogue, till exploded by The Rehearſal. A new train of dramatic writings ſucceeded, without the genius, and with all the abſurdities of Dryden. Vide Buſiris, Zara, Mahomet, Barbaroſſa, The Chriſtian Hero, &c. &c. A new Rehearſal is much wanted.

ALL FOR LOVE:

A Tragedy.

In this elaborate play, Dryden imitates Shakeſpeare; and, by that imitation, excells himſelf, though ſtill he is far ſhort of the judgment, genius, and happy expreſſion of that great maſter. How wretched our modern prologues and epilogues, compared to thoſe of Dryden? How wretched Dryden's plays, compared to thoſe of the older poets? but the taſte of every age ſeems to be happily ſuited to the talents of its cotemporary bards. We have been charmed with the quaint prologues and epilogues of Garrick; and we are daily pleaſed with the flat laboured productions of our nameleſs dramatic poets.

THEODOSIUS; OR, THE FORCE OF LOVE:

A Tragedy, by Lee.

A RAPTUROUS romantic play; it pleaſes men, women, and children, who have not formed their taſte upon the ſenſe and genius of Shakeſpeare, but on modern novels and plays.

OROONOKO:

A Tragedy, by Southerne.

THIS is the only good play in the Bookſeller's Select Collection.

MAHOMET THE IMPOSTOR:

A Tragedy, from Voltaire.

THIS Collection is wretched, but ſuited to the taſte of thoſe gentlemen called Bookſellers. I give it a place in my collection only as a patch to Shakeſpeare, and a monument, may it be ſhort lived, of bad taſte. From this hard cenſure, I mean to except the Siege of Damaſcus. It has ſome merit; and there is indulgence enough in this admiſſion; perhaps the beſt critics may blame it. But I proceed to the merits of the play in queſtion. Monſieur Voltaire could not abide Shakeſpeare, which is not ſurpriſing. They were moſt perfect oppoſites, as a man of profound abilities and wiſdom, is oppoſite to a pleaſant ſuperficial fop. A total want of genius, and even of taſte and propriety for tragic compoſition, is remarkable in every line of this piece, at leaſt in the Engliſh play; yet it has a great run at London. The general admiration of this, and many other dramatic pieces of the ſame caſt, affords full proof that we are degenerate and ſtupid. Douglas, the ſingle good tragedy of this age, was at firſt rejected at London. Mahomet, Barbaroſſa, *&c. &c.* live and flouriſh there.

THE SIEGE OF DAMASCUS:

A Tragedy, by Hughes.

THE epilogue, ſpoken by Mr. Wilks, is ſilly, and very like thoſe in vogue at preſent. The prologue, ſpoken by Lord Sandwich, is ſinely poetical, and worthy of the occaſion, and the actors.

The play, indeed, is fitter for ſuch occaſional performance, than common exhibition on the public theatre, having various beauties, and great imperfections.

THE CHRISTIAN HERO:

A Tragedy, by Lillo.

THE compoſition of this play is as full of dulneſs and abſurdity as Mahomet, and leſs intereſting in the plot.

LADY JANE GRAY:

A Tragedy, by Rowe.

I CANNOT read an hiſtorical play, without thinking of a compariſon with Shakeſpeare, by whom the characters of nature are perfectly preſerved, and yet raiſed above the pitch of nature, by the force of a great and inimitable genius.

DON SEBASTIAN KING OF PORTUGAL:

A Tragedy, by Dryden.

THIS play is full of abſurdities and unnatural flights; yet we may diſtinguiſh them as the abſurdities of a poet and a man of genius, unlike the nonſenſe of the moderns. The moral is rigorous indeed.

JANE SHORE:

A Tragedy, by Rowe.

How ſtrangely different is the Glouceſter of Shakeſpeare from the Glouceſter of Rowe. An audience of true judgment and taſte, could not bear this compariſon on the ſame theatre.

MUCH ADO ABOUT NOTHING:

A Comedy.

THERE is not, on the Britiſh theatre, a more entertaining play than this; and I always thought that Benedict was Garrick's maſterpiece, but groſsly injured by his alterations. The curious and judicious reader, who has a true taſte for Shakeſpeare's genuine works, will be in ſome meaſure amuſed, but ſtill more offended, with the modern alterations and additions which I have pretty exactly traced out on the margin of the text.* The reader will, with me, abhor the ſtage-managers, who have vilely perverted, and never once reformed, or improved, our divine author.

In Act IV. Scene 3. Beatrice, Speaking of Claudio's treachery cries out——

Beat. "Is he not approved in the height a villain, that hath ſlander'd, ſcorn'd, diſhonoured my kinſwoman! O, that I were a man! what! bear her in hand until they come to take hands, and then with public accuſation, uncover'd ſlander, unmitigated rancour—O God, that I were a man! I would eat his heart in the market-place.

Bene. Hear me, Beatrice.

Beat. Talk with a man out at a window?—a proper ſaying!

Bene. Nay, but Beatrice.

Beat. Sweet Hero! ſhe is wronged, ſhe is ſlandered, ſhe is undone.

Bene. Beat——

Beat. Princes and Counts! ſurely a princely teſtimony, a goodly count-comfect, a ſweet gallant, ſurely! O that I were a man for his ſake! or that I had any friend would be a man for my ſake!" *&c.*

* Vide *Preface.*

Here the judicious editor, inſtead of ſeeing the beauty of the break in the name of Beatrice, has altered it for that eloquent monyſyllable BUT.* By this ſample you may judge of the havock made among Shakeſpeare's other plays, and in your own library, preſerve the original author. I look on it as one evidence of degeneracy in ſenſe and good taſte, that theſe deteſtable alterations have been ſuffered, and are ſtill allowed on the ſtage. A judicious critic, yet to come, may retrench ſome parts of Shakeſpeare. The greatneſs and force of his imagination ſometimes fly into obſcurity, perhaps from defect of our ſight. But it is impoſſible both to alter and amend him. There is, in page 34th of this play, a curious alteration of the text, where the critic makes the Clown laugh moſt improperly. *Vide* Shakeſpeare's advice to players in Hamlet—"Let thoſe "that play the Clown, ſpeak no more than is *ſet down* "for them. For there be of them that will themſelves "*laugh*, to ſet on *ſome quantity of barren ſpectators* to "laugh too; though, in the mean time, ſome neceſſary "queſtion of the play be then to be conſidered. That's "villainous, and ſhews a moſt pitiful ambition in the fool "that uſes it."

THE COUNTRY WIFE:

A Comedy, by Wycherly.

THERE are wit, humour, eaſy and lively converſation, variety of character, and pleaſing adventure in this play; but there is a very unpardonable want of delicacy and decency. A lewd young fellow gains full credit to a report, that he had, by a faſhionable misfortune, loſt his virility. By this means, he cuckolds all the huſbands, and lies with all the women of the drama. There are, however, weak ſcenes in the play, improbabilities and, I think the characters both of Pinchwife and Sparkiſh are outre.

* *Vide* Bell's edition, printed in 1774, Vol. II. p. 366, "regu-"lated from the prompt books" of the two Theatres Royal in London.

To make a dance of cuckolds at the end of this play, is a judicious conduct in the author, but a shameless exhibition on a public theatre.

THE CITY WIVES; OR THE CONFEDERACY:

A Comedy, by Vanburgh.

This is one of those plays which throw infamy upon the London stage, and general taste, though it is not destitute of wit and humour. A people must be in the last degree depraved, among whom such public entertainments are produced and encouraged. In this symptom of degenerate manners, we are, I believe, unmatched by any nation that is, or ever was, in the world. There is one good line in the epilogue; but neither judgment nor moral in the play, though there are strokes of wit, and some detached scenes of humour in it.

THE SUSPICIOUS HUSBAND:

A Comedy, by Hoadly.

It is well that I am only a private critic, otherwise I could hardly avoid being torn to pieces for many offences; and, among the rest, for avowing no great admiration of this play. Perhaps, even in the small circle of readers, who may chance to meet with, and chuse to read my odd, irregular remarks, some few may not materially differ from my opinions. But as I have broke all terms of peace with the many, I desire to keep in my lurking-place, and fairly out of their sight. I have always thought that this favourite play is not founded on a real knowledge of life and manners, but upon a motely imitation of characters and incidents in other plays. Benedict, Don John, and Captain Plume, are the models of Ranger. Strickland is but an ill copy of Kitely. Meggot is a collective imitation of Marplot, Captain Brazen, Wittol, and other dramatic good natured half wits. The rest of the characters are undistinguishable, and serve only to fill up a great part of the drama; for the whole diversion lies in Ranger. Till he appears, the audience yawn. Clariſſa is Marianna, ill drawn, from Fielding's Miſer. But, though I am clear that this play cannot be juſtly eſteemed as an original piece, it has the merit of better imitation than ordinary, in our later comedy; and when the parts of Ranger and Clariſſa are well acted, it is a good entertainment on the ſtage; yet ſtill it is a poor one, at beſt, in the cloſet. And when examined with more attention and judgment than is, or ought to be employed by ſpectators, it will be found that there are only two good ſcenes in it.

THE CAPRICIOUS LADY:

A Comedy.

ALTERED FROM BEAUMONT AND FLETCHER.

Whatever in this play is lively, proper, and characteriſtic, belongs to the ancient poet. The modern part of it is motely, conſtrained, and deviates from nature moſt widely; yet it is not inferior to ſome other modern alterations of good old plays. Indeed the original, though it contains ſome excellent ſcenes, is not of a piece, and is not, on the whole, one of the beſt of Beaumont's and Fletcher's comedies. I ſuppoſe this play had a great run, and high applauſe, at Covent Garden.

THE HISTORY AND FALL OF CAIUS MARIUS:

A Tragedy, by Otway.

When I read this and other plays in which Shakeſpeare's writings are partly introduced, I always reflect on a beautiful paſſage in his Richard the Second, which Dryden has juſtly celebrated in one of his Prefaces.

" As on a theatre, the eyes of men,
" After a well grac'd actor leaves the ſtage,
" Are idly bent on him that follows next,
" Thinking his prattle to be tedious;
" Even ſo, or with much more contempt," &c.

This diſtinction is handſomely confeſſed in the prologue to Otway's play.

" Like greedy beggars that ſteal ſheaves away,
" You'll find he's rifled him of half a play.
" Amidſt his baſer droſs you'll ſee it ſhine,
" Moſt beautiful, amazing, and divine!"

THE FAIR QUAKER OF DEAL:

A Comedy.

THE ſea characters are well drawn and preſerved; there are ſome ſcenes of humour and natural converſation, but the two laſt acts fall off. The plot is neither well invented, well wrought up, nor intereſting.

SHE WOU'D AND SHE WOU'D NOT:

A Comedy, by Cibber.

THESE modern plays have ſome merit, and afford entertainment when well acted on the ſtage, but are liable to many exceptions, and juſt criticiſm, when cooly conſidered in the cloſet.

ULYSSES:

A Tragedy, by Rowe.

THE genius of Shakeſpeare formed natural characters, and converſation, and probable entertaining plots, dignified above common life, by the power of true poetry. This author has ventured to imitate his manner, but very unſucceſsfully. Though there are ſome happy ſtrains of poetry intermixed, yet, in general, the circumſtances of the plot are romantic and unintereſting. The converſation is laboured in one uniform ſtyle; and the characters, like the compoſition in modern drama, ſtudied and artificial.

XIMENA; OR, THE HEROIC DAUGHTER.

A Tragedy, by Cibber.

THIS play is below criticiſm.

BUSIRIS KING OF EGYPT:

A Tragedy, by Young.

THIS, I do think, is the moſt abſurd and ridiculous *Tragedy* in the whole of Monſieur Bell's Collection of the *beſt* Engliſh Plays; and it is written by the *great* (as they call him) Doctor Young. It is, however, hardly more eminently extravagant and outre, than another Tragedy, much admired by the many, and written by the ſame author, *viz. The Revenge.** What an audience! that failed to damn that play at the firſt hearing. Yet it lives to this day, at the diſtance of half a century, in Bell's Collection of Choice Engliſh Plays. And we are told, is yet acted with applauſe on the London ſtage. The epilogue has ſome merit.

AMPHITRYON; OR, THE TWO SOSIAS:

A Comedy,

ALTERED FROM DRYDEN,

BY HAWKESWORTH.

THIS I ſhall have bound up with Addiſon's Drummer, as a bad play by a good author; with allowance, in this caſe, that the modern reformer has made it worſe. †

* To this liſt, may be added THE BROTHERS. In one ſcene Dr. Y. introduces Perſeus imitating a paſſage in Macbeth; but the imitation is attended with ſome very ridiculous circumſtances.

† If Hawkeſworth falls behind Dryden, the latter is at leaſt as much inferior to Plautus. In the original Latin, there is a long and very pleaſing prologue, and the deſcription of a battle, in the very firſt ſcene of the play, has little to fear by a compariſon with Epic Poetry. Of Plautus, a tranſlation in five large octavo volumes, has been publiſhed, under the name of the late Mr. Bonnel Thornton, and another Gentleman. Had their book retained the Latin text, it muſt have been of value. The pretended verſion is in blank verſe, and intolerable.

EURYDICE:

A Tragedy, by Mallet.

Artificial poetry, laboured language, and romantic love are too remote from nature and Shakeſpeare to pleaſe me; yet they commonly gain a temporary applauſe from the fond many, and uninformed ignorance continues to admire. The epilogue was no doubt received with great applauſe.

" We are ſuch ſtuff
" As dreams are made of."———

THE MERRY WIVES OF WINDSOR:

A Comedy.

If there was nothing in Falſtaff's character, as our critics deſcribe it, but " rodomontades, lies, and jollity," Queen Elizabeth would never have deſired a continuation of it. But her judgment diſcerned higher qualities in it, a great meaſure of ſhrewd ſenſe, and incomparable humour. A continuation of the ſame identical character in this play, without flattening in the leaſt, is an amazing proof of the ſtrength of Shakeſpeare's genius.

AURENG-ZEBE:

A Tragedy, by Dryden.

This is by far the beſt rhyming play in the Engliſh language; yet though it has beauties, it has many abſurdities.* I give great credit to Dryden for the elegant en-

* Such as the following couplet:

" Dara, the eldeſt, bears a *Gen'rous* mind,
" But to implacable revenge *Inclin'd.*"

The lines that follow are worthy of a place in the ſublimeſt page of Lucretius or Juvenal.

" When I conſider life, 'tis all a cheat;
" Yet fool'd with hope, men favour the deceit;
" Truſt on, and think to-morrow will repay;
" To-morrow's falſer than the former day,
" Lies worſe; and while it ſays we ſhall be bleſt
" With ſome new joys, cuts off what we poſſeſt.

eomium upon Shakeſpeare, and his full confeſſion of great inferiority in his own dramatic talents.

The lines which I refer to, are in the prologue, and ſeem to me ſo juſt and beautiful, that I ſhall take leave to inſert them.

"But ſpite of all his pride, a ſecret ſhame
"Invades his breaſt at Shakeſpeare's ſacred name:
"Aw'd when he hears his godlike Romans rage,
"He, in a juſt deſpair would quit the ſtage;
"And to an age leſs poliſh'd, more unſkill'd,
"Does, with diſdain, the foremoſt honours yield.
"As with the greater dead, he dares not ſtrive,
"He would not match his verſe with thoſe who live;
"Let him retire, between two ages caſt,
"The firſt of this, and hindmoſt of the laſt."

The poetry is fine, eaſy, and agreeable, but there is ſomething abſurd, romantic, and fantaſtical, in a great part of the love, that is to ſay, in a great part of the play. Shakeſpeare never thought of love in this extravagant faſhion.

"Strange cozenage! none would live paſt years again,
"Yet all hope pleaſure in what yet remain;
"And from the dregs of life think to rceeive
"What the firſt ſprightly running could not give.
"I'm tir'd with waiting for this chymic gold,
"Which fools us young, and beggars us when old."

It is a pity that Dryden could not have ſeen the third volume of Colonel Dow's work, as that volume is, perhaps, the moſt pathetic and intereſting hiſtorical compoſition now extant. The fate of this very Dara, is, in particular, irreſiſtibly affecting. There is another book, intitled, Memoirs of Eradut Khan, tranſlated by Captain Jonathan Scott, and printed in 1786, which contains an account of the laſt year of the reign of Aureng-Zebe. Some letters written by that great monarch, a ſhort time before his death, are inſerted, and contain a humiliating leſſon to the maſters of mankind. Theſe works have not acquired the attention they deſerve; and Mr. Gibbon has gone out of his way, to ſneer at Colonel Dow. But if Mr. Dryden had ever ſeen either of them, he would at once have diſcovered the richeſt materials for tragic poetry.

ISABELLA; OR, THE FATAL MARRIAGE:

A Tragedy, altered from Southerne, by Hopkins.

ALL, or great part that is original of this play, is admirable. The fable is ſimple, probable, and very intereſting. The language is pure and proper, the characters well diſtinguiſhed and maintained, and the poetry is in ſome paſſages delightful. I ſee no modern quaintneſs, affectation, raving, or bombaſt; but there are ſo many laboured abſurdities in the laſt act, that I ſuſpect the modern managers have tampered with it.

CREUSA, QUEEN OF ATHENS:

A Tragedy, by William Whitehead, Eſq.

THERE is ſomething very ſingular in this play. The poetry is good, the language is pure and proper. There are in it no extravagant unnatural flights, no romantic love, no modern bombaſt. I can hardly find fault with any particular part of it, yet I cannot much applaud the whole.

PLAYS WRITTEN FOR A PRIVATE THEATRE:

By William Davies.

NEWS; THE MALADY:

A Comedy, in three Acts.

THE MODE:

A Comedy, in Five Acts.

THE GENEROUS COUNTERFEIT:

A Comedy, in Five Acts.

BETTER LATE THAN NEVER:

A Comedy, in Five Acts.

THE MAN OF HONOUR:

A Comedy, in Five Acts.

I HAVE ſome favour for this author, on account of his good intentions to reform a taſteleſs age, and entertain us with ſpecimens of genuine comedy. I read on, till my patience failed, and till I was quite convinced of his inability to ſurpaſs other modern dramatic writers. He talks of Moliere as a pattern of excellence, without any meaſure of his happy genius. He damns, and juſtly, our modern dramatic writers, without diſcovering ſuperior talents. In place of a pleaſant and eaſy imitation, he falls, like other modern comic writers, into a ſtudied affectation of nature. He is as fantaſtical in his inſtructions to the players, as either Mr. Bayes, or General Burgoyne.* Where he means to be either witty or pathetic, he is utterly inſipid; and particularly in the abſurdity of invented names to his Dramatis Perſonæ, he outdoes even our modern farce writers. Of this, I ſhould ſet down ſome inſtances for a monument, but indeed every one of them is remarkably fooliſh and affected. To do him juſtice, he has not much of the quaintneſs and outre which predominate, and paſs for wit and ſpirit in this age, and perhaps for that reaſon, he has failed in the ſavour of the managers of our public theatres. Travellers may find amuſement in a tranſient peruſal of his novelties.

THE GAMESTERS:

A Comedy, by Shirley.

THIS, upon the whole, is an exceellent comedy. Though the characters, in general, are looſe, there is no indecency

* This name ſounds ſtrangely for comedy, and it may be affirmed without, preſumption, that, in the beſt days of Britain, the performance of ſuch an author would hardly have been received on the Stage.

It is true that a *Cæſar* and a *Frederick* have condeſcended to write plays. But in them we vindicate ſuch vivacity as the exuberance of genius, the ſportive relaxation of a mind incapable of repoſe, and too vaſt to be compreſſed by the limits of a ſingle walk of excellence. When a field-officer performs his public duty better than any perſon elſe, the world has no pretence to cavil at the nature of his private amuſements. But when an individual has retired from the ſervice of his country, with the moſt unauſpicious circumſtances, and when, with invincible hardineſs, he once more thruſts himſelf into public notice, contempt muſt extinguiſh all reflections on his character.

in it. The plot is interesting, well wrought, and the catastrophe is highly moral. The dialogue is proper and unaffected. The characters are judiciously distinguished and supported. There is no forced wit, the bane of modern comedy and taste, and the humour is natural, characteristic, and entertaining. The evident falling off in some parts, I ascribe to modern alteration ; but I cannot exactly determine, till I have compared it with the original, which I am very curious and impatient to do. There is another play, a sort of tragedy nearly of the same title. Though it is very modern and miserably outre, it has I believe many admirers.

PHILASTER:

A Tragedy,

AS ALTERED FROM BEAUMONT AND FLETCHER,

BY WILD.

This, in so far as original, is a charming play, to be read over and over again. Sweet simplicity, and tender natural passion, distinguish it from the laboured affected strains of modern tragedy, though still far inferior to the force and genius of Shakespeare.

THE GUARDIAN:

By David Garrick, Esq.

[*From a Collection of the most Esteemed Farces.*]

How strangely different is this piece from the nature, sense, and humour of the old plays of Shakespeare, Johnson, Beaumont and Fletcher. I should score every line, and make the stuff illegible, if I took my usual method to mark by scoring, what I damn as insipid, flat, affected, or unnatural. It was received with rapture at London, and yet pleases on that stage.

THE APPRENTICE:

A Farce, by Arthur Murphy Esq.

Farce and mummery indeed ! It is not easy to conceive by what fascination of acting, this piece pleases any audience on earth; but outre is the taſte of the times. I can hardly think that Garrick had ſo little judgment, as to approve of this performance; but he knew, that with the help of his art, and the grimace of other actors, it would charm his audience, and " put money in his " pocket."

THE ANATOMIST; OR, SHAM DOCTOR:

By Edward Ravenſcroft, Eſq.

GRIMACE again, in place of good old ſenſe, and humourous nature. This too, is a favourite modern entertainment. The character of the French Doctor is natural, and ludicrous enough; the reſt is in the ſtudied, affected, low, modern taſte.

FLORIZEL AND PERDITA; OR, THE SHEEP-SHEARING:

A Dramatic Paſtoral.

SHAKESPEARE is here mangled as uſual; yet it ſhines in this Collection of modern Farces.

HIGH LIFE BELOW STAIRS:

By David Garrick, Eſq.

IT is quite inconceivable how this piece, flat and inſipid in peruſal, ſhould be ſo managed as to afford a run of entertainment on the ſtage. There is in it a juſt ſatire on the infamous licentiouſneſs of Engliſh ſervants, and a low kind of humour, moſtly affected, and wholly unnatural. The beſt part of the ſatire is levelled againſt high life, and is an awkward imitation of the incomparable Beggar's Opera.

TASTE:

By Samuel Foote, Eſq.

I VENTURE to aſſert, that this age has produced no genius for comic entertainment, but Foote alone. Yet even he is far ſhort of the ſterling humour, ſenſe, and happy expreſſion of the old poets. He was a diſſipated pleaſant fellow, and could not afford the pains or patience of forming a complete piece of regular comedy, if the Minor is not one. Yet his farces are amuſing on the ſtage, and in the cloſet.

THE UPHOLSTERER:

By Arthur Murphy, Eſq.

THE outre prevails in every character and ſcene, to pleaſe a London populace.

LETHE:

By David Garrick, Eſq.

THE ſcene which exhibits Lord Chalkſtone is good. The reſt are trivial, and quite in modern taſte.

THE DEUCE IS IN HIM:

By George Colman, Eſq.

THIS piece has uncommon merit. The plot is well fancied, and agreeably managed. The dialogue is natural and characteriſtic, without flatneſs, or that ſtudied compoſition of the poet, which appears, for the moſt part, in our modern comedy. I am agreeably ſurpriſed to find, in this very modern Collection, one piece on which I can beſtow ſuch commendation.

THE KNIGHTS.

THE plot is fooliſh enough, and the fooliſh characters are ludicrous and diverting enough, to pleaſe, very highly, a London audience.

THE SULTAN:

By Samuel Foote, Eſq.

ONE can ſay nothing of this, but, that it is nothing at all.

THE CHAPLET:

By Moſes Mendez, Eſq.

The Beggar's Opera is the only muſical entertainment of true genius in the Engliſh language, I mean of the comic ſort. The Comus of Milton is in a higher ſtyle. Whoever can read theſe pieces, or has ſeen them performed on the ſtage, and can bear with patience this, and all the reſt of our Engliſh operas,

"May juſtly be reckon'd an aſs."

I except our charming Scots paſtoral, the Gentle Shepherd, and deſpiſe all diſtinctions of South and North Britain; happy, and vain to think, that Shakeſpeare, Milton, *&c.* were my countrymen, in ſpite of ſhallow partial pride.

MISS IN HER TEENS:

By David Garrick, Eſq.

Though the characters are affected as uſual, it requires a good deal of artful grimace and foolery in the actors to make this thing ſo laughable, as it commonly is, upon the ſtage. Hardly any of our modern dramatic poets have the cloſer capacity to obſerve Shakeſpeare's divine leſſon. "O'erſtep not the modeſty of nature, for any thing ſo "*overdone*, is from the purpoſe of plays, whoſe end both "at the firſt, and now, was, and is, *to bold*, as it were, "the mirror up to nature, to ſhew virtue her own fea- "ture, ſcorn her own image, and the very age and body "of the time, its form and preſſure. Now, this *over- "done*, or come *tardy off*, though it make the unſkilful "laugh, cannot but make the judicious grieve; the cen- "ſure of which one muſt overſway a whole theatre of "others. Oh! I have ſeen plays, and heard them praiſ- "ed, and that highly, which imitated humanity abomi- "nably."

The *Decies repetita placebit* of Horace, will not apply, at leaſt in peruſal, to many of the pieces in this Collection. But travellers of ſenſe and taſte (they do not crowd our highways and inns) may find amusement in some of them. I deserve at least forgiveness from every traveller. A landlord who keeps an open house, should not be censured for a dish he likes, though an ill one at his table. But every traveller is welcome to damn me as a bad critic, if he thinks proper. I beg, once for all, that the English traveller who may chance to cast his eye on these remarks, will believe, that when I express contempt of a London audience, which I most heartily feel, I mean no reflection on THE NATION IN GENERAL, NOR THAT AUDIENCE IN PARTICULAR, but the bulk of them, who are not Englishmen, but the sweepings of every country in Europe. A part of them are undoubtedly superior judges of the English drama: but their voice is lost in the tumult of an ignorant and licentious vulgar, great and small. Time brings on their judgment to prevail; and suppresses from age to age, the fooleries past, for an endless succession of new ones. Thus, classical productions are thinly scattered through the course of time, and thus antiquity is justly valued.*

* Mr. Congreve appears to have been exactly of this opinion, with respect to the character and taste of a London audience. In a letter, dated the 9th of December 1704, he says, "Cibber "has produced a play,† consisting of fine gentlemen, and fine "conversation altogether; which the *ridiculous town*, for the "most part, likes; but there are some *that know better.*" *Vide* Berkley's Literary Relics, published in 1789. Many of Dryden's prologues and epilogues contain nothing else but abuse of his audience, whom he loudly charges with the want of candour, judgment, and common sense. The Spectator tells us, that in his age, indecency was expected in every new comedy. He adds, That, for this reason, many *ladies of his acquaintance*, were partiularly careful to attend every new play, on the first night. A notable specimen of the virtue of our grandmothers! It would be chime-

† The Careless Husband.

THE MAYOR OF GARRET:

BY SAMUEL FOOTE, ESQ.

THE ſimple Jerry Sneak, and his termagant ſpouſe, are comical characters. Jerry was created to fit the peculiar humour of Weſton the player, and probably will never be ſo entertaining, by the performance of any future actor. Major Sturgeon, a character outre, as uſual in modern comedy, ſuited the extravagant drollery of Foote, the author. The reſt is inſipid.

THE REPRISAL.

By Dr. Smollet.

THIS gentlemen had humour, and parts, of which his Roderick Random, and ſome other pieces, will be a laſt-

rical to queſtion the judgment of Congreve and Dryden, or the information of ſo intelligent and polite a writer as the Spectator.

Trinculo, in the Tempeſt, to the ſame purpoſe ſays, " Were
" I in England now, as once I was, and had but this fiſh painted,
" not an holiday-fool there but would give a piece of ſilver.
" There would this monſter make a man; any ſtrange beaſt there
" makes a man; when they will not give a doit to relieve a lame
" beggar, they will lay out ten to ſee a dead Indian."

But Cowley comes cloſeſt to the preſent point:

" Whilſt this hard truth I teach, methinks, I ſee
" The monſter, London, laugh at me;
" I ſhould at thee too, fooliſh city!
" If it were fit to laugh at miſery;
" But thy eſtate I pity.

" Let but thy wicked men from out thee go,
" And all the fools, that crowd thee ſo,
" Even thou, who doſt thy millions boaſt,
" A village leſs than Iſlington wilt grow,
" A ſolitude almoſt."

Theſe authorities, to which a thouſand others might be added, are inſerted only to vindicate the text from any ſuſpicion of improper aſperity.

ing monument. In that now before me, the characters of the Irishman and Scotsman are natural and entertaining. Heartly and the Lady are no characters at all. And to suit the ungenerous pride of a London rabble, the Frenchmen are too much debased, and treated with illiberal contempt; though Captain Lyon's concluding speech makes some amends for this fault. The songs are in the low modern style. Hearts of oak is borrowed.

THE DEVIL TO PAY:

By Charles Coffey, Esq.

COMICAL actors in Jobson, Nell, and the Lady, make this piece laughable on the stage. In private perusal, it is low, flat and absurd. There is one good song in it, page 68. and 69. The rest are execrable. Indeed, the bulk of this Collection of celebrated Farces, are such, that if you wish to have entertainment, in seeing them acted on the stage, you should never read one of them. If you want to read theatrical pieces with taste and pleasure, you must go back to the old poets. Gay's "What "d'ye Call it" is the best modern little piece or farce, but is not to be expected in a Bookseller's Collection.* That must be suited to his own and the popular taste; and so what good ones you have, fall in by mere chance.

THE LYING VALET:

By David Garrick, Esq.

WE have here a foolish plot, no natural or interesting character, and as little true original wit, or humour. Garrick, in all his pieces, copies from plays, not from nature; and yet by his great abilities as an actor, and by his art as a manager, he gained, and long maintained, a sovereign direction of the London taste.

This sort of familiar gentleman, and pert speech-making footman, are characters very current in modern comedy

* When this Collection was publishing, our critic advised the compiler to insert this piece, but his advice was rejected. Note by the Editor.

and eſpecially in the plays of Vanburgh, Congreve, and Cibber, but are not to be found in nature or real life, in the old plays of true genius.

THE VIRGIN UNMASKED:

By Henry Fielding, Eſq.

THE affected ſtyle and character prevail ſo much in this piece, that I wonder not it is in vogue. The ſongs too are wretched.

THE LYAR:

By Samuel Foote, Eſq.

THERE are ſome things diverting, but many more trifling in this piece. Extravagance and pleaſantry are blended through the whole of it. There is much good humour in the firſt ſcene, part of which has been injudiciouſly ſuppreſſed by the managers. The Footman's familiarity and pleaſantry are not unnatural, as uſual in modern comedy, and are well accounted for by the curious hiſtory of his life.

THE CUNNING MAN:

By Dr. Charles Burney.

SHAKESPEARE and Milton only had the power of conjuration. This is miſerable ſtuff.

THE OLD MAID:

By Mr. Murphy.

I NEVER ſaw the original. This may be a good piece in France, but I am ſure it is a trifling one in England.

THOMAS AND SALLY:

By Bickerſtaff.

Inſignificant, ſilly, modern ſing ſong.

CRONONHOTONTHOLOGOS:

By Mr. Carey.

A BURLESQUE on modern tragedy; in ſome paſſages pleaſant enough, but every attempt to imitate the Rehearſal has hitherto been very defective, though there is great abundance of new matter for ſuch exquiſite criticiſm and juſt ridicule. The plays of Young alone, though yet acted, and admired by many, afford more examples of unnatural flights, quaint conceits, and every ſpecies of dramatic abſurdity, than all the plays, ridiculed in the Rehearſal.

NECK OR NOTHING:

By D. Garrick, Eſq.

[*Vide* Remark on the Lying Valet.]

THE LOTTERY:

By Henry Fielding, Eſq.

FIELDING's humour makes a figure in his Romances, particularly in Tom Jones, though the quaint and outre are ſometimes to be met with. He alſo diſcovers judgment, knowledge of human life, and nature. But, in his Farces and Songs, he is generally flat and vulgar. This pert inſignificant foppery, is in the true ſtyle of modern wit. The epilogue is, I ſuppoſe, much admired at London.

THE MUSICAL LADY:

By Mr. Colman.

I SUPPOSE the charm of this piece, at London, lies in ſome perſonal imitation or mockery of known Italian ſingers. It is no doubt admired, for it is very fantaſtical, and at the ſame time very dull. The prologue is in a deſperate mode indeed.

MIDAS:

A Burletta, by Kane O'Hara, Esq.

What power of acting, music, or song! What shew of scenery can make this piece an entertainment to any audience above the age of pupillarity? When one has seen no theatrical entertainment but a puppet-shew, or a harlequin, he may be excused for being highly diverted at mere grimace, or the coarse jokes of Punch and his Wife. But I often wonder, that an audience accustomed to see the plays of Shakespeare, can endure the bulk of other tragedies; or, that the spectators of a Beggar's Opera can suffer this, and almost every one of the other comic operas in our language, to pass one night without damnation. Yet a mass of such mean musical pieces have flourished, of late years, on our theatres; sounds without sense or humour, and mere musical notes without a single spark of poetical genius.

THE CITIZEN:

By Arthur Murphy, Esq.

When our moderns try to write in the style of natural character, and conversation, they fall into a medley of insipidity and affectation. They can bear no comparison to the old poets, Shakespeare, Johnson, and Fletcher, whom they mean to imitate.

THE TOY-SHOP:

By Dodsley.

There is in this piece a mixture of quaintness with good sense and some wit; but it is so full of serious thought and studied expression, that I cannot conceive how any art of acting can make it a proper or agreeable entertaiment on the stage.

THE GOLDEN PIPPIN:

By O'Hara.

THIS is an odd, fantaſtical, muſical trifle, with ſome humour in it, if well ſung and acted; and at any rate there is much foolery.

THE ENGLISHMAN IN PARIS:

By Foote.

THIS is a leſs negligent piece, than moſt of Foote's. There is a good deal of characteriſtic humour and pleaſantry in it, very unlike the great bulk of modern comedy. And what is farce but a ſhort comedy?

THE ENGLISHMAN RETURNED FROM PARIS:

By Foote.

PROPRIETY, eaſe, and humour, diſtinguiſh Foote's prologues from the ſtudied ſtrains of his cotemporaries. The "Invita Minerva" of Horace is moſt ſignificantly expreſſed by Shakeſpeare.

"Extremely ſtrain'd and conn'd with cruel pain."

This line is perfectly applicable to the bulk of modern writing of all kinds: *Vide* Warburton, Johnſon, Gibbon, and almoſt all our dramatic pieces, except Douglas.

This play is abſurd in the plot, looſe and ill digeſted in the ſcenes, with a baſe tendency to promote national pride and prejudices, diſgraceful and baneful to England in this unhappy age. Some paſſages which the author intended to obviate this cenſure, are ſuppreſſed by the wiſe ſtage-managers. See page 111, and 116.

THE INTRIGUING CHAMBERMAID:

By Fielding.

THE part of Trick is, as uſual, outre: yet the ſingular queerneſs of a Clive, made it laughable to an audience guided more by the performance of actors, than the merit of plays. The other parts of this piece are ſo flat, that no art or grimace of acting can enliven, or make them entertaining to any audience,

POLLY HONEYCOMB:

By Colman.

This Polly is a ſad ſlut; the whole very bad as uſual. Affecting natural character and converſation, the writer falls into mere flatneſs and inſipidity. What inundations of nonſenſe are diſcharged upon this unfortunate country, in the ſhape of prologues and farces, *&c.*

THE BRAVE IRISHMAN:

By Sherdian.

Here is a moſt wretched attempt to imitate, or rather transform Moliere's play of Monſieur Pourceagnae. It is an affront on common ſenſe to publiſh ſuch trumpery as *eſteemed* pieces; and bad as my opinion is of London taſte, I can hardly think this "Brave Iriſhman" could eſcape damnation the firſt night.

THE AUTHOR:

By Foote.

There is here the beſt modern prologue which I have ſeen. Foote has a viſible ſuperiority, when he chuſes to exert it, over the herd in this Collection, in his formation of character, in humour, and in eaſe, and propriety of expreſſion. Intermixed with this merit, there is a good deal of ludicrous outre, intended, as I ſuppoſe, to ſuit the prevailing taſte of the multitude who fill the houſes, and are beſt diverted with mere grimace.

THE KING AND THE MILLER OF MANSFIELD:

By Dodſley.

There is a very good meaning, and ſomething pleaſing in this piece. The deſign and plot of it are worthy even of a Shakeſpeare's genius. His execution would have been precious indeed. But *quantum mutatus!*

THE PADLOCK:

By Bickerſtaff.

Poor enough. Yet there are worſe things in this Collection of "the moſt eſteemed Farces."

THE REGISTER OFFICE:

By Joſeph Reed.

In this piece there are a great number of laboured characters, and ſome pleaſant enough as times go.

CATHARINE AND PETRUCHIO:

By D. Garrick, Eſq.

It is very fooliſh to entitle this piece as the work of Garrick. He was utterly incapable of any thing comparable to it. Every flat and defective part of it is his. Every thing excellent, every thing that ſhines in this dark Collection flows from the divine genius of Shakeſpeare, and will delight the reader of taſte, like a paradiſe in the middle of a deſart. A ſcene of incomparable humour, in which Catharine's obedient behaviour gains a bett, or wager, to her huſband, is wholly, and moſt unpardonably ſuppreſſed. The prevailing alterations of this author's incomparable plays, afford a monſtrous proof of degeneracy and ill taſte. Garrick, a great actor, was a mere quack in dramatic poetry, and miſled the world, like their quacks in phyſic, law, politics, and religion,

CYMON:

Altered from D. Garrick, Eſq.

I allow this to be the work of David Garrick, Eſquire. Much good may it do to his illuſtrious memory, as a cobler of plays and farces.

REMARKS ON YOUNG's NIGHT THOUGHTS.

This viſionary poet

—— " Makes ſweet Religion
" A rhapſody of words." SHAKESPEARE.

—I wonder not that his ſon Lorenzo was an infidel. In this age, we have two authors prodigiouſly great in the *outre* ſtyle; one in verſe, and one in proſe; one ſerious, the other comical. They are both much admired by the multitude of readers, commonly titled by modern authors, " the reſpectable public." There is a wonderful ſimilarity in their talents, in quaint expreſſion, wild conceit, and ſtudied fetches of metaphyſical reverie. The poet is Young: The Proſe Quixote is Sterne.

In my opinion, our celebrated enthuſiaſt of this country, the Reverend Mr. Ralph Erſkine, in his *Riddles*, is leſs extravagant. I am ſure, that he ſhould at leaſt be more amuſing and tolerable either to believers or infidels, than Dr. Young in his woeful *Night Thoughts*. I know no rule of criticiſm ſo juſt, ſo material, and ſo general, as one laid down by old Horace, importing, that good ſenſe is the only true principle and fountain of good writing and taſte.

" Scribendi recte, SAPERE eſt et principium et fons."

I ſhall examine the Night Thoughts by this rule, after firſt inſerting a few ſpecimens of Ralph's Riddles.

" I'm here and there and every where!
" And yet I'm neither here nor there.
" I'm ſchool'd, though never at a ſchool;
" I'm wiſe and yet a natural fool!
" I'm poor, and yet I nothing want!
" I'm both a Devil and a Saint!"

I could quote from the Night Thoughts many ſimilar paſſages of ſubtile and fantaſtical antitheſis; but I am afraid, that the bulk of readers would take them for charming poetry. Thoſe who can diſtinguiſh quaintneſs and affectation from true ſublimity, will find ſuch paſſages in every page; nay, almoſt in every line. However, I ſhall hazard ſome ſpecimens which ſeem to reſemble Ralph's Riddles very much.

"All knowing! all unknown, and yet *well-known!*
"*Near* though *remote!* and tho' unfathom'd, *felt*;
"And though *inviſible*, for ever *ſeen!*——
"Know this, Lorenzo, (ſeem it ne'er ſo ſtrange),
"Nothing can ſatisfy, but what *confounds*;
"Nothing but what *aſtoniſhes*, is *true*†.

Speaking of man, he ſays:

"An heir of glory! a frail child of duſt!
"Helpleſs immortal! *inſect infinite!*
"A *Worm! a God!*"

The "Devil" and the "Saint" are hardly ſuch exaggerated oppoſites as the "Worm" and the "God."

The following extracts I leave, without illuſtration, to the common ſenſe of the reader. I have ſometimes quoted, and ſometimes omitted to quote the particular Night and line at which the ſpecimen may be found; but the Doctor's ſtyle is ſufficiently marked.

"Procraſtination is the *thief* of time!——
"What can awake thee, unawak'd by this,
"*Expended Deity* on human weal?

Night 4th, l. 195.

"Oh love of gold! Thou *meaneſt of amours!*

Night 4th, l. 349.

"Are paſſions, then, the *pagans* of the ſoul?

† One of the venerable ancient fathers held a very ſimilar maxim, *Credo quia eſt impoſſibile.* The name of this logician was Tertullian. A great part of his works is exactly in the ſame ſtyle. In particular, the reſt of the very paragraph now quoted, is ſo groſsly indecent, that I dare not ſhock the pious ear, by attempting to inſert it. Yet our divines, of all deſcriptions, are inceſſantly appealing to the authority of this man, who was, in every reſpect, an hundred and fifty degrees below Whiſton or Whitefield.

" Reaſon alone *baptiz'd?* alone *ordain'd*
" To touch things ſacred.——
" Oh ye cold-hearted, frozen, formaliſts!
" On ſuch a theme 'tis *impious to be calm;*
" *Paſſion* is *reaſon; tranſport, temper*, here.——

Night 4th, l. 629.

" *Devotion*, when lukewarm, is *undevout.*——
" Lorenzo! haſt thou ever *weigh'd a ſigh?*
" Or ſtudied the *philoſophy of tears?*

Night 5th, l. 516.

" Death's dreadful *advent* is the *mark* of man,
" And every *thought* that miſſes it, is *blind.*——
" *Revere* thyſelf:—and yet thyſelf *deſpiſe.*

Night 6th, l. 128.

" Man's *miſery* declares him born for *bliſs;*
" His anxious heart aſſerts the truth I ſing,
" And gives the ſceptic in *his head* the lie.

Night 7th, l. 60.

" Man's heart *eats* all things, and is *hungry* ſtill;
" More, more! the glutton crys:——

Ibid. l. 123.

" The world's all *title-page*, there's no *contents;*
" The world's all *face;* the man who ſhews his heart,
" Is hooted for his *nudities*, and ſcorn'd.

Night 8th, l. 333.

——————" Lorenzo!
" This is the moſt indulgence can afford;
" Thy *wiſdom* all can do, but make thee *wiſe;*
" Nor think this cenſure is ſevere on thee;
" *Satan*, thy maſter, I *dare call a dunce.*

Night 8th, l. 1414.

" When *pain* can't *bliſs*, heaven *quits us in deſpair.*

Night 9th, l. 497.

After all, and as ſome apology to the numerous admirers of Dr. Young, I allow that there are ſtrokes and paſſages of genuine poetry to be found, though thinly ſcattered, among the wild effuſions of this long and laboured

O ij

poem. I refer, in particular, to the firſt five lines of Night Firſt, and to the thirteen firſt lines of Night Fourth. For the ſake of juſtice to our author, the two paſſages ſhall be inſerted at full length.

Night Firſt.

" Tir'd nature's ſweet reſtorer, balmy ſleep!
" He like the world, his ready viſit pays,
" Where fortune ſmiles: the wretched he forſakes;
" Swift, on his downy pinions, flies from woe,
" And lights on lids unſullied by a tear.

Night Fourth.

" A much indebted muſe, O Yorke! intrudes,
" Amid the ſmiles of fortune and of youth;
" Thine ear is patient of a ſerious ſong.
" How deep implanted in the breaſt of man
" The dread of death? I ſing its ſov'reign cure.
" Why ſtart at death? Where is he? Death arriv'd
" Is paſt; not come, or gone; he's never *here.*
" E'er *hope*, *ſenſation* fails; black-boding man
" *Receives*, not *ſuffers*, death's tremendous blow.
" The knell, the ſhroud, the mattock, and the grave;
" The deep damp vault, the darkneſs and the worm;
" Theſe are the bug-bears of a winter's eve,
" The terrors of the living, not the dead.

From this, the writer runs wild, and continues with very ſlight and tranſient lucid intervals, to the end of the poem.

The following lines, at the beginning of Night Ninth, may be conſidered as one of the beſt paſſages in this poet.

" As when a traveller, a long day paſt
" In painful ſearch of what he cannot find,
" At night's approach, content with the next cot,
" There ruminates, a while, his labour loſt;
" Then cheers his heart, with what his fate affords,
" And chants his ſonnet to deceive the time,

" Till the due ſeaſon calls him to repoſe:
" Thus I, long-travell'd in the ways of men,
" And dancing, with the reſt, the giddy maze,
" Where *diſappointment* ſmiles at *hope's* career,
" Warn'd by the langour of life's ev'ning ray,
" At length have hous'd me in an humble ſhed;
" Where future wand'ring baniſh'd from my thought,
" And waiting, patient, the ſweet hour of reſt,
" I chaſe the moments with a ſerious ſong.—
" Song ſoothes our pains; and age has pains to ſoothe.

The following detached lines, among others, diſplay the ſpirit of poetry, blended with conceit, and affectation.

" How rich! how poor! how abject! how auguſt!
" How complicate, how wonderful is man!"

And again, ſpeaking of Narciſſa:

" Early, bright, tranſient, chaſte as morning dew!
" She ſparkled, was exhal'd! and went to heav'n."

REMARKS UPON A JOURNEY THROUGH THE CRIMEA TO CONSTANTINOPLE:

In a Series of Letters from the Right Honourable Elizabeth Lady Craven.

I WAS tempted to purchaſe this book, price one pound four ſhillings, becauſe it partly deſcribes foreign countries where I have lately travelled. The fine female author prattles agreeably, and in a ſort of good modiſh Engliſh language. But ſhe does not over-load her readers with material information. Her converſations with emperors, princes, and embaſſadors, have no tendency to excite envy in the minds of inferior people.

PHILOSOPHICAL DISSERTATIONS:

By J. B. Eſq.

" ELABORATE and little ſignificant" is a very general character of modern authors, both ſerious and coimcal. I am afraid that David Hume, that able apoſtle of infidelity, gains ground by the incapacity of his antagoniſts.

MORAL TALES:

Translated from Marmontel.

I WONDER not that these tales are in vogue, for they are very absurd and romantic. There is only one which I have read with satisfaction, viz. "The Wife of Ten "Thousand." It is, I think, wrote in a better style, with more propriety, character, and interest, than any of the rest.

ANCIENT HISTORY:

Translated from Rollin.

THIS work, in the original, is full of weak and frivolous observations, which become still more flat by a bad translation. However, it contains information for the intelligent, and has otherwise merit enough to please the unlearned.*

There is manifest absurdity in Rollin's application and explanation of prophecies. Rollin himself was certainly a weak superstitious man. This character has recommended him to the admiration of many, indeed to the multitude of modern readers, both male and female. He very seriously ascribes to God, all the extravagant mischiefs done by Alexander the Great, and finds out that he is *clearly* described in the prophecies of Daniel, by the

* In a preface to this volume, Rollin intimates that if Quintus Curtius had lived before the age of Quintilian, he would certainly have appeared in his catalogue of Roman Authors; and Mr. Gibbon, has remarked, that "those who place him under "the first Cæsars, argue from the purity of his style, but are "embarrassed by the silence of Quintilian, in his *accurate* list of "Roman Historians." The passage referred to is in the tenth book of Quintilian's Treatise on Eloquence. Of Roman Historians he has named only *four*; and adds "Sunt et alii scriptoris boni: "sed nos genera degustamus, non bibliothecas excutimus."— "There are other good historians, but we are not here discus"sing the merit of libraries; we only touch slightly on the dif"ferent kinds of authors."

Ram, and the He-goat. To convey a true idea of his character, he should be called Alexander the great *Madman*; and to characterize Louis le Grand, we should call him Louis the great *Coxcomb*. To Julius Cæsar, to Henry IV. of France, to Peter of Russia, and to Frederiek, we may allow the title of Great, without a similar addition.

Rollin tells us, that "Alexander was dear to others, "because they were sensible that he was *before hand* "with them in affection." His soldiers were like all the herd of mankind in all ages, exceedingly fond of vain extravagant men of rank and power. The Roman soldiers were fond of Nero, and the Swedes of our modern great madman, Charles the Twelfth.

KEYSLER's TRAVELS.

"Much ado about nothing," is the character of this, and a great many of our modern books. Probably the translation does injustice to the original, and makes it appear more trivial. At London, the trade of printing and publishing books is often a mere piece of quackery.

THE LIFE OF SAMUEL JOHNSON, L. L. D.

By James Boswell, Esq.

If this biographer's judgment was in full proportion to his vivacity, and singular diligence, he would have given a much shorter and much better book. There are some good materials, but——

Apparent raræ nantes in gurgite vasto.

I own I grudged my two guineas, till I read Johnson's excellent Letter to Lord Chesterfield, which I think well worth the money. There are other good letters from him, and there are curious, and sometimes very sagacious answers to slender suggestions and questions by Tom Davies, Tom Tyers, Joe Warton, and certain other companions of this extraordinary man. Upon the whole, from a patient perusal of this book, I am much reconciled to Johuſon's character. With ſuperior talents, I think, that though exceedingly vain, he was a good natured man; and that his prejudices againſt poor Scotland, were not ſo irrational and unjuſt as I formerly imagined.

Is there not a fable of intimate friendſhip, between a ferocious Lion, and a lively Terrier? What ſays Peter Pindar to this, is he ſilenced, or is he ſatisfied?

VOYAGES D' ITALIE ET HOLLANDE:

Par M. l' Abbe Coyer. Paris. 1775.

I HAVE conceived ſuch an idea of an Abbe, that if he turns author, I think he muſt write in this ſtyle and faſhion; pert, flippant, pretty, with little ſenſe and no ſolidity.

AN INQUIRY INTO THE BEAUTIES OF PAINTING:

By Daniel Webb, Eſq. London 1760.

THERE is merit in this Treatiſe; but it is more learned and ſcientific in the matter, than elegant in the compoſition.

A VOLUME OF PLAYS:

As performed at the Theatre, Smoke Alley, Dublin, 1785.

A SELECT collection of ſing-ſong farces, in high reputaion, though without genius, ſenſe, or humour.

I. THE DUENNA:

THE run of this piece has been great; compoſed in imitation of the charming Beggar's Opera, without any ſufficient or juſt reſemblance.

II. THE AGREEABLE SURPRISE.

THIS is worſe than the other; feeble, fooliſh, fantaſtically improbable, and unnatural. It ſurpaſſes my comprehenſion, how the grimace of actors can make ſuch things pleaſant to any audience on earth.

III. LOVE A-LA-MODE:

A Comedy.

WITH a good deal of the favourite *outre*, we find in this piece, more ſenſe, humour, and character, than in moſt of our farces.

IV. *The* POOR SOLDIER:

A Comic Opera.

THIS piece touches the bass-string of vulgarity itself, affected simplicity, and unmeaning sing-song; yet it had a vogue. I have scored many passages which no patience can bear.

ON THE

DRAMATIC WORKS OF PHILIP MASSINGER:

4 vols. 8vo. *London* 1761.

THE few who can taste and relish the fruits of genius will find them here, but thinly scattered. Old Horace, the only perfect critic of my acquaintance, the sensible and elegant Horace, says, *Interdum bonus dormitat Homerus*,* and again, *Non ego paucis offendar maculis.*† These texts are applicable to Shakespeare, and to Shakespeare alone, of all our dramatic poets. He supports the dignity of his singular genius through the great bulk of all his plays, though he sometimes, but rarely sinks, and produces obscure, trifling, or superfluous passages. On the contrary, the bulk of Massinger's writings in Tragedy are flat and diffuse, and he rarely shines, hardly in any one whole scene together. His beauties, though genuine, are as rare as the imperfections and faults of Shakespeare. In comedy, he is more successful; and the reader of taste will find a due reward, even for the perusal of his Tragedies. He will discover golden ore in the mass of dross; a commendation inapplicable to any tragedy our age has produced. I except the Douglas alone.

THE VIRGIN MARTYR:

A Tragedy.

IT is astonishing what beauties there are in this old play, and what deformities.

* "Sometimes honest Homer nods."

† "I am not offended by a few blemishes."

II. THE DUKE OF MILLAN:

A Tragedy.

Of this play the Editor obſerves, that the fable in general greatly reſembles the tragical ſtory of Herod and Mariamne. He adds, "The modern play of that name is "more uniform and conſiſtent than this, but, in my opi- "nion, has not ſo many fine independent paſſages." It is, indeed, perfectly modern. This has many beauties, and nature ſhines in it; as affected poetry and laboured dulneſs characterize Fenton's play. In Act II. this Editor cenſures Maſſinger for permitting the Dutcheſs to deſcend from her dignity to make ſport for the galleries. The old poets repreſent human failings and paſſions in characters of the higheſt rank, for which they are cenſured by our refined modern critics. Thus they condemn the divine Shakeſpeare, a poet, by nature, above the reach of all critics, for the moſt exquiſitely fantaſtical humours in the character of his Cleopatra; and they prefer the artificial, laboured, affected character of Cleopatra, by Dryden. After theſe remarks, it is needleſs to add, that I conſider Maſſinger, as in this inſtance, perfectly defenſible. The publiſher is right, that there is a degree of genius in his old poet, but I think he ſometimes miſtakes the droſs for the golden ore, and *vice verſa.* In the ſimilies of this poet, there is commonly a want of that clearneſs and apt propriety which always attend the poetical ſimilies of Shakeſpeare.

III. THE FATAL DOWRY:

A Tragedy.

The laſt act of this play has more beauty and uniformity than any of the reſt, and is, I think, in Maſſinger's ſtyle altogether. It is a thouſand pities that this author had not more judgment. He had great parts and powers of dramatic compoſition.

THE MAID OF HONOUR:

A Tragi-Comedy.

If there was a modern genius, but there is none, to reform the plot, to refine the groſs parts, and to make the whole of a piece with the ſuperior paſſages of this play, it would deſerve a much better ſtage than the preſent Engliſh one. It is in its original ſtate unfit for any ſtage. On this play a few verſes have been inſcribed to the author, by a horribly quaint fellow. He has many companions on Parnaſſus.

THE CITY MADAM, AND THE NEW WAY TO PAY OLD DEBTS.

Contain fine and rich, though neglected materials, for excellent comedy. The biographers of our ſtage, inform us that Shakeſpeare was an intimate friend to Maſſinger, and that he occaſionally aided him, of which I imagine that the beſt judges of Shakeſpeare, may trace inſtances.

THE WORKS OF HORACE, TRANSLATED INTO ENGLISH PROSE:

By Charles Smart, A. M.

The ſenſe and humour of Hoarce, are as little underſtood by this tranſlation, as his poetry.

OBSERVATIONS ON THE PUBLIC LAW OF SCOTLAND:

By Gilbert Stuart, L. L. D.

Affected language and unmeaning ſpeculation, without perſpicuity, without matter, without ſolid judgment, but of a piece with the bulk of modern books, which never will be ancient.

THE REGENT:

A Tragedy, by Bertie Greatbeed.

This applauded tragedy is worſe than any thing of the kind I have ſeen. No ſpark of genius, taſte, or ſenſe, all *Invita minerva;* all quaint laboured fuſtian. *O Tempora!*

THE GENTLEMAN DANCING MASTER:

A Comedy, by Wycherly.

Some ſcenes of this play deſerve our approbation. But there are many unnatural converſations and quaint double meanings quite in the character of fantaſtical comedy, and falſe wit; ſuch were the firſt rate wits of Charles the Second, and they would be great wits ſtill. Singular abſurdities paſs to this day for humour and diverting comedy. *Vide* The Agreeable Surpriſe, and many more. Did Wycherly write only to pleaſe a fooliſh audience, or had he ſo little ſenſe, as to fancy this matchleſs foolery true comedy? Such another complication of abſurdities can only be found in ſome of our modern admired plays and farces.

Much has been ſaid above reſpecting the preſent ſituation and management of the London Theatres. To ſhew that abſurd exhibitions are not confined to them alone, the following obſervations, communicated by a Gentleman from London, a few months ago, may afford an agreeable diverſity of amuſement to the reader.

"Though I go to few public places, yet what is called "*puffing* is carried on here to ſuch extravagant perfec-"tion, that I was induced, by repeated advertiſements "in the news-papers, to go to Aſtley's, to ſee the whole "houſe melted into tears by the affecting delicacy with "which Mr. Aſtley's ſuperior genius conducted *the flight* "and *capture* of The Royal Fugitives. The King and "Queen of France who did not appear to have ever ſeen "company in a ſtate of ſeparation from Boxes, Pits, and "Galleries, were at firſt in a moſt furious hurry; but "when the King perceived the Dauphin and Madame E-"lizabeth approaching, his royal feelings quite overcame "him. In their better days, his Majeſty and his daugh-"ter the Princeſs, had both been Tumblers; he there-"fore, in a paroxyſm of grief, ſeized the Princeſs juſt "above the elbows, and without quitting his hold toſſed

" her up as high as his head. He did not mean to throw " her Royal Highneſs over his head, but merely to bring " her face into contact with his own. After going through " the ſame ceremonies with the Dauphin, all the Royal " perſonages joined hands, and in a ſlow and meaſured " ſtep marched to the muſic, uſing great circumſpection, " and many geſtures peculiarly ſuited to their own ideas " of the occaſion. Upon the whole, there can be no doubt " that had the King and Queen of France been as com- " pletely diſguiſed on the continent as they are here, they " would not have been ſtopped in any part of Europe."

There is here no deſign of repreſenting a London audience as, by nature, inferior in taſte to the reſt of mankind. In every part of the world, the mob are much the ſame and in no part of the world can ſuch trumpery be admired by ſpectators, who deſerve a better title.

THE FRIEND.—ANCIENT AND MODERN.

If any truth could ſtrike us with ſurpriſe,
Which happens every day before our eyes,
The firſt of wonders is, that all pretend
To ſeek to value, to deſerve a friend;
And yet that ſcarce a couple can agree,
In this plain query what a friend ſhould be.
The prating preſes of an ale-houſe knot,
Thinks human wiſdom center'd in the ſpot.
The ſlave of learning poring out his eyes,
Pities the plowman, nature made as wiſe.
The ſot ſeeks him who every care can *drown*,
The bruiſer him who knocks a bully down.
Each terms, in turn, his company the beſt,
And properly deſpiſes all the reſt.
  Diſaſtrous truth compells us to declare,
That common friendſhip is as light as air,
That all its pleaſures ſeldom pay the pains,
That half the riſk will balance all the gains;

Nay, pious Young, expiring at fourſcore,
He who ſo fondly ſung its charms before,
Forgot the peers, he once was proud to praiſe,
Forgot the prieſts with whom he ſpent his days,
Forgot his *quondam* fav'rites of the quill,
And juſt one tradeſman mention'd in his will.
But though your boſom-friend may prove a rogue,
One comfort ſtill, depend upon your dog.
He with eternal patience bears the yoke,
And licks your hand juſt lifted for a ſtroke.
Nor will he for a bribe betray his truſt,
But thinks he's well rewarded with a cruſt.
No toil, no danger will your cent'nel fly,
For you he lives, for you he's proud to die;
One generous thought ſubliming all the reſt,
Glows in his grateful, his intrepid breaſt;
Yet could he ſee how meanly you deſpiſe
Superior worth in ſuch a low diſguiſe,
Th' indignant brute would act his maſter's plan,
And ſink in want of honour like a man.
'Tis but a bitter comedy to trace
The woeful writhings in your patron's face,
When fondly catching ſome unwary word,
You hint what help you know he can afford;
With how much confidence you dare depend,
On the fine feelings of ſo firm a friend;
That well you know before ſix months have run,
No living mortal for a doit ſhall dun.
Then with domeſtic miſery fill his ears,
Your children trembling, and your ſpouſe in tears;
And beg he'll condeſcend to plead your cauſe,
And for one day ſuſpend the turnkey's paws;
Deſcribe the jail, and importune relief
With all the earneſt eloquence of grief.
Behold his features freezing in a grin,
To hint the tenderneſs that glows within;
From gay to grave, in half a minute ſour,
He vows relief lies far beyond his power.—

" I have a world of work on hand to-day,
" And muſt at ſix attend upon the play;
" My ſoul takes fire at ſuch a ſcene of love,
" For who like Jaffier can our pity move;
" And yet when Belvidere begins to weep,
" Some poor unfeeling blockheads fall aſleep:
" Though ſhe's ſo ſweet, pathetic, and ſublime—
" I'll hope to ſerve you at ſome better time.
" Theſe yelping brats have made your ſpirits fail,
" Shylock, I'm ſure, wont bury you in jail.
" You ſay the priſon is a horrid place,
" But faith 'tis not ſo horrid as your face;
" And after all this lamentable rout,
" No man goes in, but ſoon or late comes out.
" The cells, you cry, are cramm'd with putrid air,
" Depend upon't you ſhan't be buried there;
" And when you catch the fever of the houſe,
" The doctor for a fee will ſet you looſe,
" By ſwearing that unleſs they let you go,
" They muſt, ere long, a winding ſheet beſtow.
" Beſides, you know, that all the nation ſwear,
" Some raſcals never thrive till they go there;
" There, oft the tradeſman feathers well his neſt,
" And there the righteous from their labours reſt.
" And if you're really nabb'd, pray let me hear,
" By George! the news will harrow up my ear.
" But if you 'ſcape the cage I hope to ſee
" My honeſt friend ſome night, next month, at tea.
" At tea, remark, for this new tax on wine
" Is horribly oppreſſive when we dine;
" And I muſt now be wiſer than before,
" And teach œconomy to guard my door:
" My fond good nature has been often bit,
" 'Tis more than time to learn a ſpark of wit,
" And were I juſt as ſilly as to lend
" But half a crown to every bankrupt friend,
" In fourteen days my whole eſtate muſt fly,
" And for my hounds one loaf I could not buy.

"Of corn my hunters only can devour,
"As much as fattens all our pariſh poor.
"Good bye—The ponies to my coach are put,
"In this damn'd weather who would walk a-foot."
And then ACHATES turns upon his heel,
And leaves you to reflect on what you feel.
And then you find how far you were beguil'd,
And gueſs his gracious meaning when he ſmil'd;
And ten to one your conſcience will declare,
That you have ſpurn'd ſome poor dependent's pray'r;
That had you fill'd your benefactor's place,
Yourſelf had juſt perform'd a part as baſe.
For moſt of us are but invidious elves,
Our narrow hearts feel only for ourſelves;
Thoſe few whom candour ſcruples to deteſt,
At friendſhip laugh as loudly as the reſt.
 But, mark ſome fop untrain'd to ſerious thought,
Who cannot have that ſenſe he never bought,
Who ne'er has wander'd through misfortune's maze,
Nor wanted ſycophants to ſound his praiſe,
Whoſe falſe good nature floats upon the whim,
That all mankind admire and copy him;
With fooliſh, honeſt ardour, he'll exclaim,
That all my end is merely to defame;
That theſe mean murmurs muſt ariſe from art,
The ſpecious croakings of a guilty heart.
For though but half were ſerious, which I tell
That this fine world would be the porch of hell;
Whereas, a drove of bright divines atteſt,
That all below muſt happen for the beſt.
Unhappy novice! and dar'ſt thou pretend,
Thou who ne'er knew'ſt diſtreſs, to know thy friend?
Go then—Thy thouſands with theſe friends divide,
And quick repentance ſhall confound thy pride.
Thoſe envied bleſſings on the mob beſtow,
Which our plump parſons call *vain things below;*
Though not one ſaint among them will refuſe
To pick up the laſt farthing of his dues;

The partners of thy purſe will melt away,
Like ice diſſolving in a ſummer's day;
Then the vile farce of friendſhip ſhalt thou find,
And curſe, with me, the baſeneſs of mankind,
And play old Timon's tragedy once more,
As fifty thouſand fools have done before.
'Twas thus when Socrates began to build;
" When ſhall this hamlet with true friends be fill'd?"
Was all the arch old man reply'd to thoſe
Who wonder'd why no prouder pile aroſe.
Thus too—While Greece his eloquence ador'd,
And Perſia's tyrant trembled at his ſword,
While in the vulgar's eye he ſign'd to ſhine,
Wiſe Pericles let his preceptor pine.
No friend appear'd, a morſel to ſupply,
The Newton of his age lay down to die. *
But lo! his worthy pupil comes at laſt
And begs his benefactor not to faſt;
" And why, dear father, would you not reveal
" Your wants to me, who all your ſorrows feel."
Inſulting lie! more ſhocking than the wrong
Of letting the old martyr ſtarve ſo long.
For when I feel ſincerely for your woes,
And really mean to help you to repoſe;
I read at once your wiſhes in your eye,
And when I can, at once, your wants ſupply;
But ſhall not baſely make my betters bend,
Nor in the BEGGAR wiſh to ſink the FRIEND.

HORACE, LIB. I. ODE XVIII.

DEAR Harry you cannot do better
  Than cover your fields with the vine.
How happy am I when your debtor
  For a bumper of excellent wine!

* Anaxagoras, a Greek aſtronomer, of diſtinguiſhed merit.

The care that is cutting your boſom,
  Before an old flaggon muſt fly;
The roſe to be ſure cannot bloſſom,
  When the buſhes are wither'd and dry.

The coward encourag'd with liquor,
  On the mouth of a cannon will run,
The curate look briſk like his vicar,
  And the laureate will laugh at his dun.

The ſurly for once are good fellows;
  The graveſt are gay for a time;
Then do you believe, what they tell us,
  That cracking a bottle's a crime.

As April when painting the furrows,
  Drives winter away to the pole;
Champaign, by diſpelling life's ſorrows,
  Relaxes the froſt of the ſoul.

But the ſot, who would always be drinking,
  Will very ſoon ſee to his coſt,
That want muſt attend want of thinking,
  And his friends with his money be loſt.

The hoſt, who has rifled his pocket,
  Will ſhow him the way to the door,
And bully like Peachum or Lockit,
  Unleſs he can anſwer his ſcore.

Of all vile deteſtable vermin,
  The vileſt on earth or in hell,
At leaſt thus their pigeons determine,
  Are ſuch as have liquor to ſell.

For when a young fool full of money,
  Is galloping into the mire,
They pillage his hive of the honey,
  And leave him to beg or expire.

HORACE, LIB. I. ODE XXIII.

DEAR Chloe, you fly from my love like a fawn,
In ſearch of her mother along the wild lawn,
When each ruſtling breeze makes the fugitive ſtart,
And each falling leaf gives a wound to her heart.
Young, timorous, innocent, Chloe like you,
She fancies the hounds have her always in view.
But tell me, ah! tell me, dear beautiful maid,
For what is my charmer of Damon afraid;
Do I like a panther approach to deſtroy,
Your preſence, your ſmiles, muſt I never enjoy;
Remember at leaſt, that you're fairly fifteen,
And 'tis (let me ſay ſo) full time to be ſeen.
And, O! could you gueſs what I feel for your ſake,
That little proud heart ſome compaſſion would take.
In pining for Chloe I paſs the long night,
Or wake with a ſigh from ſome dream of delight;
In vain would I run to a ball or a play,
For nothing can pleaſe me when Chloe's away.

THE COMFORTS OF MARRIAGE:

A TALE.

WHEN Cinna earn'd but twenty pounds a-year,
No dunning tradeſman Cinna had to fear.
In debt to nobody, his heart was gay,
He look'd no farther than the current day;
His income juſt allow'd a decent coat,
An alehouſe ramble coſt him but a groat.
From him no barber had long bills to ſeek,
He clear'd with every claimant once a-week.
At night he drank ſmall beer, and ſmok'd, and read,
And ſlipt as ſober as a nun to bed.

He ſhunn'd the ſex. His fortieth year began
Before he durſt eſſay the pleaſures of a man.
Nay, when December chill'd the world with froſt,
That month, when monks and maidens murmur moſt,
When the cold ſheets were freezing to his ſkin,
Like Ruth no laundreſs at his heels crept in;
No drab to groping conſtables could tell,
That he, good man! had made her centre ſwell.
His blabbing tongue no pious aunt could fear,
On him no bawd beſtow'd her wanton leer.
At him, no cuckold bent the budding horn,
Wenching, in every ſhape, he held in ſcorn.
Surpriſing fact! in ſuch a rampant age,
So pure a ſaint deſerves a brighter page.
Alas! how very ſeldom we have ſeen
The virgin fort reſiſt us till fifteen.
But love of change ſtill haunts the human breaſt,
Thus Indolence itſelf grows tir'd of reſt.
The ſot has now and then a ſober fit,
Miſers, by times, extravagance admit.
The veteran may ſhake with childiſh fear,
And ſurgeons have been ſeen to ſhed a tear;
By turns the fooliſh follow Wiſdom's rules,
By turns, the wiſe behave themſelves like fools.
Though Fortune ruſhes in her richeſt tide,
We ſigh for ſome enjoyment yet untry'd;
In ſearch of novelty our fancies tire,
Gaze at the moon, and ſtumble in the mire.
And thus the hero of the preſent ſong,
Having ſo long gone right, at laſt went wrong.
His wages trebling, Cinna took a wife,
That precious balſam for the wounds of life;
But Care was quickly painted on his brow,
He found himſelf in debt, he knew not how;
Such heavy, daily, damnable demands,
A guinea never halted in his hands.
His penſion mounted to five hundred pounds,
And this you'll ſay, magnificently ſounds;

And ſwear the man muſt very ſoon be rich,
Unless this his ſpouſe feels the true ſpendthrift itch.
With nine pert puppies yelping at his tail,
To talk of ſaving makes his patience fail.
Maids, midwives, milliners, and heav'n knows what,
Keep Cinna barer than a tar's old hat.
On pariſh rates, tithes, laces, lodging-rent,
Tea, china, claret, half his funds are ſpent;
Thrice nine and thirty couſins have implor'd
That help, his purſe, they cry, can well afford.
His precious rib has ventur'd to declare,
"'Tis vulgar on one's legs to take the air."
In vain poor Cinna vows himſelf behind,
Plays, balls, and fiddlers, fill my lady's mind;
And, as no man of ſenſe expects to ſee
Two females, two whole hours at once agree,
Ten times a-day his ſpouſe and ſervants brawl,
His dear deſcendants every ſecond ſquall;
His bed, his ſhirt, they ſteep in midnight ſtreams,
Pox, worms, and meaſles, haunt his morning dreams.
Each day commences with a cloud of bills,
For taylors, nurſes, ſpelling-books, and pills;
To-night more cradles he muſt buy or borrow,
And a twelfth ſexton's fee pay down to-morrow.
And though, ye rakes, may think he ſhould rejoice
To quit expence, vexation, toil, and noiſe;
What agonies convulſe a father's breaſt,
While Innocence is writhing into reſt?
  Thus, to his fatal coſt, hath Cinna found,
That wedlock's holy joys are juſt a ſound;
That peace will end, where happineſs begins,
And wives are the grand ſcourge of human ſins.

THEOCRITUS, IDYLLIUM XXX.

When Venus ſaw her ſwain
Expiring on the plain,

She ſummon'd all the loves,
And bade them ſearch the groves,
And bring the briſtly boar,
Whoſe teeth the fair Adonis tore.
The Cupids flew the foreſt round,
And ſoon the bloody ſavage found.
His fury for to check,
One tied him by the neck;
Another, with his bow,
Began a drubbing to beſtow.
Slowly pac'd the boar along,
He knew that he was in the wrong,
And trembled to be ſeen
By Love's avenging queen.
In words, like theſe, her paſſion burſt:
"Of all brutes, thou moſt accurſt,
"Why didſt thou gaſh my lover's thigh?
"Why let on him thy vengeance fly?"
The cunning boar had laid his plan,
And, very humbly, thus began:
"A brute, O Venus, would you hear,
"By your ſacred ſelf I ſwear,
"I ne'er intended to deſtroy
"The lovely, much lamented boy.
"But, when I ſaw his beauteous face,
"(I own it to my ſad diſgrace)
"At once I kindled with deſire,
"And all my boſom was on fire.
"I thought it the ſublimeſt bliſs
"To catch, at leaſt, a ſingle kiſs;
"I ran to touch his ſnowy thigh,
"But—what a luckleſs wretch am I!
"Now, charming Venus, if you will,
"The lover of Adonis kill;
"Or, if your goodneſs let me live,
"Theſe tuſks a ſacrifice I give;
"And, if it be too little, pray
"Cut my clumſy lips away."

Venus believ'd the tale, and ſo
Bade her Cupids let him go.
The grateful beaſt reſolv'd to ſtay,
And follow'd Venus from that day;
And, a juſt penance to impoſe,
Struck out the teeth that caus'd her woes.

A TRITE TRUTH.

When by ſome perjur'd worthleſs rake,
A frail fond virgin is outwitted;
Her rivals ſuch an uproar wake,
As if ſhe ought not to be pity'd.

Mere envy makes their venom burſt,
They view the rogue with palpitation,
And would, kind creatures! if they durſt,
Afford him inſtant occupation.

But, if he's rich, and gayly dreſt,
They ruſh like moths around the candle;
And pleaſure heaves each pouting breaſt,
Which he prepares to preſs or handle.

They ſhrink, indeed, to let him ſee
Their ſtraight and finely taper'd limbs;
For though the heart is always free,
The head with affectation ſwims.

Their very toes are taught to ſpeak;*
To whet temptation they'll retire,
And while he follows, raiſe a ſqueak,
That harmony may fan his fire.

How charmingly the boſom ſwells!
How ſweetly they defy his vaunting!

* "Nay, her foot ſpeaks."
Troilus and Cressida.

Each look, each amorous murmur, tells
  For what their balmy tongues are panting.

His presence is for ever sought,
  And WHY our maidens may determine;
Shall we mispend one serious thought,
  On servile tyrannizing vermin,

Who persecute without remorse,
  The helpless victim of despair;
But welcome, as a work of course,
  The robber with a wanton stare.

The girl whose petulance runs mad,
  O'er the perdition of her sister,
Is but a hypocrising jade,
  Who rages—that the sportsman miss'd her.

THE WORLD AS IT GOES.

Of those we call the great, how very few,
The path to greatness happily pursue;
By dear experience every day we find,
That riches commonly degrade the mind;
That he, who train'd through want's instructive school,
Had prov'd a man of sense, becomes a fool;
As dirt on all beneath himself looks down,
Nor feels for any sorrow but his own.
  Nor these alone our total censure claim,
All men are but *another and the same*;
And he who most at human folly rails,
Always in some grand point of wisdom fails.
Let us, my friend, the varied scene survey,
Sketch out some features of the passing day;
And while the grinning world our faults declare,
Shew half the species have an equal share.

While one both ſoul and body riſks for wealth,
The helpleſs lord of thouſands begs but health;
The luſty plow-boy wants a handſome wife,
His hen-peck'd ſire in ſecret curſes life.
The young regret the prudence of the old,
While age, with terror, feels the blood run cold;
The virgin pines her brittle toy to crack,
The teeming ſpouſe expires upon the rack;
While poor foot-paſſengers are quite bemir'd,
The jolting coach her ladyſhip hath tir'd;
The ſober proſe-man would be proud to rhyme,
The hungry bard deplores his loſs of time;
And while his groom would gladly ſtorm his bride,
His *Honour* ſnores, an wool-pack by her ſide;
Nor kindles when her eye with paſſion ſwims,
Nor gives the receipe for female whims.
The bagnio-cully cannot ſtamp an heir,
The beggar's aſs-loads wring his heart with care.
Beſides, each inſtant that we croſs the ſtreet,
A troop of jolly wanton girls we meet,
Who cannot find one ſilk that's fit to wear,
Yet age, in rags, with ſcornful ſilence hear.
The admiral ſhares fifty thouſand pounds,
The gunner fifty groats, and fifteen wounds.
For half a fidler's ſalary per week,
His curate, when to publiſh or to ſpeak,
Supplies the roſy dean with ſermons and with Greek.
Though parching Spring denies an ounce of grain,
And putrid Auguſt rots their hay with rain;
Though ſome fox-chace their harveſt hath deſtroy'd,
Or ſome tithe law-ſuit their whole caſh employ'd,
Whether his bond-men can or cannot pay,
His Grace wrings out his rent, at each term day;
While law the juſtice of his claim inforces,
To pamper concubines, and hounds, and horſes;
To buy his pimp a ſeat for ſome pure borough,
To bet on dice to-night, or on the turf to-morrow.

Q

Thus goes, and thus hath always gone the world,
Folly and Vice in one ſtrange hodge-podge hurl'd.
To hope amendment were the height of madneſs,
Apoſtleſhip diſſolves in ſober ſadneſs:
And Truth, concludes where an old bard began,
"Who'd be that ſordid, wretched thing, call'd man?"

THE PHILOSOPHER.

A CERTAIN Philoſopher lives in this town,
  Whoſe merit Melpomene means to diſcloſe;
To whom every fact in all Nature is known,
  But what lies immediately under his noſe.

His tongue, when you meet him, like thunder is loud,
  And Folly and Lazineſs keep him as poor:
I cannot think what makes the pedant ſo proud,
  Or why that pale face is eternally ſour.

The Cynic, this morning, was trying his wit,
  And plaguing a cobler, a plain merry man;
The fellow who felt himſelf terribly bit,
  Flung his awl on the floor, and got up, and began:

"What ſignifies learning without common ſenſe?
  "Or, why do we read what we cannot digeſt?
"Your ſtudies produce neither honour nor pence,
  "But that horrid cough which is rending your breaſt.

"The end of all books is to better the heart,
  "Or with new ideas enlighten the head;
"And the Sage had done wiſely in driving a cart,
  "Whom nobody living laments when he's dead.

"You prove to a ſecond, at what time of day
  "Achilles and Hector began to engage;
"You call them poltroons, yet have nothing to ſay
  "When your doxy finds proper to fly in a rage.

" You teach us a ſure way for winning of wealth,
" And yet (who would think it) your elbows are out;
" And while you are telling us how to keep health,
" Each joint in your carcaſe is wrung with the gout.

" You know that Queen Beſs was a virgin moſt true;
" That Mary, her victim, deſervedly died;
" But how many pots to the landlord we're due,
" Or one, or a dozen, you cannot decide.

" When you look at the ſky you can ſay, to an ell,
" In how wide a circle old Saturn ſhould run;
" But no duck or partridge as yet ever fell,
" Nay, gueſs'd at your aim when you levell'd a gun.

" You ſtate to a ſhilling the national debt;
" A plan for its payment you long ſince made known;
" But, with all this preciſion, I'd take you a bet,
" You never ſhall know the amount of your own.

" You ſpend half your life-time in poring on books;
" What a mountain of wit muſt be cramm'd in that ſkull!
" And yet, if a man were to judge by your looks,
" Perhaps he would think you confoundedly dull.

" More happy, by far, is the clown at his plow,
" Who never attempts what he cannot attain,
" Than ſuch a capricious haranguer as you,
" With mad metaphyſicks tormenting your brain.

" And what is the value of Newton or Locke?
" Do they leſſen the price of potatoes and corn?
" When Poverty comes can they ſoften the ſhock,
" Or teach us how hunger is patiently borne?

" No *innate ideas* can mend a bad crop;
" No ſquaring of circles can temper the ſky;
" Then all ſuch wild vagaries promiſe to drop,
" Or tell us in what does their excellence lie.

"'Tis very like folly to wear out our eyes,
"In gueſſing the diſtance and bulk of the ſun;
"I fear that a cat would be fully as wiſe,
"To inquire when, and wherefore, balloons were begun.

"A ſmall ſhare of learning may ſerve us while here,
"The farce of exiſtence will ſoon have an end;
"And without the fatigue of deep thinking, 'tis clear,
"That age and infirmity muſt make us bend.

"You try to convince us that love is a crime,
"That filling a bumper is arrogant folly,
"That no man of ſenſe would take patience to rhyme,
"That the Bible, forſooth! has forbid to be jolly.

"But I would not give one fond embrace of my laſs
"For all the queer ſecrets Sir Iſaac explor'd;
"Nor part with my fiddle, nor flinch from my glaſs,
"Or the beef, or plumb-pudding that ſmokes on my
"board.

"The tranſit of *Venus* your paſſion employs,
"In ſtaring at *Sirius* you loſe the long night;
"A tranſit more tender enhances my joys,
"When Polly impells me to plunge in delight.

"Her boſom, her clean taper'd ancles, diſplay
"More eloquent charms than a limb of the moon:
"When virginity ſoftens, ſhall manhood cry Nay;
"Ye Gods let me ſhrink to an oyſter as ſoon!"

THE FAIRY QUEEN:

A TALE.

Of all the knights accuſtom'd to reſort,
From Cambria's wide domains to Arthur's court,
The hardy Lonval was excell'd by none,
For ſtill in danger's van, his valour ſhone.

Thro' twice ſix fields, where drench'd with Saxon blood,
In war's grim front, victorious Arthur ſtood;
The dauntleſs champion conquer'd by his ſide,
And, whether with his lance, he turn'd the battle's tide;
Or the keen falchion haſted from its ſheath,
Thick dealt his wounds, and every wound was death.
When peace return'd, his manners were as mild,
As if with blood, his arms were undefil'd;
From rivals, not himſelf, his praiſe began,
And foes who fear'd the hero, lov'd the man.
  But monarchs have, alas! too much to mind,
And Lonval, this ſad truth was taught to find;
The king forgot the proweſs of his ſword,
Nor what in war he ſpent, in peace reſtor'd:
For glory, not for hire, his blade he drew,
And ſcorn'd, like others, to demand his due.
His ſcanty fortune by degrees grew leſs,
Nor did his comrades lighten his diſtreſs,
But rather view'd him with diſdainful eyes,
For poverty both rich and poor deſpiſe.
This Lonval felt; nor would the ſoldier's pride
Submit to ſue for what might be deny'd.
  Boiling with indignation and diſguſt,
In royal faith determin'd ne'er to truſt,
Our knight, one morning, mounted on his horſe,
And o'er the fields purſu'd his ſolitary courſe.
He meant ſome diſtant region to explore,
And ſerve his proud ungrateful prince no more.
To Arthur his deſign he dar'd not tell,
Nor bade one ſordid ſunſhine friend farewell;
Content to live, nor yet afraid to die,
He left his native land without a ſigh.
He knew no fondneſs for that ſpot of earth,
Where nature thruſt him naked into birth;
And why ſhould he forbear the world to range,
Who forfeits nothing by the hardeſt change?
  On the third noon, while paſſing through a wood,
Before his eyes a large pavilion ſtood.

Two lovely damſels dreſs'd in rich array,
Approaching with a ſmile bade Lonval ſtay.
They caught his bridle with a courteous air,
Told him to leave his courſer to their care;
And ſaid their princeſs who his worth admir'd,
His much lov'd preſence in her tent requir'd.
The knight amaz'd at what he heard and ſaw,
Alighting, enter'd with reſpectful awe.
The lady roſe to meet him, and her face
From every feature beam'd celeſtial grace.
With accents ſweeter than the Syren's ſong
She wonder'd he delay'd his route ſo long;
Then preſſing by the hand the bluſhing knight,
(No lily as her own was e'er ſo white)
Into a ſpacious hall ſhe Lonval led,
Luxurious plenty on the board was ſpread.
She warm'd his courage with a bowl of wine,
He ſought no ſecond call to reſt and dine.
His brain with ſuch oppreſſive pleaſure ſwims;
The fairy's graceful height, her finely moulded limbs,
Each look, each motion, ſets his ſoul on fire,
And every vein is raging with deſire.
  Few words are wanted here to intervene;
You all foreſee the ſequel of the ſcene;
And only this remains for me to tell,
That gallant Lonval play'd his part ſo well,
That in a trance of joy his Dido ſwore,
She ne'er had known felicity before.
" My glorious veteran," the fairy ſaid,
" Long have thy matchleſs feats been ill repaid,
" And did not deſtiny my heart oppoſe,
" This day ſhould pour my vengeance on thy foes;
" Thy thankleſs chief ſhould tremble in his blood,
" And ſhe-wolves litter, where his halls had ſtood.
" What ſcorn and miſery his meal attend,
" Who pines upon the bounty of a friend?
" Again to Arthur's caſtle thou muſt fly,
" This purſe in plenty ſhall thy wants ſupply.

" To wealth, like thine, each ſuitor ſhall give place,
" And ſordid beauty wear a welcome face;
" And when thy breaſt with generous paſſion warms,
" When love, or glory, vindicate their charms,
" When fond deſire is flaſhing in thine eye,
" Or thy brow darkens, and the valiant die,
" This ring, thrice preſs'd, that inſtant ſhalt thou ſee,
" Thy guardian, viſible to none but thee:
" I only charge thee to conceal my flame,
" Nor dream I ſhall endure a rival dame.
" A faithful ſpy thy boſom I'll explore,
" Then dread the fairy much, the female more."
The amorous queen embrac'd him and withdrew;
The ſplendid viſion vaniſh'd from his view.
Mounting his ſteed, he ſaw with glad ſurpriſe
Arthur's tall battlements in proſpect riſe;
And by the fairy's aid ſo quick return'd,
To prove his grateful heart, with ardour burn'd.
At court arriv'd, the ſplendor of his gold,
Ten thouſand tongues with ſpiteful wonder told,
Nor need we ſay how faſt his friends increas'd;
How kindly he was call'd to every feaſt;
What deep attention every virtuous maid,
And wailing widow to his wiſhes paid.
But Lonval met their proffers with diſdain,
And love and friendſhip ſped their ſhafts in vain.
For 'twas his daily care on ſome pretence,
To laviſh more than double their expence.
Himſelf, his conſort choſe it ſhould be known,
That Lonval had abundance of his own.
Yet no brave comrade, honeſt, old, and poor,
Retir'd without his bounty from his door.
Now, what a fatal farce is human joy;
How ſeldom fortune ſmiles but to deſtroy.
For Arthur's Queen, Geneura was her name,
Had heard, long ſince, of Lonval's martial fame;
His manly form excited fond deſire,
And all her boſom glow'd with wanton fire.

But when ſhe ſought her paſſion to reveal,
The haughty ſoldier ſcorn'd to hear her tale;
Nay, raſhly vow'd that far ſuperior charms
Were at his will, devoted to his arms.
To jealous rage Geneura's fondneſs turn'd,
And all her breaſt for bloody vengeance burn'd:
Now in the monarch's preſence ſhe appears,
Her locks diſhevell'd, and her eyes in tears.
" And is it thus," ſhe cries, " in Arthur's court,
" That Arthur's queen becomes a traitor's ſport?
" A wretch of yeſterday, on pity fed,
" Who madly dreams to ſtain his ſovereign's bed."
And then ſhe tun'd a melancholy tale,
Of luſt outrageous, and reſiſtance frail;
With what ſtern virtue ſhe oppos'd the cheat,
How quick her ſcreams compell'd him to retreat;
Laſt, and moſt inſolent, to crown the whole,
What far more lovely miſtreſs ſway'd his ſoul.
Uxorious Arthur, prone to be deceiv'd,
The mournful clamours of his dame believ'd,
And had the laws allow'd to vent his wrath,
Our hapleſs knight had met immediate death.
But this deny'd, he choſe the ſole reſort,
To call his barons to a general court.
Lonval himſelf was ſummon'd to attend;
Next morn, an hundred chiefs the lofty hall aſcend,
And though a party in the ſuit confeſt,
The prince, in perſon, ranks above the reſt.
A knight appears, who to the queen belongs,
Begins her cauſe, announces all her wrongs,
And then, to cloſe the lecture, claims aloud
The juſt atonement of a traitor's blood.
Lonval, too late, diſcover'd to his coſt,
The double ruin of his amorous boaſt.
Nor would the fairy now attend his ring,
Nor could he hope to ſoothe his furious king.
Death he deſpis'd, but then to leave a name
Of guilt behind him, blaſted all his fame.

Nor with lefs agony his honour mourn'd
The fairy's generous love ungratefully return'd.
" I ftand not here your pity to implore
" For one," he faid, " who values life no more.
" Nor fhall I with harangues harafs the court,
" The plea of innocence is plain and fhort:
" Geneura knows on what a vile pretence
" She at my conduct chus'd to take offence.
" But having now, by fatal rafhnefs loft
" A love more godlike than the world can boaft,
" All leffer evils I muft blufh to dread,
" Pour, then, the royal vengeánce on my head:
" That grateful Arthur may with triumph tell
" His fate, by whom fo many Saxons fell."
No doubt, the reader muft expect to hear
That Lonval's doom was inftant and fevere;
That every orator had fold his vote,
And every venal placeman ftrain'd his throat;
That all obfequious to the monarch's nod
Were vain, like modern peers, to kifs the rod;
That this fam'd maxim fway'd the patriot throng,
A king of Britain never can do wrong.
With what a tone of fenfe the precept founds!
On this our happy conftitution founds;
And all agree who ruminate the cafe,
The fuperftructure's worthy fuch a bafe.
No premier with excife oppres'd us then,
Our anceftors, 'twas well, were wifer men.
No baron kept the key of Arthur's ftole,
Or for a paltry garter pawn'd his foul.
No jockey ftatefman to Newmarket ran,
Or hir'd, at Weftminfter, a bludgeon clan.
No fenate fang the virtues of a whore,
Or tax'd tame Albion for a gambler's fcore.
No courtly judge, or perjur'd jury dar'd
A ftrumpet's name from infamy to guard.
No vicar of a tithe-fuit chofe to prate;
No pettifogger fuck'd the vitals of the ftate.

What ſtrange reverſe to all we ſuffer now,
When every curate can arreſt your plow;
When judges tell us truth's a mortal crime,
And proſtitution virtue's true ſublime;
When ſeats in parliament, what precious ware!
Are bought like ſtalls for cattle at a fair;
When ſtill the more extortion grinds us down
With louder notes of joy, our wrongs we drown.
A tax on burials who would dare diſpute,
When 'tis to pay a bankrupt's birth-day ſuit.
Behold the laſt remains of common ſenſe,
By hell-born ſuperſtition hooted hence;
How is that bubble, human reaſon, ſhamm'd,
While every ſaint believes his brother damn'd,
For points of faith too ſhocking to be nam'd,
Which nothing ſhort of bedlam could have fram'd;
Now Shakeſpeare's ſacred page is fritter'd down
To pleaſe that motley maſs we call the town;
While ſing-ſong operas our ears have tir'd,
And Foote, and all his farces, are admir'd.
The candid court met Lonval at his word,
Inquir'd what matchleſs dame he thus ador'd,
And proffer'd a reſpite of twenty days,
For time to prove the juſtice of his praiſe.
And ſhould his miſtreſs, by the ſenate ſeen,
Eclipſe, in their account, the Cambrian queen,
They frankly would diſmiſs the whole affair,
If otherwiſe, for death, he muſt prepare;
Mean time confinement was the culprit's doom,
In the lone anguiſh of a dungeon's gloom.
The term elaps'd, no rival dame appear'd,
And every feeling heart for Lonval fear'd;
A dark ſuſpicion fill'd the public breaſt,
Geneura's motives were not deem'd the beſt.
Though ſtill a punk of far inferior rate
To fifty queens of very modern date;
'Twas thought ſhe often held her huſband cheap,
And ventur'd, by the bye, the lover's leap.

The chieftains were conven'd, and Lonval brought
Before them, but in vain an anſwer ſought;
The court proteſted he was much to blame,
Who ſtill refus'd to tell the lady's name.
Their verdict, now, was ready to be paſt,
And this unlucky day had been his laſt,
When lo! a blaze of lightening burſt around,
And ſubterranean thunder rock'd the ground;
While ſuddenly, on their aſtoniſh'd ſight,
Advanc'd a beauty more than mortal bright.
Her form, her mein, unrivall'd all atteſt;
Tumultuous rapture throbs in every breaſt.
"I come, my lords, an injur'd knight to aid,"
(With modeſt dignity the fairy ſaid)
"Though, ſince he raſhly vaunted of my love,
"'Twas needful his fidelity to prove.
"A wanton woman is below my wrath,
"But ere her generous victim ſuffers death,
"Since nothing elſe can ſave my huſband's life,
"Till once you judge the perſon of his wife,
"Say—might my fond embrace an hour employ,
"Or ſoothe a warrior's boſom into joy!"
She ſpoke: The council in one voice declar'd
No earth-born daughter could be here compar'd.
Arthur himſelf acknowledg'd that the knight,
By ſuch a choice, was nobly in the right.
Beyond the ſtairs which to the caſtle lead,
The ſtranger queen had left her ſnow-white ſteed.
She mounted: Lonval, ſmiling, vaults behind,
And off they fly, more rapid than the wind,
For thoſe far diſtant, but delightful plains,
Where, on her native throne, the fairy monarch reigns.

STRUT:

A CHARACTER.

WHEN STRUT begins to read a book
Which all the world has recommended,
His ſole intention is to look
For ſome pretence to turn offended.

And, ſhould the author be a friend
Whom we reſpect and patronize,
To downright ſcolding he'll deſcend
While Bedlam ſparkles in his eyes.

Converſing but to kindle ſtrife,
Rewarding homage with diſdain,
The total pleaſure of his life
Ariſes from inflicting pain:

And did the law your father hang,
He kindly would inquire the cauſe,
On *ropes* eternally harangue,
And pay your patience loud applauſe.

An uſeful leſſon to beſtow,
Provokes his ſordid thankleſs pride;
For STRUT himſelf pretends to know
More than all mankind know beſide:

And though he very fully feels
The force and weight of what you ſay,
Conviction ſullenly conceals,
And ſnaps and wrangles half a day:

And when he can no longer fly,
Like Puſs at bay, the chace he'll turn,
His previous arguments deny,
And your ſtrange *deafneſs* gravely mourn.

Conſcious how little he has read,
The fight he'll force you to begin;
And, hearing all that you have ſaid,
Steals up materials, and ſteps in.

Silence would wake his utmoſt wrath;
Yet mind this all important rule,
'Tis better far to ſave one's breath,
Than quarrel with a peeviſh fool;

Whoſe heart ſuſpicion makes her prey,
Whoſe tongue eternal ſpite defiles,
Who liſtens only to betray,
Nor ever but at miſchief ſmiles:

A bankruptcy, a rival's death, *
A reputation to deſtroy;
And his own conſequence to breathe
Completes the climax of his joy.

To hint the mildeſt mortal's worth
Provokes a ſtorm of contradiction;
He drags your ſlighteſt follies forth,
And proves your virtues all a fiction:

But with ſome "jolly, ſurly groom,"
The viper's bite muſt be delay'd;
He cringes till you quit the room,
And then the black arrears are paid.

His moral merit you ſhall hear:
He hates a wench, drinks only water;
And, but from *intereſt*, or from *fear*,
Sincerely ſcorns to flinch or flatter.

* It is uſeful to know what ſhocking characters *may* poſſibly exiſt in ſociety. Some years ago, a Gentleman was thrown from his horſe, and report ſaid that he was killed. "Ha! Is it ſo? Is "it ſo?" exclaimed * * *; "that muſt be of vaſt ſervice to ſome-"body; but I *have no connection with any of his clients*."

R

ON THE NOVELS OF Dr. SMOLLET.

For the talent of drawing a natural and original character, Dr. Smollet, of all Engliſh writers, approaches neareſt to a reſemblance of our inimitable Shakeſpeare. What can be more chaſte, amuſing, or intereſting, than Random, Trunnion, Hatchway, Liſmahago, Pallet, the Pindarick Phyſician, Tom Clarke, Farmer Prickle, Strap, Clinker, Pipes, the Duke of Newcaſtle, and Timothy Crabtree? The laſt is indeed a cloſe imitation of Sancho Panca, as Morgan is partly borrowed from one of Shakeſpeare's Welſhmen; but ſtill both are the imitations of a great maſter, not the tame copies of a common artiſt. Matthew Bramble is a moſt eſtimable portrait of a country gentleman; and admirably contraſted with his ſiſter Tabby. This novel was written when its author was declining both in health and fortune; yet he diſplays all the ſpirit and vivacity of Roderick Random; and in ſome paſſages, ſuch as that reſpecting the Smith's widow, is irreſiſtibly pathetic. All which paſſes on board the Thunder, is a ſeries of almoſt unexampled excellence. The night ſcene in bedlam, in Sir Launcelot Greaves, is drawn with uncommon force of judgment and of fancy. In the ſame publication, the ruin of Captain Clewlin and his family, enforces, with aſtoniſhing eloquence, the madneſs and infamy of paternal tyranny, and the delicious raptures of paternal tenderneſs. In the character of honeſt Bowling, Smollet, if any where, excells himſelf: The Captain's ſpeech to his crew, when about to engage a French man of war, is ſuch a maſterpiece, that, in reading it, we feel a ſort of involuntary impulſe for a broadſide. The phlegm of an old lawyer is happily illuſtrated in the conduct of Random's grandſather, and forms the moſt ſtriking contraſt imaginable to the ferocious benevolence of the naval veteran. The diſappointment of the maiden aunts, on opening the old man's will, is infinitely natural and amuſing. The entertainment in the manner of the ancients, affords a ſtrange ſpecimen of the learning and abilities of its author. The oration of Sir Launcelot to an election mob, is in the true ſpirit of Cervantes. The knight elucidates, with exquiſite ſenſe, humour, and propriety, the miſerable farce of repreſentation in parliament; and the inſolence of a rabble, incapable and unworthy of a better government, is in harmony with the conviction of every reader. With ſo much merit, Dr. Smollet had likewiſe imperfections. His oaths and execrations are indecent, and unneceſſary; and the adventures of Lady Vane ought to be expunged from the pages of a claſſical author. In this age, many gentlemen publiſh volumes of criticiſm, and attempt to illuſtrate the human mind upon metaphyſical principles. In their works, it is uſual to cite paſſages from poets, and other writers in the walk of invention; yet it is ſingular that they have ſeldom or never quoted Smollet, whoſe talents reflect honour on his country, and who, next to Buchanan, is by far the greateſt literary genius of whom North Britain has to boaſt. The admiration of the public beſtows an ample atonement for the ſilence of our profeſſed critics. His volu mesare in every hand, and his praiſes one very tongue.

POLITICAL QUERIES.

The Engliſh language has been exhauſted in panegyric upon the virtues and abilities of the preſent miniſter. We have likewiſe ſaid a great deal more than was neceſſary about the *execrable* coalition. For my own part, I muſt conſider it as a very mortifying circumſtance that an enlightened nation ſhould depend upon the talents of any ſingle individual for the conduct of its affairs. There muſt certainly be a miſerable defect *ſomewhere*, in the principles of ſuch a government. Indeed, our legiſlators have committed a variety of egregious blunders, and almoſt every day enlarges the liſt. The tax upon pedlars was the only tax, I ſuppoſe, ſince the beginning of the world, which was avowedly intended to extirpate the object of taxation. The neceſſary conſequence was, that in South Britain, at leaſt, a very uſeful and induſtrious claſs of men were reduced to beggary. Had we been informed that *Nadir Shaw*, or any other Oriental deſpot, had invented a tax for the purpoſe of exterminating its object, we ſhould naturally have exclaimed, that *this was the extremity of oppreſſion!* In the preſent caſe, however, we were ſatisfied with a few fine ſpeeches about the immaculate morality of the miniſter, and the profligacy of an abandoned coalition; for with this laſt topic the greater part of miniſterial ſpeeches, for ſome years paſt, have ended, with whatever ſubject they ſet out. The ſhop-tax ſupplies another of many good reaſons why the preſent miniſter cannot hope to be remembered with regret by poſterity. My only reaſon for preferring him to his political antagoniſt is, the external decency of his deportment. We have never ſeen him at the head of an election mob, ſpreading terror and confuſion through the ſtreets of a great city; we ſhall never be obliged to pay his arrears for dice, for race horſes, or for concubines. His enemies have very fooliſhly attempted to turn into ridicule the beſt part of his character. But there is a peculiar degree of duty of this ſort incumbent on the governors of a great nation, ſince their bad example may have the moſt ruinous conſequences.

The following queries are humbly ſubmitted to the attention of the public.

Query 1ſt. Whether it be true, that not many years ago, the greateſt part of the manufacturers of ſtarch in Scotland were reduced to bankruptcy? and whether it be alſo true, that all this ruin was owing to an abſurd and oppreſſive mode of enforcing the exciſe laws, adopted about that time, and that the few who eſcaped were ſaved from deſtruction merely by a timely relaxation in the mode of executing theſe laws? And whether all this did not happen without any alteration of the law itſelf?

Query 2d. Whether it be true that there is twenty times

lefs foap manufactured in this country than there was five years ago; and whether many of the manufacturers have not retired with their capitals into England to avoid approaching bankruptcy, and carry on their manufactures there, where the excife laws are executed with far lefs rigour?

Query 3d. Whether the tax on agents before the Court of Seffion, and upon folicitors in the inferior courts of law, is not grofsly iniquitous? A licence cofts five pounds a year to an agent, who does not perhaps clear twenty pounds by his practice; while an agent who clears a thoufand pays only the fame fum.

Query 4th. Whether it is not a notorious fact that the excife laws are making a rapid progrefs in the final deftruction of Scottifh breweries, and feveral other manufactures? Whether the number of brewers in the city of Edinburgh is not diminifhed by one half within the laft fix years? Whether fix or eight breweries, in the Canongate of Edinburgh, are not at prefent lying wafte, which were lately poffeffed by reputable tradefmen, who have been driven from their profeffion by the weight of the excife fceptre. Is there not one tenement of this fort, for which the proprietor ten years ago refufed thirteen hundred pounds, and which at prefent ftands unoccupied, though the landlord has offered to fell the whole premifes for four hundred pounds?

Query 5th. When falt is employed for curing herring, we are told that the duty is to be remitted: Whether the numerous and expenfive formalities, practifed by officers of excife, *only in this part of Britain*, do not render this indulgence totally ufelefs? Whether this circumftance has not hitherto prevented the fuccefs of every attempt to promote the fifheries on this coaft? and whether if not removed, it will not fruftrate the humane views of the patriotic fociety which at prefent exifts for the promoting of fifheries? In fhort, there appears to be no end of fuch queries; but I hope I fhall live long enough to fee an end to a part of the encomiums on the father of the horfe-tax, and the creator of revenue farmers in Britain.

In this liſt of queries there is a wide variety of omiſſions, for we have hardly a manufacture in this country which has not, at one time or other, been reduced to the brink of ruin within theſe few years, by the ſevere oppreſſion of revenue laws. It is true that both parts of the united kingdom are making rapid advances in wealth and population; but this is not in conſequence of *good*, but in ſpite of *bad* government. We are no more to thank Mr. Pitt for the general improvement of the country than we are to blame him for the preſent cold ſummer weather. On ſome occaſions he may have acted in the beſt manner that circumſtances would permit, but is he the only perſon capable of acting ſo? My cenſure is levelled, not at the man, but at the wretched ſpirit of faction which pervades this iſland. One half ſuppoſe Mr. Pitt the only perſon capable of preſerving us from ruin; the other half, equally judicious, imagine that the ſaviour of three kingdoms is only to be found in a ſtable, a gaming-houſe, or a bagnio. Yet in ſpite of many faults, Mr. Fox has often deſerved the gratitude of his country.

EDINBURGH, *June* 21. 1791.

ON FEMALE FRAILTY.

FROM PLAUTUS.

FOND boys may fancy, if they pleaſe,
  That marriage is a happy ſtate;
And, could the ſex avert diſeaſe,
  Might bear exiſtence with a mate.

Her wonted want of thrift and ſenſe
  Is yet the leaſt of Madam's failings;
For what vexation, toil, expence,
  Succeed to her inceſſant ailings.

Diſcretion, elegance, or wealth,
  My humble wiſhes dare not ſeek,
Would but my ſpouſe enſure her health
  Six hours, at leaſt, in every week.

ON HARD DRINKING.

If you who hear this deathlefs ode,
Where Pindar glows in every line,
At midnight never range abroad,
To foak the effence of the vine;
No gout fhall ever rack your toes,
Nor lamp poft bounce againft your nofe.

Nor fhall you to the bagnio roam,
Nor on the roundhoufe run afhore,
Nor plunging through the kennel home
Kick your dependents to the door;
Nor fhall your brains at breakfaft ache,
Nor fhall your nerves at thirty fhake.

Had Noah when his box was landed,
Inftead of bidding bumpers flow,
Behav'd as common fenfe demanded
And taught his fons to weave and plow;
Their father had not turn'd their jeft,
But doz'd with decency at leaft.

Had this old tar been truly wife,
And burn'd his poifonous plantation,
One root of almoft every vice
Which fills the world with devaftation,
Perhaps he might have liv'd to fee,
Ham had a founder head than he.

A FRAGMENT.

There liv'd, in former days, an honeft man,
Who did not figure on our modifh plan;
His coat was homely, but his credit found,
He paid with twenty fhillings in the pound.

He manag'd what had been his father's farm,
No currish landlord could his peace alarm;
An hearty welcome made the stranger glad,
For Hunger never wanted what he had.
He did not, like the wits of later days,
Consume his time on magazines and plays,
But fancy'd every minute worth his care,
Methusalem, he said, had few to spare.
And if, at eve, he felt a wish to read,
Isaiah, Job, and Moses, lin'd his head;
Strong common sense from Solomon he drew,
And at the ninetieth reading found him new.
When Joseph and his worthy kin were met,
His soul too, soften'd, and his cheeks were wet;
He felt a kind of pleasure in his grief,
While the tears gushing gave his heart relief.
Ruth's tender tale was often on his tongue,
And pleas'd in age, as it had pleas'd him young.
On mystic points he did not much inquire,
Nor pertly dar'd defy eternal fire.
Truths out of kenn the goodman let alone,
Nor thought it ever meant that all things should be known.

HORACE, LIB. I. ODE XXVII.

Why should my friends when they're drunk,
  Make such a terrible noise!
Will gentlemen brawl like a punk
  Pelted with dirt by the boys.

When valets convene in a cellar,
  Dividing their vails over gin;
If the landlady's pert, they may tell her,
  The liquor is dear of a pin.

They may batter her bottom pell mell,
  Kick up a sandalous pother;

And finiſh the farce very well,
  With pounding the bones of each other.

When members have met in *the houſe*,
  Our national honour to ſave,
They're heartily welcome to chouſe,
  Each patriot in turn as a knave.

But when men of faſhion agree,
  To paſs in good humour a night;
The rabble would bluſh, did they ſee
  Their betters beginning to fight.

A PARALLEL BETWEEN RICHES AND POVERTY.

FROM THE GREEK OF RHIANUS.

An ancient bard had reaſon to complain,
That all mankind are ignorant and vain;
Nor in proſperity their pride repreſs,
Nor with calm dignity ſupport diſtreſs;
To thoſe below them with contempt behave,
To thoſe above them act the downright ſlave.
  Thus, he who is in want of daily food,
Feels no bold courage animate his blood;
Nature to him no beauties can diſplay,
He curſes fate and ſhuns the light of day.
The rich, in public, tell aloud their mind,
The poor, in ſervile ſilence, ſlink behind.
"Chill Penury" each generous thought controuls,
And freezes all the ardour of their ſouls.
Nor ſhould we rail at the corrupted times,
'Tis Poverty which fills the world with crimes;
For very few begin to rob or ſteal,
Till once they've fear'd the want of many a meal.

If halters only ſor the rich were made,
Ketch ſoon might ſtarve, or ſeek a better trade;
His office merely keeps poor rogues in awe,
For great men's crimes are ſanctified by law.
To what I ſay, exceptions will be found;
But 'tis a common caſe the world around.
The great adopt a ſurer, ſafer courſe,
They neither break a ſhop nor ſteal a horſe;
They ſeldom pick a purſe, or forge a note,
Or point a piſtol at a coachman's throat.
Yet all to vice are equally inclin'd,
Their miſdemeanours vary but in kind;
The poor dare only cheat, the rich oppreſs,
The firſt muſt hide, the laſt avow ſucceſs;
The bluſhing footpad plunders in the night,
The *noble* felon dares the noon-day light.
And ſure of mortals, the moſt fooliſh thing,
Is, for the moſt part, what we call a king;
Vile ſycophants, devoted to his will,
Define his right to conquer and to kill;
And ſome poltroon, who, bred among the poor,
Had ſcarce dar'd thruſt a vixen from his door;
Commits whole empires to the ſword and flame,
Dreaming deſtruction dignifies a name.
But inſtant vengeance treads upon his heel,
And all his pride inflicted makes him feel.
Survey that claſs with an impartial eye,
How few have died as wiſe men wiſh to die;
Though fools may deem the day of vengeance paſt,
Guilt in repentance, always ends at laſt.

NOTHING NEW.

Unhappy is the bard who ſighs
For ſolid friendſhip with the great,
Since every effort which he tries-
Will prove his plan a bitter cheat.

By a long furfeit of fuccefs,
  The heart grows hard, the fancy light,
And all approaches of diftrefs,
  Derange the vifion of delight.

In vain your eloquence would plead,
  No words the fordid foul can alter;
'Tis better far to beg your bread,
  Or make your exit in a halter.

CRITICAL REMARKS ON SOME OF THE MOST EMINENT HISTORIANS OF ENGLAND.

THOUGH we are now in the clofe of the eighteenth century, the hiftory of this ifland has never been ftudied with proper attention. That portion of it, in particular, which precedes the Reformation, feems, at prefent, buried in profound neglect. For this misfortune, fufficient reafons may be affigned; an hundred and fifty years were wafted in theological frenzy, or in defeating the tyranny of the houfe of Stuart; and a modern compiler of general hiftory is ftrongly tempted to rufh with precipitation over the remoter periods, and to referve his abilities and refearch for thofe later fcenes, in which a reader of the prefent day is more heartily interefted.—On fome of thefe modern authors, a few candid obfervations may repay a perufal.

The name of RAPIN is now almoft forgotten; and Mr. Hume, in the end of his Englifh Hiftory, has branded him as an author "the moft defpicable both in ftyle and matter." The cenfure is invidious, and unjuft: His work contains an immenfe multitude of interefting circumftances, wholly omitted by the Scottifh author. From his perfonal fituation, a claffical compofition was not to be expected. He wrote a more complete General Hiftory of England, than had ever appeared in this country; and whatever be his faults, it would be ungenerous to deny his uncommon merit.

SALMON made an eſſay on the ſame ſubject. Though ſhort, it contains much information, which is not to be found in more voluminous hiſtorians of England. His own reflections are brief, lively, and ſenſible. It is uſual to repreſent Richard III. as deformed and decrepid; yet theſe very authors inform us, that he unhorſed and killed with his own hand the ſtandard-bearer of Henry VII. who was reputed to be the ſtrongeſt knight in the rebel army. The inconſiſtency of theſe two ſtories is pointed out by Salmon. He has left behind him no work of very ſuperior value, yet he muſt have been an author of ſuperior abilities; for, without becoming tireſome, he has written more than moſt of us have read.

The ſame remarks apply with equal juſtice to Dr. SMOLLET. The immenſe bulk of his writings proves that he compoſed with greater facility than ordinary men are able to converſe. By his own account, in the expedition of Humphry Clinker, it appears that he very often wrote merely for wages; and on ſuch occaſions, nothing above mediocrity can with reaſon be demanded. The continuation of his Engliſh Hiſtory, from 1748 to 1764, is a mere catchpenny chaos, without even a ſpark of merit. There is great reaſon to believe that he, or rather his journeymen, copied at random from ſomebody elſe, moſt of the quotations and references arranged with ſo much parade on the margin of his text.

GUTHRIE has left behind him more than one ponderous fabric on Britiſh hiſtory. He had ſenſe, learning, candour, and induſtry. He had an original manner, and wiſhed to think for himſelf: But to elegance, he was an entire ſtranger, and to that happy choice of circumſtances which forms an inſtructive hiſtorian; he was often familiar without perſpicuity, and prolix without completeneſs. No writer is at preſent leſs popular. A geographical grammar has been printed under his name; but it is generally underſtood, that he had no ſhare in its compoſition.

In point of ſtyle, Mr. HUME may be ſtudied as a perfect model. Pure, nervous, eloquent, he is ſimple without weakneſs, and ſublime without effort. In the art of telling an humorous ſtory, he can never be excelled; and when he choſe to exert himſelf, he was even a conſiderable maſter of the pathetic: But it was his misfortune to deſpiſe accuracy of reſearch, and fidelity of citation. He was a bitter Tory; and while detection flaſhed in his face, he commonly adhered to whatever he had once written. His account of the houſe of Stuart is not the ſtatement of an hiſtorian, but the memorial of a pleader in a Court of Juſtice. He ſometimes aſſerts a poſitive untruth, contradicted by the very author whom he pretends himſelf to be quoting; but more commonly gains his purpoſe, by ſuppreſſing the whole evidence on the oppoſite ſide of the queſtion. His conduct in the controverſy with Mr. Tytler, can hardly be defended: And his injurious treatment of Queen Mary of Scotland is not more diſguſting than his farcical panegyrics on the virtues of her poſterity. When we examine Mrs. Macaulay's performance on the ſame period, we meet with a profuſion of intereſting intelligence, of which the mere reader of Hume has not the moſt diſtant conception. The Scottiſh hiſtorian gives but ſhort and partial excerpts from the writers of the times. His female antagoniſt, on the other hand, gives large extracts from the original writers; and though to a ſuperficial eye, her work aſſumes an air leſs pleaſing and claſſical, what is loſt in elegance is fully repaid in authenticity. He is a zealous advocate for the ceremonies of the Church of England. He cenſures thoſe brave and able men who reſiſted and defeated her uſurpations; and to whom we are, at this day, indebted for our liberties. He attempts to prove, that Epiſcopacy is preferable to Preſbyterianiſm, and that Laud may be vindicated for perſecuting the diſſenters. Had Mr. Hume been ſerious in this opinion, he might have deſerved an anſwer. But on turning over to his Eſſays, we are ſurpriſed by the moſt ſtupendous and unbluſhing contradiction. One chief end of his metaphyſical writings is to extinguiſh every ſentiment of religion. The ſame Court, therefore, which ſent Baſtwick and Prynne to the pillory, would, with far leſs injuſtice, have ſent our hiſtorian himſelf to *a more decided ſituation*. What are we to think of a profeſſed infidel defending the barbarous inſolence of the prieſthood?

Mr. Hume has expreſſed much indignation at that memorable act of juſtice, the execution of Charles I. His two elder ſons ought to have ſhared the ſame fate. Their annals are diſtinguiſhed by endleſs uſurpations, plots, rebellions, and maſſacres; by two foreign wars, and a revolution. We cannot but obſerve with the honeſt Dutchman, that their predeceſſor "was quite another man." Had Cromwell ſurvived but for ten years longer, we ſhould have heard no more about the poſterity of "The Holy Martyr."

James I. butchered Sir Walter Raleigh, without the form of a trial. Mr. Hume tells us that, this meaſure "was eſteemed an inſtance of the utmoſt cruelty and injuſtice;" and his vindication of James is one of the moſt elaborate paſſages in his whole work. The beſt of his arguments appears to be, "that no jury would have found Raleigh guilty!"

At the ſentence of Lord Bacon, Mr. Hume adds, that James "conferred on him a large penſion of eighteen hundred pounds a-year, and employed every expedient to alleviate the weight of his age and misfortunes." This penſion would have been equivalent to ſix or eight thouſand pounds Sterling at the preſent day: And as his Majeſty had nothing of his own, it muſt have been transferred from the pockets of his ſubjects. The tranſaction at beſt could have but reſembled an apprentice interfering with his maſter's till; a compariſon which applies to moſt other examples of royal munificence. But the fact is, that Bacon, from the time of his ſentence, lived as he died, in beggary. On this point, the reader may conſult Mrs. Macaulay and her authorities.

Mr. Hume has canted much about the death of Strafford, and claims the merit of having shed some "generous tears" on that subject. All that he says, put together, is not worth a single expression of honest Pym! When Strafford, then a leader of Opposition, for the sake of a place at Court, deserted the public cause; "you have left us," said Pym, "but we shall not leave you while your head is on your shoulders," and he kept his word.

No part of our historian's performance has been more controverted, than that relative to Queen Mary. Perhaps the next age may consider her conduct in a light equally different from her present accusers and her apologists. I would meet the former on their own ground, and frankly reply, that the brutal insolence of Darnly to his wife, his sovereign, his benefactress, deserved ten deaths; and that Mary, if connected with the conspirators, was at worst, but an executioner of justice. If she wanted to depose and destroy Elizabeth, still the ruin of her country, the massacre of her friends, the loss of her kingdom, her liberty, and her child, justified her revenge. Let us, for example, suppose that Mr. Hume had been confined in one of the dungeons of the Holy Office at Lisbon, and that he had obtained a chance of escaping. *Query*, Would he have refused freedom, for fear of injuring the inquisitor who arrested him? Surely he could not have scrupled at knocking out the brains of the whole fraternity? Many modern historians, and among others, Mr. Hume, have fallen into the practice of quaint wiredrawn portraits. The virtues and literary genius of James I. for instance, are expanded by our author into a quarto page, which can be regarded but as waste paper. As a man of taste, Mr. Hume is often extremely singular. He affirms that Shakespeare "was totally ignorant of *all* theatrical art and conduct; that it is in vain we look either for continued purity, or simplicity of diction; and that he cannot for *any* time uphold *a reasonable propriety of thought*." There is much more to the same purpose.

Mr. Hume, in common with most of our historions, has omitted to give an account of his materials. A judicious reader, when he ſees them perpetually referred to, will aſk who is Froiſſart, and who is Rhymer? Till the acceſſion of the houſe of Tudor, his narrative is abrupt. For example, the reign of Edward III. extended to almoſt half a century, and is one of the moſt buſy and memorable in ancient or modern annals. It is compreſſed by Mr. Hume within an hundred octavo pages, while the reign of Elizabeth alone fills one of his largeſt volumes. His warmeſt admirers muſt allow, that he betrays a wide diſproportion of parts in the execution of his plan: But in truth, it was by far too extenſive to be completed by any ſingle pen. It was neceſſary to write a book of a ſaleable ſize. As an epitome of Engliſh Hiſtory, it is too large; but as a complete hiſtory, it is by far too ſhort. We often ſee whole folios printed on the antiquities of a ſingle town, or a ſingle country pariſh. Why then ſhould we think it tireſome to read twenty or thirty volumes on the national hiſtory of our anceſtors? Mr. Hume, like many men of eminence, has performed too little, by attempting to perform too much; yet his writings afford univerſal and laſting pleaſure. The diſtinctneſs of his manner, and the acuteneſs or plauſibility of his general obſervations, caſt a veil over the errors and deficiencies of his narrative.

On the ancient hiſtory of England, few writers have thrown more light than the famous FROISSART. His chronicle commences with the acceſſion of Edward III. and ends with the death of Richard II containing a period of ſeventy-three years. Like almoſt every other writer, he has numerous and obvious imperfections. But what Plutarch has remarked of a paſſage in Xenophon, may with equal juſtice be applied to this author. Froiſſart does not deſcribe a march, a battle, a ſiege, or a purſuit, but he places them before our eyes. By the firſt ſtroke of his artleſs, yet magic pen, we are tranſported into the tumult of action, and forward to forget that we continue in the cloſet. He has not indeed attempted the higher walks of eloquence. He is neither a Thucydides nor a Salluſt, nor does he difplay the judgment and accuracy of Polybius; but he deferves to be termed the Xenophon of his age. Replete with materials, it is true that he has inferted a multiplicity of particulars, which are no longer interefting at the diftance of four centuries. But wherever his fubject rifes equal to his abilities, full, without redundancy, intelligent and inftructive, without oftentation, he charms us by that pathetic fimplicity of manner, that minute but happy felection of circumftances, which animates the page of the admired Athenian. Nor is it the leaft honourable part of his praife, that he appears to have been entirely diverted of national and of perfonal prejudice, and that without any veftige of parade or affectation, he frequently difcovers the traces of a feeling heart. The candid reader will forgive this tribute of refpect. While hourly oppreffed with a frefh multitude of infipid compilations from compilations, we are in the moft ferious danger of forgetting the very exiftence of thofe ineftimable writers from whom our whole fources of information are originally derived. Of the many fhip-loads of treatifes on Roman affairs, which Englifh, and ftill more, French idlenefs has dragged into light, a numberlefs majority make not the moft diftant approaches to claffical merit; and yet of the greater part of Greek and Roman hiftorians, an entire and decent tranflation will be fought for in vain in either language. After fuch mournful evidence of our ftupidity, it is hopelefs to add, that an accurate verfion of Froiffart would be an important acquifition to the literary world.

His memoirs exhibit a beautiful portion of feudal hiftory; and a liberal mind will obferve with peculiar pleafure, that they are not deformed by the madnefs of theological rancour. They do not exhibit the horrid farce of nations exterminating each other for antiquated fyftems of faith, in the wildeft degree abfurd, or abfolutely unintelligible. This venerable veteran was not to difguft us by the detail of controverfies and of martyrdoms, where learning is frivolity, and fortitude at beft but the frenzy of ignorance; nor were a cock-fight and a card-table, a maſquerade and an horſe-race, to limit the amuſements and ambition of a brave and proud nobility. The Black Prince never condeſcended to become arbiter in the quarrels of a band of jockies, of fiddlers, or of ſtage dancers.* Neither his father nor his fellow-ſoldiers would have admired his magnanimity. Glowing with the moſt exalted ſentiments of perſonal independence and heroic fame, it was to vindicate the importance of his family, or the beauty of his miſtreſs, that the knight couched his lance, and ruſhed into the field. The rough, but manly features of the ſoul, diſplayed an intereſting dignity: The paſſions blazed into their wildeſt effort; and though reaſon and humanity cannot always approve, the tear of ſenſibility atteſts that we admire.

HORACE, LIB. V. EPODE XV.

'Twas night; the ſilent moon ſhone clear
  Amid the ſtarry ſkies,
When you, my love, preſum'd to ſwear
  By Jove whom you deſpiſe.

* Beccaria tells us, that it was lately the cuſtom for Italian barbers to write upon the ſign above their ſhop doors, "Boys gelded here in the neateſt manner." On reading this, we raſhly infer, that ſuch artiſts muſt be the very dregs of mankind. But, thoſe who encourage the practice are certainly far more culpable.

We are juſt now [January 1791,] informed by the daily papers, that there has been a numerous meeting of our nobility, at London, with a Prince at their head, to conſult about rebuilding the Opera Houſe, and that an hundred thouſand pounds will be wanted. It would be in vain to remind ſuch people, of the ſuperior propriety of paying off their tradeſmen, or of abating a year's rent to a diſtreſſed tenant. A Roman ſenate, aſſembling to deliberate about the cookery of Domitian's mullet, † formed a leſs prominent object of ridicule.

† See Juvenal, Sat. IV.

And while my charming trait'refs ſpoke,
  Her arms enclos'd me round,
As we have ſeen the ſolid oak
  By twining ivy bound.

You promis'd, while the wolf ſhould tear
  The tender lambs away;
While ſailors, through the main ſhould ſteer,
  My raptures to repay.

But now, my faithleſs fair, believe,
  Horace ſhall act the man;
Nor will he, for your coyneſs grieve,
  But ſtrike a bolder plan.

Addreſs ſome fair ingenuous girl,
  From pride and falſehood free;
And when your fancy takes a whirl
  And drives you back to me:

For well I know your preſent ſwain
  Shall ſoon your coldneſs mourn;
Then will I, heedleſs of your pain,
  Be merry in my turn.

THE PROGRESS OF MERIT.

When nature, clapping up in haſte a head,
For want of brain, pours in a pound of lead;
When learning cannot pierce the ſolid ſcull,
And lady mother owns her darling dull,
Though creeping prudence his repute may ſave,
'Tis two to one, the blockhead is a knave.
The paltry rotten thing he calls his heart,
Would fain ſupply the want of ſenſe with art;
And ſuch a man has far the faireſt chance
In fortune's ſlippery turnpike to advance.

The dunce who doats on antiquated rules
Ensures applause from all the mob of fools;
For every solemn ass helps on his brother,
Like mites in cheese, they crowd by one another.
If you, kind Sir, dissent from what I say,
For one lax moment listen to my lay;
Perhaps the muse your wisdom will persuade
That merit's wrong'd in almost every trade,
That excellence supreme is oft a curse;
The conclave hardly could have coin'd a worse.
When fate has gifted some superior mind
With sense above the rabble of mankind,
If genius in the cause of truth engage,
And strike at error sanctified by age,
With fearless eye wide nature's field explore,
And shew how little folly saw before,
And boldly charge the reigning sons of art,
With the rash ardour of an honest heart,
From every side the trump of slander's blown,
And the whole herd of pedants hunt him down:
Into broad day each trivial error's brought,
While dulness shudders at a daring thought:
On merit's head their mean revenge is hurl'd,
And what can one man do against a world?
The youth who labours to acquire a name,
Must never seek a pure bye-path to fame;
For instance, should he traffick in the laws,
His pen must vindicate the vilest cause.
His tongue must learn to wrangle and dispute,
Where every common rascal would be mute;
That white is black, and black is white, he sees,
Conviction always rising with his fees.
And as a bawd hires out her fiend-like train,
The baser sophist prostitutes his brain;
For every knave says all which can be said,
Nor blushes to exult in such a trade;
In short, a counsellor can seldom rise,
Who truth or falsehood scruples to disguise.

Nor can the flip-flop faculty proclaim
That candour always points their path to fame.
When fome poor man who ftrives to force his way,
Through this fine world on fifteen pence a day,
Who fees ten healthy brats about his board,
For whom he's envied by fome heirlefs lord,
By heavy labour, and by fcanty food,
Has loofen'd all his nerves and thinn'd his blood,
When the fierce fever ftops his fcanty pay,
And fhakes the crumbling tenement of clay;
When all the father wrings his foul with fear,
And the fond hufband foftens in a tear;
His ancient rules the fexton's friend obferves,
He fweats, cups, bathes, bleeds, blifters, purges, ftarves;
Secundum artem all his rage he vents,
And half his gallipots, are eas'd of their contents.
A ring of females babble out his praife,
And watch his eye, and lick up all he fays.
" I cannot promife; but—pray—hope the beft,
" With water-gruel try to cram his cheft.
" There's too much *vigour* in the patient's veins;"
Then fhakes his head, but cannot fhake his brains.
And oft when men of more than common fkill,
Who fcorn alike the julep and the pill;
Who but a tragic farce believe their trade,
Who dare not choofe to poifon and be paid;
When fuch men fmiling, at difcordant rules,
Reject the trafh they fwallow'd in the fchools;
Nor with vile drugs the patient's paunch diftort,
But, fure that hunger muft require fupport,
On wholefome victuals roundly bid him dine,
And brace the fyftem with untainted wine;
The folemn homicides foon bear him down,
Ten thoufand falfehoods fill the trembling town;
And fages fent to fave the human race
Reap the reward of danger and difgrace.
The toils of Sydenham and Harvey read,
What clouds of darknefs burft on either head!

The rising sun of science was o'ercast,
But truth, though slowly, may prevail at last.
An honest parson, let him do his best,
Can hardly fail of censure from the rest.
Thus, when great Conyers* tore the veil aside,
Expos'd the bloody progress of their pride,
And mark'd what dreadful mischief they had done
That this poor world no blacker curse had known;
An host of maniacs rose in Heaven's defence,
And all assail'd the page of common sense.
What, though in argument the gown-man fail,
One certain road to conquest is to rail:
The modern saint must labour to ascend,
By twining texts to serve his party's end;
First of the van, the holy champion flies,
And loudly tells each methodist he lies;
That Satan long has panted for his soul,
And ne'er receiv'd a felon half so foul;
That the Great Judge of nature will rejoice
To hear the damn'd send up a doleful noise;
That rigid justice in the pit below
For want of *faith* inflicts eternal woe;
That smoking brimstone fills each Quaker's nose,
And guilt forbids Socinians to repose.
Had thrice five hundred of that bawling tribe
Whom not even mitres into peace can bribe;
Who fire mankind to fight for empty names,
And preach up love, and set the world in flames;
Had they descended with the *Royal George*
We had been too well eas'd of such a scourge.
Behold his fate who by plain merit tries
In physic or divinity to rise.
The faculty must kill, the clergy damn,
Lest the pert vulgar vow their trades a sham.

* The Reverend Dr. Conyers Middleton, the celebrated librarian of Cambridge; a man who deserves to be entitled the Shakespeare of theologians.

And many a worthy man we may believe,
Whofe confcience can't become an arrant fieve,
Who fcorns with polemicks to plague his head,
Nor pores on Celfus, but in fearch of bread,
With honeft anguifh acts the parfon's part,
And deals cathartics with a trembling heart.
Attorneys who adhere to common fenfe,
Who fcorn to fcribble in a rogue's defence,
Who are without a bribe the poor man's friend,
The public *tafte* are certain to offend:
A crowd of clients cannot hope to fee,
Nor twice a term to touch a handfome fee;
Though Chatham's genius from the tomb fhould ftart,
To teach them all the magic of his art.
And though fome parafite may chance to rife,
Like Boileau, by reciting fervile lies,
The pupils of Apollo, 'tis confeft,
Are almoft all but beggars at the beft.
Thus Jaffier's father faw his morfel fail,
And Taffo ran diftracted in a jail.
Dryden did fomething worfe than beg his bread,
And Spenfer figh'd to flumber with the dead.
Butler, poor man! fupported life with pain,
While Chatterton renounc'd it with difdain.
The long fucceeding numbers who can name,
But all were fick of hunger and of fame.
Though men of tafte may liften to his lays,
And fools fatigue him with infipid praife;
No brother of the quill will condefcend
To be the poet's, ftranger's, young man's friend.
Their cold hearts cannot give effential aid,
They dare not afk him if his dinner's paid.
His little wants no critic fhall fupply,
His patrons pity, praife, and let him die.

HORACE, LIB. IV. ODE IX.

And ſo, you fancy all the rhymes
  Your friend ſo fondly would recite,
Will neither pleaſe the preſent times,
  Nor give poſterity delight?

You ſay that Shakeſpeare has attain'd
  The boldeſt height of claſſic praiſe,
And every bard ſhall be diſdain'd
  Who cannot emulate his lays:

But, though his fearleſs flaſh excells
  The pompous elegance of Rowe,
When Shore her tender ſtory tells,
  We feel our tears begin to flow:

Though Zara force not awful wonder,
  Like Proſpero's enchanted iſle,
When Congreve's Ben begins to blunder,
  Can gravity forbear to ſmile?

Though Butler offers no pretence,
  Or to the tender, or ſublime,
Yet, what a blaze of wit and ſenſe
  Burſts through the rubbiſh of his rhyme!

And thus, though Swift could ne'er pretend
  To paint the ravings of a Lear,
Yet when the Dean predicts his end,
  The proudeſt Cynic ſteals a tear:

For every word Old Wagſtaff ſays
  Deſcribes him in a light ſo true,
That, with one general burſt of praiſe,
  We give the Drapier all his due:

Nor ſhould you damn one all at once
  For eking ſome inſipid pages,

Though Fathom's father ſeems a dunce
Tom Bowling ſhall endure for ages:

Though Dryden's farces be forgot,
How ſweet Cecilia's numbers roll!
And Otway woeful nonſenſe wrote,
But ſtill Monimia melts the ſoul.

ON IDLENESS:

FROM THE FIRST BOOK OF SPENCER'S FAIRY QUEEN.

The chariot of the queen † now mov'd along,
With ſix poſtilions, a ſtrange motely throng.
The maſter-groom was mounted on an aſs,
And ſlow the beaſt, and ſlow the rider was;
His looks betray'd the dulneſs of his ſoul,
His clothes were ſhabby and his ſhirt was foul.
His ſtockings folding down his ancles hung,
From a capacious mouth loll'd out his tongue.
The loſs of buttons kept his boſom bare,
His eyes ſtood fixed in a vacant ſtare.
His only pouch, his cards and dice preſerv'd,
His ſpouſe had broke her heart, his children ſtarv'd.
Left by his father with a large eſtate,
His folly ſoon had forc'd the frowns of Fate;
If want of care can rank us with the bleſt,
He of all mortals happineſs poſſeſt.
Reflection never wrung his heart with pain,
Nor ſtirr'd the ſtanding puddle of his brain;
From danger of a jail though never free,
Surety for all who ſought his help was he.
His pooreſt friend had lent him more or leſs,
For every day produc'd ſome new diſtreſs;

† The Poet is deſcribing the chariot of Pride; and Idleneſs, Gluttony, Avarice, &c. are perſonified as her poſtilions.

When tradeſmen bawl'd, he huſh'd them with a ſong,
Nor gueſs'd if their demands were right or wrong.
And when his breeches got an hundredth rent,
He laugh'd to ſee his taylor's patience ſpent.
Nor health in early walks the ſloven ſought,
Nor knew the nobler exerciſe of thought;
By day he ſtroll'd the current lie to hear,
And loung'd, and gam'd, and read the gazetteer.
And when the liſtleſs day began to cloſe,
With brother vagrants, ſoak'd his ev'ning doſe.
He never went to ſleep till twelve at night,
Nor twice in twenty years roſe with the riſing light,
But always eat his breakfaſt in his bed,
Unleſs compell'd to ſteal before he fed.
The want of toil his uſeleſs nerves unbrac'd,
And purſe, and perſon, ſunk with equal haſte;
The dream of reformation died in words,
That precious fruit which Idleneſs affords.

ON WRANGLING.

Some ſilly fellows have a way
Of contradicting all you ſay;
And ſeem to fancy converſation
Invented but for diſputation.
As puſs, with briſk erected ears,
A ſcratch behind the wainſcot hears;
So theſe are always on the watch,
Your ſlighteſt ſlip with triumph catch;
And ſhould you venture a defence,
Deplore your want of common ſenſe.
  Such vipers, (for they cannot claim
A kinder, or a better name,)
Betray, in ſpite of all their art,
A ſhallow head, a worthleſs heart.
  Six ſerious words are juſt enough,
To anſwer all their ſaucy ſtuff.

" That's your opinion, 'tis not mine,"
And thus the combat you decline.
To them, and all mankind, be civil,
But fly them as you'd fly the devil.
If e'er you dare to take a wife,
And wish to shun eternal strife,
Seek one who never shall presume,
To start a paradox from Hume.
Ten thousand quibbles he contains,
Fit only to confound her brains.
Nor let her learn to talk by rule,
Nor *reason* till she turns a fool;
Nor ever quote a pointed phrase,
Nor quit her wheel to pore on plays.
Teach her, and cite the holy Paul,
That spinsters never ought to brawl;
That silence proves her manly spirit,
And prompt obedience forms her merit.

A DREAM:

FROM THE LATIN OF BUCHANAN.

THE morning star had shed his parting ray,
The dawn's gray smile announc'd approaching day;
The swain began his endless toil to curse,
The wakesome bantling battled with its nurse.
Smoke from the chimney top essay'd to rise,
The lark melodious warbled up the skies;
The barn-yard cock led down his female train,
The rooks embodied pour'd across the plain.
Rats from the cupboard hasted to retire,
And curs and cats throng'd round each kitchen fire.
My careful spouse the curtain-lecture clos'd,
With solemn wonder why her servants doz'd;
As if invaded by ten thousand fleas,
Or china crack'd had robb'd her soul of ease,
Or some shrewd sister wrong'd her of a groat;
Or bought perhaps too fine a petticoat,

From my embraces to the floor ſhe ſprung
And the whole houſe with wholeſome proverbs rung.
Not half ſo loudly, when he fears a wreck,
The ſurly boatſwain pipes all hands on deck,
When darkneſs hides the deep, the rigging rends,
The pumps are choaking, and the hull deſcends,
The pilot headlong from the rudder's thrown,
And all the raging ocean ruſhes down.
Myſelf more lazy, lay awake a bed,
When ſudden heavy ſlumber ſeiz'd my head,
And, all at once, before my frighten'd eyes,
The father of Franciſcans ſeem'd to riſe.
His waiſt was bound, as uſual, with a cord,
His back, the abſence of a ſhirt deplor'd;
A cowl conceal'd his cloſely ſhaven crown,
And o'er his brawny ſhoulders flow'd a gown.
His roſy cheeks, and his round bulky cheſt,
Proclaim'd the ſymptoms of a mind at reſt.
In his right hand a crucifix he bore,
And in the left, a dreſs like that he wore.
My joints, and every ſinew ſhook with fear,
When thus the ſacred leeoh addreſs'd me with a ſneer.
" No more let midnight rambles wrong your health;
" Reſign, dear George, the raſh purſuit of wealth,
" From reaſon's impious eminence deſcend,
" And through the quagmire faith your footſteps bend.
" Fear, hope, and grief, and joy, alike are vain,
" The warmeſt pleaſure terminates in pain.
" This fooliſh world no proſpect can diſplay,
" For which the wiſe loſe would a ſingle day;
" Accept our garb, celeſtial cares attend,
" Chant, hymns, count beads, and at our altars bend."
My courage rallied while the phantom ſpoke,
And thus on his harangue, I boldly broke:
" Let others vaunt their fortitude of face,
" My careleſs temper ſhudders at grimace.
" Whatever fortune proffers, good or ill,
" My thoughts, I always told, and always will.

" The novice, who preſumes to fill your gown,
" Muſt caſt his freedom and his conſcience down.
" Let thoſe deteſted hypocrites who can,
" Abjure the generous feelings of a man,
' Force from their cheeks the honeſt bluſh of youth,
" And tell us they promote the cauſe of truth:
" That to perdition we muſt all be driven,
" Unleſs impoſtors point the way to heaven.
" Go—bid old women croke your ſtupid hymns,
" Shall I in dirty ſackcloth wrap my limbs,
" And like a ſavage madman waſte my days?
" Can bedlam propagate our Maker's praiſe?
" Could paradiſe be gain'd by this pretence,
" I'd frankly dare the worſt, with men of ſenſe.
" Whatever of ſalvation you declare,
" 'Tis ſeldom that a monk obtains a ſhare.
" Biſhops, indeed, are jolly honeſt fellows,
" Keep doxies of their own, nor drive old fumblers jealous;
" On pimps and paraſites their bounty pour,
" Nor quaff their Bourdeaux with a grin ſo ſour.
" But leaving fanaticks to cant and pray,
" They game and wench all night, and gormandize all day.
" Reſerve the gown, you value as a prize,
" Till ſome more hungry candidate ariſe.
" I'm no knight errant of eternal bliſs,
" Nor ſhall for the next world torment myſelf in this.
" Yet, if you wiſh me happineſs divine,
" Mark what Elyſium I prefer as mine.
" Of ſome rich mitre, conſtitute me lord;
" Your belly ſhall be cramm'd for ever at my board."

ON THE ABUSE OF TIME.

We always find ſo quick the moments run,
That life is ended ere 'tis well begun.
The bubble Hope is bought with ſo much pain,
That few wiſe men would wiſh to live again.

The dulleſt mortal breathing ought to know,
We're only in probation here below;
And former hours, in vice or folly paſt,
How ſolemn, and how terrible, the laſt.
Yet ſpite of all religion can reveal,
And all conviction forces us to feel,
How vile an uſe do many make of time,
How frequent, how deplorable the crime!
  The early hunter ruſhes to the chaſe,
What brutal joy is painted in his face,
When fifty half-ſtarv'd dogs with open throat,
Ruſh on a hare that's hardly worth a groat?
  Some give their nights, and wiſh to give their days,
To hear unletter'd vagrants mangle plays;
Deform the ſcene pathetic Otway drew,
And ſpout in Shakeſpeare's name, the traſh he never knew.
From galleries, and pit, applauſe is roar'd,
While common ſenſe turns pale at every word.
  See how yon ſoakers puſh the glaſs about,
And forfeit half their lives to gain the gout,
On ſober Prudence break each vulgar jeſt,
And all the man is buried in the beaſt.
A Daniſh doit,* a Patagonian flower,
Demoliſh oft an academic hour.
The liſt of human whimſies is ſo long,
To tell the tithe would tire a Frenchman's tongue;
Let all defend their foibles as they pleaſe,
Exiſtence was not lent for ends like theſe;
No race, no cock-pit, their ambition fir'd,
When Phocion and Pelopidas expir'd.
  Far other pleaſures all their thoughts employ,
Superior ſallies of untainted joy;
Who rifle the remains of Greece and Rome,
And trace in ages paſt, the fate of thoſe to come;

* Twenty-ſix quarto pages, beſides ſeveral prints, have been expended upon "the PENNY with the name of Rodbertus IV." See Archæologia, Vol. V. p. 390.

Who to the toil of thinking dare ſubmit,
Drink the rich ſtream of Smollet's fearleſs wit;
Revere in Swift, the wonder of his age,
And love and ſtudy Gay's facetious page;
A few like theſe, would partly fill the void
Of thoſe Tertullian's diſciples deſtroy'd.

HORACE, LIB. I. ODE XXIX.

I WONDER, Harry, what delight
You feel in ſeeing raſcals fight;
Or how poor mortals dare be proud,
Of daily ſhedding ſo much blood.
The beſt excuſe that can be made,
For ſuch a vile, inhuman trade,
Is, when a man of virtue draws
His patriot ſword, in Freedom's cauſe;
But who can give a right to you
To ravage Bengal or Peru?
The hunter calls, the blood-hounds fly,
And guiltleſs millions are to die.
Our hirelings, give me leave to ſay,
Fight not for principle, but pay.
Ruffians, impatient of repoſe,
For what have they to gain or loſe?
And tell me, when the war is ended,
Can they ſuppoſe their fortunes mended?
They ſtill muſt pay their pot of ale,
Or ſee, full ſoon, their liquor fail.
The beardleſs enſign ſhakes his cane,
And they muſt bear the beau's diſdain.
But let the bully dare a ſtroke,
Or hazard one inſulting joke,
On ſome poor man who toils for bread,
The clown will break the coxcomb's head.
What, for ſo many thouſand years,
Has fill'd the world with blood and tears,

But restless bedlamites, like you,
Who scorn'd to settle at the plow?
The black record of ancient times
Is full of nothing but their crimes;
The rank they bear in modern days
Can add but little to their praise;
By whom was Corsica opprest?
A herd of cut-throats at the best;
Pizarro did no more than you
Practise upon the poor Gentoo.
 And who, alas! will now deny
That Tiber's bed may soon be dry,
That muddy Nile may backwards flow,
And boiling Ætna vomit snow;
Since you, a man of sense and thought,
Who such a world of books had bought,
Forsake felicity at home,
And all the wits of Greece and Rome,
To ramble round this wretched globe,
To burn, and butcher, steal, and rob.
'Tis thus the royal forces act,
(Let Impudence deny the fact;)
Our beggar'd loyalists can say
What sums your Tartars made them pay;
And when Culloden's glorious field,
Had forc'd ill-fated Charles to yield;
Who but the Devil would have done,
What they did, when the day was won?
 What is, in short, a volunteer?
Five words will make the matter clear;
A lazy lounger who engages,
For ten times less than hangmen's wages,
In spite of Nature's plainest law,
To murder men he never saw;
And thus he proves his public spirit,
What worth such heroes must inherit?
 Since Israel, by divine command,
Set out to clear the promis'd land;

With ſpecial orders not to pity,
But raze or burn each impious city,
Pound every pregnant mother's bones,
And daſh her infants on the ſtones,
Though war has ne'er again his forehead
Inſcrib'd with characters ſo horrid,
Through all the feats of Rome and Greece,
The tale is always of a piece.
The luſt for pillage, rapine, blood,
Was ardour for the public good;
But not one ſingle war in ten
Was made to ſave the rights of men;
So many bouts are loſt and won,
Such endleſs, mutual, miſchiefs done;
That Juſtice, bluſhing at the ſight,
Swears neither party can be right.
Lay down your ill-directed pride;
Go home, take care of your fire-ſide;
And, if you hate a peaceful life,
Provide, betimes, a loving wife.

HORACE, LIB. I. ODE XXXIII.

Do not, dear Ned, ſo gravely mourn
The falſehood of the fair;
But all your ſervile verſes burn,
Before they take the air.
I muſt, upon my ſoul, deſpiſe
A lover who ſincerely ſighs.

The pretty prattling fools are proud,
To give their betters pain:
But, when our angels are allow'd
Full leiſure to diſdain;
We read in each relenting face,
They would, but dare not, turn the chaſe.

'Tis not your men of ſenſe or wit,
  Who win their wavering hearts;
You muſt, the female taſte to hit,
  Aſſume a Coxcomb's arts:
    At every ball be ſure to ſhine,
    And laugh at fools who cringe and pine.

Then Madam's pride will take alarm,
  To ſee her pow'r diſdain'd;
And then ſhe'll ſummon every charm
  To get the rover chain'd:
    And then the fort's within your reach,
    You may, at pleaſure, ſtorm the breach.

THE PATRIOT.

Whatever rank we hold among mankind,
Wiſdom will recommend a ſteady mind.
Though fleeting fortune bid her bounties flow,
Mark how content the beggar halts below.
He ſees contending kings for ſafety fight,
And peaceably enjoys his humble right.
His heart is light, full cheaply is he fed,
And each barn-floor can ſerve him for a bed.
You muſt not, then, the poorer rank deſpiſe,
Becauſe they cannot to your height ariſe.
Born to your fortune, they had ſhone like you,
Hume, bred a plowman, might have held his plow;
And common ſenſe had ſurely ty'd his tongue,
Admitting Moſes and the clergy wrong.
"How many men fine poets might have made
"Whoſe wit (ſaid Locke), lies buried in a trade."
Milton, a cobler, had not ſung the ſkies
But rail'd in rhyme at Biſhops and Exciſe.
The puns of Swift had forc'd ſome vulgar ſmiles,
And ſpread his fame through ten or twenty miles.

And tender Otway from the liſt'ning crowd,
Had ſtole a ſigh for "Orphans in the Wood."
Perhaps the very boy who drives your cows,
Could bear great Dryden's laurel on his brows,
And feels within his breaſt that ſacred fire,
Which we, too late, in Chatterton admire.
For oft our talent in oblivion lies,
Till ſome reverſe of fortune bids it riſe.
Thus had not virtue rous'd a tyrant's wrath,
More had not taught us how to ſmile at death.
Thus had not Shakeſpeare ſhot at Shallow's deer,
Ophelia's fate might ne'er have forced a tear,
The Prince of bards had calmly comb'd his wool,
And paſt, perhaps, with pedants for a fool.
Aſtoniſh'd nations had not hail'd his name,
And Engliſh wit had wanted half its fame.
  But as good ſenſe forbids you to diſdain
The homely plowman plodding o'er the plain,
Ten thouſand thouſand hackney'd tales atteſt,
That mankind's maſters are at war with reſt.
Does fond ambition all your ſoul employ,
Let this reflection every wiſh deſtroy;
" That happineſs the great have ſeldom known,
" And leaſt of all that man who wears a crown."
While Sully's hero made his people bleſt,
Domeſtic miſery ſtabb'd the monarch's reſt;
And what embitter'd, what deſtroy'd his life?
A ſtrumpet's malice and a madman's knife.
'Tis a trite truth that ignorance alone,
Make us repine at ranks above our own.
Remark my lord, his carriage, and his gout,
And bleſs your fortune, you can walk about.
Nature to moſt is equally ſevere,
And death ſoon ends each vain diſtinction here;
The rich, the poor, the mendicant, the king,
Return to the ſame duſt from which they ſpring.
Nor by the faithful ſhould it be forgot,
Omniſcient goodneſs fixes every lot.

And when you murmur at the part that's given,
What are you but a mutineer to heaven.
And what wife man would fhew his rage in vain,
Or madly bite an adamantine chain.
Here common fenfe for once at leaft combines,
With the grave cant of orthodox divines.
You hear with patience all I have to fay;
But ftill ambition bears your heart away.
You cannot think felicity complete,
Unlefs you fhare the glories of the great.
" And fure," you cry, " 'tis quite a different thing,
" To cringe as lacquey, and command as king.
" Who would not wifh to figure in the HOUSE
" What fond applaufe my talents might produce."
For every freak, fome fond excufe we find,
Does public fpirit really fire your mind?
No longer ftrain your lungs in each debate;
Are you concern'd what broker pawns the ftate.
Your talk will never turn one factious voice,
Each patriot has already fixed his choice.
In vain Demofthenes himfelf might bawl,
One luft for plunder rages through them all.
Or fhould by chance an honeft man go there,
No living foul would fancy him fincere.
Both fides would wonder what the Quixote meant,
And tell him he difgrac'd the meffage he was fent.
School-boys alone would dream of fuch a part,
No fenator fpeaks fairly from his heart.
Through right and wrong his fide he muft defend,
Or elfe be branded as a faithlefs friend.
Statefmen at beft, are actors in a play,
This is in fact the language of the day.
And would you rifk fame, fortune, health, and eafe,
Merely to herd with partifans like thefe.
Then raife no more a vile election mob,
To tell them how the great the nation rob;
Thefe apron'd patriots, railing from below,
Would copy, if above, their betters now.

Nor weakly fancy that ſuch ſordid crimes,
Reflect uncommon ſcandal on the times.
Such was the ſcene in every ſeſſion paſt,
Were the ſame ſelfiſh vermin firſt and laſt.
The premier knows the price of every man,
And cools as many patriots as he can;
But in all this he drives at nothing more,
Than Carthage, Rome, and Athens did before;
And let for once this happy truth be told,
The world appears to mend as it grows old.
For though like them we daily vend our votes,
No more our placemen cut each other's throats.
No courtier now by ſtabbing would ſucceed,
Shrewd poliſh'd perfidy ſupplies its ſtead,
   We'll ſtate the caſe which ſince old time began,
Has rarely happen'd to one ſingle man;
That all your actions meet ſupreme applauſe,
That matchleſs talents gain the nobleſt cauſe,
That grateful nations hail your ſpotleſs fame,
And vanquiſhed tyrants tremble at your name;
Even ſuch a patriot finds his fate ſevere,
And learns what ſcanty peace awaits him here.
In vain to public juſtice will he truſt,
See good Camillus humbled in the duſt.
But why through ancient annals would we roam,
When full conviction may be found at home.
   Thus generous Hampden all the world admire,
But had he liv'd to ſee the laws expire,
To ſee his ſenate from their grandeur thrown,
And Cromwell's majors make the realm their own;
Hampden, perhaps, had ſcrupled at the zeal,
Which led him to protect the public weal,
In freedom's aid provoke the careleſs crowd,
And drench whole kingdoms in a crimſon flood.
   When Blenheim's hero bow'd the Gallic pride,
Trode down the fop, who juſtice had defy'd,
And ne'er was leſs than victor in the field,
And ne'er aſſail'd a fort which did not yield;

What ſums were ſpent triumphal piles to raiſe?
How many a bard was penſion'd in his praiſe?
We hail'd his progreſs for a length of years,
And claſs'd him firſt by far of Europe's peers;
And was not this felicity complete?
Could ſuch a favourite fear reverſing fate?
One ſerious moment from your dreams deſcend,
And trace this heir of glory to his end.
Repenting all that ten campaigns had done,
At once we quitted what our arms had won.
His goſſip ſovereign ſpurn'd the haughty chief,
The plunder'd nation hiſs'd him as a thief;
Pride, anguiſh, indignation, ſhook his brain,
The dotard trembled at the martial train.
Nor wealth, nor titles, could afford him eaſe,
Nor all his treaſures buy domeſtic peace.
The man whoſe fame had rivall'd Greece and Rome,
Crawl'd a poor idiot cuckold to the tomb.
  Nor need I to your common ſenſe ſubmit,
How dear we purchas'd the renown of Pitt.
An hundred precious millions were paid down,
To ſhelter thoſe who ſince our name diſown.
Nine years the nation bled in every vein,
Twelve years we pauſe, and lo! we tilt again.
A ſecond hundred millions are expended,
To vanquiſh thoſe we juſt before defended.
Had Clive, and Wolfe, and Granby, kept at home,
And ply'd the plow, the anvil, and the loom,
We might, no doubt, have fail'd of martial fame,
But public credit had not been ſo lame;
The debts of England had long ſince been paid,
And all its millions multiplied in trade.
Our naval heroes with the utmoſt eaſe,
Of every foe had fairly ſwept the ſeas;
And all who know ſound policy muſt own,
This our true road to riches and renown.
  When ſome ſmall ſtate, where peace and freedom find,
A refuge from the madneſs of mankind,

Where no attorney picks the poor man's purſe *,
And blameleſs curates heſitate to curſe;
Where guiltleſs doctors modeſtly declare,
That the beſt pills are exerciſe and air;
Where no proud tyrant tears the crop away,
And bids his vaſſals tremble and obey;
Where every ſwain with frugal plenty bleſt,
Protects, and is protected by the reſt;
'Tis there thoſe awful ſcenes of worth ariſe,
Degen'rate ages hear with juſt ſurpriſe;
And ſcarce believe a ſoldier can be proud,
To ſeal the rights of mankind with his blood.
'Twas thus, of old, her brave immortal pair
Freed ſervile Thebes from bondage and deſpair,
Led forth her ſons to conquer or to die,
And taught proud Sparta's proudeſt chief to fly.
But in our days 'tis quite another ſcene,
When hirelings fight and know not what they mean;
And they, forſooth, are in purſuit of glory,
And they would purchaſe fame in future ſtory.
How wretched is the fool who breaks a limb,
To pleaſe ſome miniſter's atrocious whim,
To buy their ſtupid huzzas from the mob,
Or ſhield rapacious pedlars when they rob.
Then you, my zealous, but miſtaken friend,
To this tempeſtuous virtue put an end.
In vain you hope old England to reform,
Retire without the vortex of the ſtorm;
Enjoy contentment at your own fire-ſide,
And ſmile at all the poor purſuits of pride.
Nor in your mind let that mean maxim enter,
That our whole pleaſures in ourſelves ſhould center.
To all the world be uſeful where you can,
A worthy heart forms half the happineſs of man.

* To Britons, this circumſtance may ſeem romantic; but it takes place in Switzerland. Many peaſants in that country have never once heard of a law-ſuit.

ON THE IMPORTANCE AND ORIGIN OF DRESS.

THE rich avoid and laugh at thoſe
Who cannot purchaſe coſtly clothes;
Their valets play that very game,
(For both at bottom are the ſame)
Survey the value of your coat,
And gueſs if you be worth a groat,
Before they'll condeſcend to ſay,
Their maſter may be ſeen to-day;
And we may honeſtly confeſs
Their wit in judging by one's dreſs;
For truly, as the world now goes,
Your beſt friend's Sunday ſuit of clothes,
If to an honeſt broker ſold,
Are worth his friendſhip ten times told;
And let not this provoke his pride,
An otter's hunted for it's hide,
The lovely form that wakes our woes,
No deeper than *the ſurface* goes;
We kill the beaver for his clothing,
But know his carcaſe good for nothing.
From cinnamon we peel the ſkin,
The wood is hardly worth a pin.
  But ſince the great contemn as traſh,
All mankind who run ſhort of caſh,
Suppoſe ſome beggar with a ſneer
Silencing thus, the ſaucy Peer.—
" With Anſon I had loſt a leg,
" Ten years ere I began to beg;
" Nor was my ſervice dearly bought,
" A flogging paid each month I fought;
" And after all your haughty tattle,
" 'Twas men like me who won the battle;
" Had we, poor fools, refus'd to go,
" Your Lordſhip had, for ought you know,

" For ever from our iſle expell'd,]
" A beſom in the Baſtile held.
" My taylor at the time I ſet,
" Has always been paid off as yet;
" And nobody can think I ſhun,
" Or dread the viſits of a dun,
" Though ſome allege, that half a ſcore
" Have long beſet a certain door.
" I'm ſure I could not ſhow my face,
" To ſell my country for a *place*;
" Or take my principles by rote
" From ſtateſmen who can buy my vote;
" Or throw thoſe victuals to my hounds,
" For which the poor would plow my grounds.
" The gentry need not be ſo proud,
" Of what they call their noble blood;
" For when Miſs Eve in Eden ſpan,
" Our common parentage began;
" And then as to your ſplendid dreſs,
" Your betters have been ſerv'd with leſs.
" When Power Divine a garden planted,
" Adam got all that Nature wanted;
" And had not Madam and the Devil
" Put matters off their proper level,
" Had ſhe refus'd to taſte his fruit,
" And tweak'd the ſerpent by the ſnout,
" Your Lordſhip at this very day,
" Made *perfect* as divines would ſay,
" In Paradiſe had planted kail,
" With not a rag to hide your tail;
" And not a penny in your purſe,
" How fine a world before the curſe!
" Your pantry could not then have boaſted
" A ſingle joint of boil'd or roaſted;
" And butter'd cabbage at the beſt,
" Had ſerv'd your Saintſhip for a feaſt.

HORACE, BOOK II. ODE IV.

DEAR Frank, you need not be afraid,
To court a poor, but honeſt maid.
The ladies tell you to be nice,
In order to ſupport their price.
By birth, and finery, and wit,
A thouſand fools are daily bit;
And learn, when counting every coſt,
They ſhould have ſomething elſe to boaſt,
Than a gay, pert, expenſive girl,
Deſcended from a Duke or Earl.
   In acting thus, you do no more,
Than what the wiſe have done before.
Old Abram left old Sarah's arms,
To feaſt on Hagar's jolly charms.
Kind Jacob, when his mates beſought him,
Aſcended every girl they brought him †.
Moſes, when turn'd of eighty, led
A jetty virgin to his bed.
Fond Ruth accepted from her ſwain,
The pill that cures a widow's pain.
For once at leaſt a Soldier's dame,
Extinguiſh'd holy David's flame;
And, when he could no longer harm,
A trull was hir'd to keep him warm.
   Nor dread that Phyllis will diſgrace
The honours of your ancient race:
For now a days it is confeſs'd,
Nobility's a Gothic jeſt.
The vixens who at Phyllis rail,
If better bidders chance to fail,

† The life of this Patriarch, as recorded in the Old Teſtament, diſplays a juſt and beautiful picture. It is one of thoſe productions which we never tire of reading. The complaiſance hinted at in the text, might afford an uſeful leſſon to the ſordid petulance of our modern dames.

In ſpite of all the din they make,
At which your prudence ſeems to quake,
To-morrow may their footmen wed,
Or be with barbers caught a-bed.
But who like Phyllis would diſdain,
The fond alluring hope of gain;
And which of all her rivals, pray,
So neat an ancle can diſplay;
Such ſnowy arms, ſo fine a waiſt,
Such innate elegance of taſte.
Her feet! by George, I muſt be bled,
Or kiſs the carpet which they tread;
And then, the radiance of her eyes!
I feel the maddeſt raptures riſe;
And ſcarce ſhall think for half an hour,
I'll ſoon be turn'd of ſixty-four.

THE NEWSPAPER:

OR,

A PEEP AT THE LITERARY WORLD.

LET me with Tartars on a ſtallion dine,
Freeze at the pole, or pant below the line,
Or row the galley of ſome pirate Moor,
Or ſoak in brandy with a Ruſſian boor,
Or hold the bottle when two butchers box,
Or bet my Bible on Lord Squander's cocks;
Rather than ſit in ſilence, while the men
Whoſe lives reverſe the precepts of their pen,
Whoſe characters are ſcorn'd, preſum'd to prate
On friendſhip, honour, and the devil knows what.
  Learning itſelf is now extremely ſcarce,
And buying claſſics but a ſolemn farce.
No Greek or Latin plague Pompoſo's head,
And can he reliſh what he cannot read?

Mæonides may pour his lofty ſtrain,
But Hector conquers—Helen weeps in vain.
Though Boyle, and Bacon, on his ſhelves are plac'd,
From freſher moderns has he form'd his taſte;
Through half their title page he dares not toil,
But pores on C——d, Rocheſter, and Hoyle;
Or nods o'er Pamela's profound harangue,
Or ſpouts French catches with a naſal twang;
Or ſtudies in the Journal of the day,
The plot and prologue of the laſt new play.
  Nay, when he would eſſay to think or write,
What mice the mountain uſhers into light;
As whether Swift his chaſtity preſerv'd,
Why Lee went mad, and whether Otway ſtarv'd;
Why Addiſon was hen-peck'd by his wife,
And ſteep'd in port the poſtſcript of his life;
Goldſmith how ſlow, how rapid Fielding wrote,
How cheaply Steele his Tatler eſſays bought,
Why beaſtly Johnſon ne'er a nightcap wore,
Why Pope was peeviſh when his lungs were ſore,
Why flannel ſhirts in winter he put on,
And ſtew'd and pick'd his lampreys to the bone,
Was proud with traſh the poſt-office to cram,
And made wry faces while he ſipp'd a dram;
Why Dryden in a club of fools grew dumb,
What Cambridge beadle pepper'd Milton's bum;
How ruſtic Shakeſpeare could not ſpell his name,
And ſpurn'd both poſthumous and preſent fame;
While that tremendous trump'ry, term'd his notes,
Whole reams of volumes in ſucceſſion blots;
Where page on page a pedant can afford,
To fix the ſpelling of one worthleſs word.
  To royal ſcenes another gooſe quill ſoars,
A Charles, an Edward, or an Henry's whores;
Or ſtrains the pureſt diction to expreſs,
The wit and chaſtity of virgin Beſs;
What gowns, and ruffs, and farthingales ſhe wore,
How well ſhe danc'd, and box'd, and rhim'd, and ſwore;

Her maids of honour with a knife would hack,
And ſprain her chaplain or her viceroy's back.
What ſpotleſs honour warm'd each James's heart,
How well poor Mary play'd a veſtal's part;
How many pregnant wives at once fell dead,
When Common Senſe knock'd off the martyr's head;*
How well Dutch William lov'd a plate of peaſe,
And if John died by prieſtcraft or diſeaſe.†
Another band of yet ſuperior ſkill,
Trace valiant Arthur's march from hill to hill;
Can tell within ten minutes at the moſt,
When Canute landed on the Kentiſh coaſt;‡
How many ruffians Cumbria's ſceptre ſway'd,
What vile hobnails a Mercian hammer made,§
When firſt Mancunium from a pig-ſtye turn'd,
When firſt in Saxon chimnies charcoal burn'd;
Whether from Wales or Galloway the route,
Of Noah's grandſons for Ierne ſet out;||
What crowns of gold the kings of Munſter wore,
Ere Sparta's cuckold touch'd the Trojan ſhore.
The feudal Sage at learned length deſcribes
The generous virtues of the German tribes,
With what pure freedom they beſtow'd their votes,
What calm delight they cut each other's throats;

* See a moſt *pathetic* paſſage on this ſubject in Mr. Hume's Hiſtory of Charles I.

† Archæologia, Vol. IV. p. 29. et ſeq.

‡ Ibid. Vol. VIII. p. 106. et ſeq.

§ Ibid. Vol. III. p. 35. See a diſſertation on the antiquity of horſe ſhoes; and another, ibid. p. 39. "On ſhoeing of horſes among the ancients." Alſo "Obſervations on ancient ſpurs." Ibid. Vol. VIII. p. 43. et ſeq.

|| Ibid. Vol. I. p. 49. An antiquarian attempts to prove that Britain was NOT firſt inhabited by any of the deſcendants of Gomer; an important diſcovery! For the circumſtance mentioned in the next couplet, ſee Ohalloran, and ſome unaccountable facts very well atteſted in the Archæologia, Vol. II. p. 32.

How cheerfully they quaff'd the ſocial horn,
And held all arts but homicide in ſcorn.
Nay, when to age their force began to yield,
Nor death had chanc'd to meet them in the field;
Then as the climax of their martial whims,
O'er ſome tall precipice they broke their limbs.
What ſpacious room for admiration here,
How much leſs lovely a Norwegian bear!
From this bright ſource two antiquarian eyes
Can ſee the liberties of England riſe;
On ſuch a topick was it not worth while,
Twelve hundred lively quartos to compile?
In latter times he paints a knighted pair
Couching the lance to prove their doxies fair;
Tells how each vaſſal on his wedding night,
Reſign'd the lover's to the baron's right;
Whether a wretch from bondage who had fled,
Or by his noſe, or ears, was homewards led;
Whether when reeling headlong round his houſe,
A Norman pirate ever kick'd his ſpouſe;
Facts pour on facts, a moſt important ſtore,
We have not time, nor patience, to run o'er. *
Argus had wanted eyes enough to glance
On half your tours through Italy and France;
Nine thouſand tomes, a ſcanty computation,
With ink, and nonſenſe, overwhelm the nation.
Sermons—but here, mayhap, I ſhall be told,
The very title makes your blood run cold;
That though whole tons are printed every day,
No mortal cares a fig for what they ſay.
Our ſober anceſtors, whoſe nerves were ſtrong,
Could hear, with tranſport, lectures twelve hours long.

* On this ſubject the reader may conſult Whitaker, Strutt, and other popular writers. It was thought needleſs to crowd the bottom of the page with quotations. By the way, Mr. Whitker ſeems very often poſſeſſed of what he himſelf calls "an amiable credulity of ſpirit."

Additions to his Defence of Queen Mary, p. 117.

How ſadly ſince have matters been derang'd,
How ſoon old Slyboots our revolt reveng'd;
On Death, and Judgment, when divines enlarge,
What modern muſcles chuſe to ſtand the charge?
Now with this world ſo wofully perplex'd,
We ſcarce find time to ponder on the next.
Nay, ſome abandon'd profligates declare,
We'd judge to the moſt purpoſe when got there.
· Unleſs another Omar ſhall ariſe,
And with ten thouſand bonefires gild the ſkies,
The ſurface of our globe muſt ceaſe to hold
The monthly mountains into calf-ſkin roll'd.
The quack, attorney, critic, and divine,
All in peculiar paths pretend to ſhine.
The bladder one informs you how to probe,
The next, in ſpite of Tyburn, how to rob;
A third would cenſure works he cannot ſpell,
A fourth engraves a folio map of hell.*
One the whole pugiliſtick art diſplays,
From brawny Broughton, down to Johnſon's days;
Where to defend, attack, to fall, to cloſe,
To ſplit the jaw bone, or to pound the noſe.
Your patriot ſhews the miniſter a fool,
Your half-pay captain how to ſlaſh by rule.
One quarto teaches how to break a horſe,
One how bad parſnips may be turn'd to worſe;
From Cambden topographers take the hint,
And every pariſh ruſhes into print.
Read Burke's eternal letter to an end,
Or crack-brain'd Boſwell on his tour attend;†

* The Editor has actually ſeen ſuch a map, in the front of a large volume, tranſlated, if he has not forgotten, from the original of a German. The well known map of Spiritual Navigation, may be conſidered as a counterpart.

† The degrees of contempt are not infinite, and a character acquires ſtability, by being placed at the bottom of the ſcale.

Pope, bury'd in the mire of Warton's ſkull,
So trite, perplex'd, impertinent, and dull; *
Or Warburton's divine legation bore,
And all the "ſacred" ſcenes of Hannah More;
Thoſe letters Lady Wortley never wrote,
Or Craven's ſcrawls ſo innocent of thought,
Or Joſeph Marſhall's jaunt, where by the bye,
Through four thick volumes every word's a lie; †
Or modeſt Bellamy's important tale,
So archly fitted for a bagnio ſale;
Where the pert harlot, ſpouting fooliſh plays,
In place of infamy demands our praiſe;
Or honeſt Mirabeau's hiſtoric ſpy,
To which a halter only ſhould reply;
Or poor Rouſſeau's unfortunate detail,
Of all that bedlam bluſhes to unveil; ‡
Thoſe five portentous tomes about a fiddle,
Nor Oedipus nor *Hawkins* could unriddle;
Or the bright anthems of our birth-day bard;
If yet one verſe the barber's tongs have ſpar'd;
Piozzi's chat, the noveliſts of Lane, ||
That paragon of peerage, Lady Vane;
Or Anna Yearſeley's admirable note,
Sweet as the warbling of a ſcreech owl's throat; §
Then with contemptuous pity ſhall you ſay,
How much good paper has been caſt away!

* See above, p. 38.

† No ſuch perſon ever exiſted.

‡ See his Confeſſions, in four or five volumes.

|| An eminent London bookſeller who advertiſes for MSS. We cannot blame him for ſelling what we chuſe to buy.

§ This is the Briſtol milk-woman. Her reception juſtifies the remark that "Wonder, uſually accompanied by a bad taſte, looks "out only for what is uncommon; and if a work comes abroad "under the name of a Threſher, a Bricklayer, or a Lord, it is "ſure to be eagerly ſought after by the million."

Introduction to Sheridan's Life of Swift.

That paper which (a far ſuperior uſe)
Might well have ſerv'd our honeſt Mother Gooſe,
Or Bunyan's Progreſs to the world to come,
The Seven Wiſe Maſters, Whitfield, and Tom Thumb.
Sagacious Elphinſtone! thou bard divine!
Did ever dulneſs eke ſuch traſh as thine?
Who has not heard where Engliſh works are nam'd,
What precious metre thy ſage wit has fram'd?
Skilful alike to cenſure and to praiſe,
An arch ſpectator of Rome's darker days,
Long Martial charm'd the world, and charms it ſtill,
But what a monſter iſſues from thy quill!
While all our boys are cruelly perplex'd,
What volume is the verſion or the text;
Admiring which of theſe can be the tongue,
In which, for plumb-cake, they have pled ſo long.
How ſtrangely Gordon hath diſtorted thee,
Couldſt thou, ſtern Tacitus, revive to ſee;
See Senſe and Grammar from thy page retire,
Thy pathos buried, and thy force expire;
That force, which if to Homer's it muſt yield,
Like vanquiſh'd Ajax, ſlowly quits the field;
Thy Spartan period in dull length extend,
Through viler proſe than Whiſton ever penn'd;
How like an eagle pouncing on her prey,
Would thy keen talons drag him into day;
And toſs the bungler down the gulf of ſcorn,
The laughing-ſtock of ages yet uuborn.
Such precious facts from Learning's fountain pour,
To vamp the volumes of the vacant hour;
Far ſooner ſhall I in the Herald read,
What ſchemes are hatching in the Premier's head;
Why laſt night's privy council ſat ſo late,
What ſhare each member bore in each debate;
What the Grand Turk when not a ſoul was near,
Whiſper'd one morning in the Muſti's ear;
Why Upper Egypt to revolt intends,
Why France, and Corſica, continue friends;

Whether, when ninety lagging years run out,
A Pope has dy'd of ratſbane or the gout;
What ſhops with port his majeſty ſupply,
Or how well ſeaſon'd his laſt Glo'ſter pye;
Why the Mogul ſtruck of his Viſier's head,
Why fools tranſlate before they learn to read;
Where with the moſt convenience mares are bled,
What dutcheſs with her barber's caught a-bed;
What jocky dukes are juſt arriv'd in town,
How oft Mendoza knock'd poor Humphries down;
What ſaving project Sherry has to broach,
What azure ſattin lin'd ſome bankrupt's coach;
How tennis and quadrille diſſolve his gold,
His ſtud how dearly bought, how cheaply ſold;
How young 'Squire Bubble on his private ſtage,
Eclips'd all parrots of the preſent age;
How tenderly Miſs Tumbledown behav'd,
How Chamont ſcamper'd, and Monimia rav'd;
And how their audience, while Champaign run o'er,
Extoll'd the farce, below contempt before;
With what refinement Pacherotti ſings,
How nimbly on the ſaddle Aſtley ſprings;
Of ſapient aldermen with turtle gorg'd,
Of invalids for tippling porter ſcourg'd;
What widow wiſhes for an active mate,
When Charger covers at the loweſt rate;
What lottery-office deals the richeſt ſhower,
What a French pedagogue demands per hour;
The price of waſh-ball, lavender, and hops,
What reſurrections follow Maredant's drops;
And how all mortal, and immortal ills
Shrink from the ſight of Leake's venereal pills.

We need not ſigh for Plautus or Moliere,
The Whitehall poſt ſupplies their purpoſe here;
Dulneſs itſelf would ſmile at the review,
And Zion's ſage acknowledge *ſomething new*.
Figures ſo rapid on the canvaſs riſe,
Such happy groupes the gazetteer ſupplies!

2

Who but with raptures of refpect muft hear,
That fix grey ponies fmoke beneath a peer;*
What banker's clerk at Dover has been ftopt,
What chopping baftard in a privy dropt;
What generous foes avoid to fire with ball,
What taylor's wife hates footmen when they're tall;
His bride what porter in a rope has bought,
What player pimps, what parfon's forg'd a note;
Where teeming maids retirement may enjoy,
What quacks a fœtus in the womb deftroy;†
Rats how to kill, and butterflies preferve,
What tools are penfion'd, and what patriots ftarve;
How fome rafh family the world can fpare,
Was beggar'd for the murder of a hare;
And how fome wretch want now compels to beg,
Pick'd berries till a man-trap crufh'd his leg;
Or fhot the pigeons that deftroy'd his corn,
And from his ploughfhare was to Bridewell torn;
Why tars with Anfon who went round the world,
Were down a ftinking hold in handcuffs hurl'd;
What heirefs with her father's groom was feen,
O'erleap each toll-bar 'twixt and Gretna Green;
What dotard with a wench of twenty-one,
In queft of cuckoldom to church hath gone;
Of Fortune's envy, what a fatal proof,
When an old nail run through Sir Peter's hoof;
Or where, with venifon, laft Monday kill'd,
Your paunch for half a guinea may be fill'd.
Facts more important ftill, they oft difplay,
When vice triumphant, blunders into day;

* Juvenal mentions a Roman conful who drove his chariot by moon light; but adds, that at the expiration of his office, he would drive it in broad day. Such men juftify the remark of Luther, "A ftone knows its ftone; and an afs knows that he's "but an afs."

† In Forfter's elegant account of one of Cook's voyages, there is inferted a copy of an advertifement to this purpofe, with fome reflections on its nature and tendency.

What Lord Chief Juſtice a harangue has made,
To prove 'tis wrong to call a ſpade a ſpade,
And better wide from guilty truth to ſteer,
Than plunge in Newgate's offals for a year;
What borough-candidate contriv'd to ſpend
All he was worth, and all his friends would lend;
With pedlars, chimney-ſweeps, and butchers din'd,
With tuns of porter every tavern lin'd;
Danc'd with each bumpkin beauty of the town,
Pledg'd every toaſt, drank all his pledges down;
Whole troops of bruiſers to the Huſtings brought,
And miſs'd his purchaſe by a carman's vote.
  But moſt of all we're happy in the hour,
When Fox and Pit their vocal thunders pour;
When ſome exciſe act into rags is torn,
And mutual taunts are dealt with mutual ſcorn.
What ſtrength of lungs and logic are diſplay'd!
A ſcene where Tully might have learn'd his trade;
What rich embelliſhments the farce would bear,
But 'tis full time to finiſh our career.

A CHARACTER.

Of men in whom North Britain's bleſt,
  On whom the poor depend for bread;
There's one, we frankly may atteſt,
  The world could ſcarce ſupply his ſtead;
That he, in Friendſhip's walk, hath ſhone,
Like Hannibal in arms, unrivall'd and alone.

Let ſickneſs kill his ploughmen's cattle,
  Or Auguſt rot their crops with rain,
He does not flog them into battle,
  Arreſt, impriſon, and diſtrain;
No grinding ſtatute is diſtorted,
But every tear wip'd off, and every nerve ſupported;

While ſome whole clouds of pigeons breed,
To pick the farmer's wheat when ſown,
And ſixty pair of blood hounds lead,
To tread the ripen'd harveſt down,
And ſtrip the cow-herd's only coat,
Who ſells a partridge worth a groat.*

Ye dire diſpenſers of the peace,
On every human right who trample!
From forcing our abhorrence, ceaſe;
And follow his ſublime example.
No more ſhall nations pray, and hope,
To ſee your worſhips dangle in a rope.

Ye Pharaohs of this generous age,
Who ſcourge your vaſſals to diſtraction!
Can ye, by venting fruitleſs rage,
Feel his tranſcendent ſatisfaction,
Who cloſes life as he began,
Exiſting but to aid the miſeries of man.

When Socrates ſought alms in vain,
Had ſuch a friend adorn'd his flock,
No care had gall'd Aſpaſia's ſwain†
About the purchaſe of a cloak;
His teacher's every wiſh had been
Supply'd that inſtant 'twas foreſeen.

* "John Jeſſop was fined at the Public Office, Bowſtreet, in five "pounds for being concerned with Newton, who was fined laſt "week in the ſame ſum for ſhooting a cock pheaſant. He could "not pay, and was ſent to the Correction Houſe for three months." *Vide* London Papers, November 1789. So much for ENGLISH Liberty! Query, What loſs would enſue to ſociety, if all the wild-fowl in Europe were exterminated?

† Aſpaſia was a woman of the town, and Socrates frequented her houſe to learn the beauties of rhetoric from HER converſation.

Could I, in all its charms, expreſs
  How bright a ray his boſom pierces,
Genius might envy my ſucceſs,
  And Candour vindicate my verſes.
The mite of virtue, in the world,
To Lethe ought not to be hurl'd.

A benefactor to mankind,
  More frank, more tender, and more true,
Exhauſtleſs Dryden never feign'd,
  His darling Shakſpeare never drew;
Nor Chatterton had begg'd in vain,
Nor Butler met, from him, with thankleſs cold diſdain.

Thus having ſlightly ſketch'd his worth,
  I've now the medal to reverſe,
Trump all his human frailties forth,
  All which a Bozzy would rehearſe;
And ſing the ſad reſolves of Fate,
That he ſhould ne'er approach the glories of the great!

Firſt, then, he wants (we can't deny)
  All the moſt ſplendid marks of wealth,
He watches, with an Alfred's eye
  His time, his money, and his health;
T' oblige all mankind ſeems as willing,
As though he were not worth a ſhilling.

Nay, worſe, he has not rear'd a ſtud,
  Nor gives the jockey crew protection;
Nor forces perjury to bud,
  By carving votes for an election;
But rarely ſpeculates in cocks,
Or gallops eighty leagues to ſee two butchers box.

He knows, moſt dully, what he's doing;
  Nor builds, and plants, and feaſts for ever;
Nor throws a farm-houſe into ruin,
  To clear his proſpect to the river;

The charm of ſolitude can prize,
Nor from *himſelf* affrighted flies:

And though his talents are refin'd,
Without a grain of affectation,
And, had their maſter ſo inclin'd,
Might long have reap'd our admiration,
And near all-matchleſs Frederick's name
Have rank'd his literary fame;

Like him he prints no terſe octavos,
To prove his tenderneſs and taſte;
Nor hires two hundred thouſand bravoes,
To lay a peaceful empire waſte.
Sages, and heroes, if ye can,
Make haſte to copy ſuch a man.

And when he's gone where Phocion went,
That breaſt compaſſion warms no more,
And crouds their *ſelfiſh* ſorrow vent
Who never ſympathiz'd before,
Some happier muſe a right may claim,
To give Poſterity his name.

MEMOIRS

OF THE LIFE, CHARACTER, AND WRITINGS OF GEORGE BUCHANAN.

This author was born at a village in the pariſh of Killerne, and county of Dumbarton, about the beginning of February 1506. The chief incidents of his life are related with modeſt brevity, in a memoir written by himſelf, about two years before his death, and commonly prefixed to his works. His ſuperior genius burſt through the darkeſt clouds of indigence and misfortune. In every country where he ſucceſſively reſided, his abilities inſpired men of letters with admiration. "Bu-

" chananum omnibus antepono*," was the expreſſion o Queen Elizabeth. " Georgius Buchananus," ſays De Thou, " vir in genii felicitate, et ſcribendi facultate, " quod ejus ſcripta ad omnem eternitatem victura vel " fatente invidia teſtantur, noſtra ætate incomparabi- " lis."—" For an happy genius, and the talent of com- " poſition, no writer of our age has been comparable to " George Buchanan. Of this we have full evidence from his " works, which, even by the confeſſion of envy, ſhall endure " to all eternity." " Sed quo te," ſays Gilbert Gray, " piaculo ta ceam Buchanane? aut quo præconio cele- " brem unicum muſarum hujus ævi decus?" " With what " blame ſhould I paſs in ſilence over thee, O Buchanan! " or in what ſtyle of panegyric ſhall I celebrate the only " ornament of the muſes in our age." " Sane aurea," ſays Quenſtedt, " ejus et cum omnibus priſcis com- " paranda poemata, jure merito omnium verſantur ma- " nu." " His verſes are deſervedly in the hands of eve- " ry one. They are indeed ineſtimable, and may be com- " pared with the beſt poems of antiquity." In the Scali- gerana we are told, that "Buchananus unus eſt in tota Eu- " ropa omnes poſt ſe relinquens in Latina Poeſi." " Bu- " chanan alone has *left all Europe behind him* in Latin po- " etry." In a ſhort poem inſcribed to our author, Julius Scaliger, one of the moſt able and moſt arrogant ſcholars of his age, compares himſelf to a magpie, and pronounces Buchanan to be " Deus litteratorum," " the God of the " learned." He tells him that he had been born on the ſummit of Parnaſſus, that he had been foſtered in the boſom of Calliope, and that, by her ſacred inſpiration, he had been deſtined to bear away the praiſe of excellence from every nation that cultivated the learning of Rome. Andrew Melvil, Theodore Beza, Joſeph Scaliger, Charles Utenhovius, Adrian Turnebus, Archbiſhop Spotiſwoode, and a multitude of other writers of different nations, have celebrated our author, as an amiable man, an accompliſh-

* " I prefer Buchanan to all." Walpole's Catalogue of Royal and Noble Authors, Vol. I. p. 39.

ed ſcholar, and above all, as a poet of unrivalled beauty. Atteſtations of this nature in Engliſh, French, Greek, and Latin, have been laborioully collected by Ruddiman. They fill thirty-two cloſe printed quarto pages in Burman's elegant edition; and we are at the ſame time told that ſuch quotations might be extended to infinity. We have alſo a catalogue of the different impreſſions of his works, at Edinburgh, London, Paris, Amſterdam, Leyden, Frankfort, Utrecht, Leipſic, Lyons, Geneva, and other cities on the continent, preceding the year 1715; and either detached portions, or entire editions, of his works had been publiſhed in his original language an hundred and twenty times, beſides numerous tranſlations. "Vivit adhuc," ſays Thomas Smeton, "et utinam diu vivat, orbis terrarum, non Scotiæ tantum decus Georgius Buchananus." "There yet lives, and long may he continue to live, "George Buchanan, the glory, not of Scotland only, but "of the world." In a letter to De Thou, Grotius diſtinguiſhes as the father of modern dramatic poetry, "Scotiæ "illud numen," "that divinity of Scotland."* Our author was of a careleſs, frank, independent diſpoſition; and as poverty, or rather a neglect of money, did not permit him to purchaſe applauſe, nor his temper to court it, we may preſume that the veneration of his cotemporaries was perfectly ſincere. Their ſentiments have been amply ratified by poſterity. "Poetarum ſui ſeculi facile prin"cepst†," has been the encomium beſtowed upon him for two centuries by the general conſent of Europe. "In his im"mortal poems," ſays Biſhop Burnet, "he ſhews ſo well "how he could imitate all the Roman poets, in their ſe"veral ways of writing, that he who compares them will "be often tempted to prefer the copy to the original. "There is a beauty and life, an exactneſs, as well as a "liberty, that cannot be imitated, and ſcarce enough "commended. His ſtyle is ſo natural and nervous, and

* "Tibi hæc mittuntur, qui poſt Scotiæ illud numen redivivam "nobis reduxiſti Tragoediam."

† "Unqueſtionably the firſt poet of his age."

" his reflections are ſo judicious, that he is juſtly reckon-" ed the greateſt and beſt of our modern authors."* His panegyriſts of the preſent day are numerous and ſanguine. Dr. Beattie, in his moſt ingenious eſſay on the utility of claſſical learning, obſerves, that " the Latin poems " of Buchanan have been long and univerſally known and " admired." " He was," ſays one of his editors, " ſo " great a maſter of the elegance of the Latin language, " that he became an author, rather than an imitator, ſo " that the blood of every Roman poet ſeems to have flow-" ed in his veins†." " The happy genius of Buchanan," ſays Dr. Robertſon, " equally formed to excel in proſe " and in verſe; more various, more original, and more " elegant, than that of almoſt any other modern who " writes in Latin, reflects, with regard to this particular, " the greateſt luſtre on his country." Of citing ſuch atteſtations there would be no end. " The name of " Buchanan," ſays the late Dr. Samuel Johnſon, " has " as fair a claim to immortality as can be conferred " by modern Latinity, and perhaps a fairer than the " inſtability of vernacular languages admits." " His " Pſalms," ſays Dr. Stuart, " in which he has em-" ployed ſo many kinds of verſe, diſplay admirably the " extent and univerſality of his mind, the quickneſs and " abundance of his fancy, and the power and acuteneſs " of his judgment." " Nullum ego," ſays Burman, " ſi " ab anti quioribus deceſſeris, celebrari unquam audivi " aut legi, qui cum Buchanano contendere poſſit." " If " you except the ancients, I have never heard or read of

* *Vide*, Hiſtory of Reformation, Vol. I. Book 3d. and a paſtoral charge by the ſame author. The above are a few detached ſentences. The original paſſages were too prolix for an entire inſertion.

† " Tantus erat Buchananus Latinitatis et elegantiæ artifex, " ut potius auctor quam imitator, utque omnium poetarum ſan-" guis ejus venam compleſſe videatur." *Vide*, Preface to an edition of his verſion of the Pſalms, printed at Edinburgh, in 1737.

" any celebrated writer, who could rival Buchanan." A ſhort review of his perſonal hiſtory ſeems neceſſary to make an account of his writings intelligible.

When a boy, he was ſent to ſtudy at the univerſity of Paris. On his return to Scotland, he inliſted as a common ſoldier in the French troops then in this country. When about eighteen, he became connected with John Major the hiſtorian, and accompanied him in a journey to Paris. Where he obtained employment as a teacher in the college of St. Barbe. He next engaged himſelf with the Earl of Caſſilis, and with him he returned a ſecond time to Scotland, after an abſence of about ten years. He then undertook the education of one of the natural ſons of James V.* In 1539, a quarrel with the Franciſcans drove him out of the kingdom. Paſſing through England, he ſettled as a public teacher at Bourdeaux. Here his fame as a poet became diſtinguiſhed; and his four tragedies were acted with applauſe. Indeed, as he died when Shakeſpeare was but eighteen, we may believe the aſſertion of Grotius, that he was the firſt dramatic writer of his day, After a reſidence of three years at Bourdeaux, he ſeems to have returned to Paris. In 1547, on an invitation from John III. of Portugal, he went into that kingdom. He was, not long after, caſt into the inquiſition, where he lay confined for about eighteen months. At laſt he obtained leave to embark for England, where he landed in 1552. In January 1553, he ſailed for France. In 1554, he accom-

* It has been ſaid a thouſand times over, that he was appointed by James V. preceptor to his ſon, who was afterwards Earl of Murray. Upon reading the dedication of the Franciſcan, which is inſcribed to the Earl of Murray, it will be obſerved, that this baſtard ſon, as Buchanan calls him, whoever he was, could not have been the perſon to whom this dedication was addreſſed. That pupil is twice mentioned, and always in the third perſon; and Mr. Man, upon the authority of Leſlie, informs us, that he was another James Stuart, who died in 1558. Vide Man's Cenſure and Examination, &c. p. 349. a book of which I ſhall take farther notice in another place.

panied into Italy Marſhal Briſſac, by whom he was received into an intimate friendſhip. In his family he continued till 1560. In 1563, he returned to Scotland. In 1565, he again viſited France, for the purpoſe of ſuperintending the printing of his verſion of the Pſalms. This voyage ſeems to have terminated his excurſions to the continent.

He was made Principal of St. Leonard's college, in the univerſity of St. Andrew's; an office which he afterwards found it neceſſary to reſign, on being appointed preceptor to James VI. In 1567, he was elected Moderator of the General Aſſembly of the Church of Scotland. He was likewiſe promoted to be Director of the Chancery, a member of the Privy Council, and keeper of the Privy Seal. His Hiſtory of Scotland was printed juſt before his death, which happened at Edinburgh, on the 28th day of September 1582. He was buried in the church-yard of the Grayfriars. "Foreign nations," ſays Dr. Stuart, "as well as his own countrymen, were filled with the "utmoſt admiration of the genius of Buchanan;" yet his grave has never been diſtinguiſhed by a tomb-ſtone.

Before I proceed to any critical remarks on his writings, it ſeems proper to take ſome notice of the reproaches which have been caſt upon his memory. Dr. Stuart, in his late Hiſtory of Queen Mary, informs us, that "She invited Buchanan from France to Scotland, with "a view that he ſhould take the charge of the education "of her ſon; and *till James ſhould be of a proper age to* "*receive inſtruction*, ſhe appointed him to be chief maſ-"ter in St. Leonard's college, in the univerſity of St. An-"drew's. Her generoſity did not ſtop here. She granted "him a yearly penſion of five hundred pounds *, payable "out of the Abbey of Corſragwell. The commiſſion for "this gift is ſtill extant, and is dated upon the 9th day "of October 1564." Dr. Stuart infers, in the harſheſt terms, that Buchanan was a monſter of ingratitude.

* Our Author ſhould have added *Scots*.

Our author returned to Scotland, in the year one thousand five hundred and *sixty-three* *. His Franciscan was published by himself in June one thousand five hundred and *sixty-four*, as appears from a dedication to the Earl of Murray, dated at St. Andrew's. The Queen was not married till 29th July, one thousand five hundred and *sixty-five*, and James, *the intended* PUPIL was born upon the nineteenth of June one thousand five hundred and *sixty-six*. Hence it would seem to follow, that the Queen of Scotland provided a preceptor for her son, about three years before his birth; and at least eighteen months before her marriage with his father.

Such are the absurdities implied in the accusation as stated by Dr. Stuart. His information, as he himself has told us, is wholly derived from Ruddiman; whose tremulous conjecture of a royal invitation from France, is founded on a typographical error. Buchanan, in his own account of his life, says, that in the year one thousand five hundred and *sixty-five*, he was appointed preceptor, not to a child unborn, but to "Jacobum Sextum Scotorum "regem." This expression proves incontestibly that "Sexagesimo *quinto*," was a mistake of the pen, or of the press. Ruddiman himself startled at the wild inconsistency of this date, proposes to read "Sexagesimo "*nono*," and this his *second* conjecture is confirmed by an act of the Privy Council past in 1569, and which he has inserted at full length. In this act there is no reference to Buchanan, as having been *formerly chosen* preceptor to the prince. The Privy Council, merely with a respectful notice of his abilities, select him for the execution of that office †. The pretended invitation from France by Mary vanishes into smoke. Besides, Buchanan was a

* "I have proved in the notes on his life, that he returned to "his own country in 1563." Ruddiman's Answer to Logan, p. 79.

† Dr. M'Kenzie, says, that he was elected on 20th August 1567, by a meeting of the nobility at Edinburgh. But he is a loose, inaccurate writer.

heretic of the moſt deteſted deſcription, and certainly one of the very laſt perſons upon earth, whom the Queen would have ſuffered as preceptor for her ſon.

Ruddiman advances no evidence to prove that Mary deſired Buchanan to quit France, on account of a pupil not yet exiſting. It is true that our author was in France in 1565, and the reaſon of his voyage was undoubtedly to print his verſion of the Pſalms, which was at that time committed to the preſs by Henry Stephens. But this accidental event, has not the moſt diſtant connection with the point in queſtion.

The ſecond charge is, that Mary appointed Buchanan to be chief maſter in St. Leonard's college. In the year 1753, Mr. James Man, of Aberdeen, publiſhed an acute and learned examination of Mr. Ruddiman's conduct, as editor of Buchanan. In that book, he has quoted the original Latin words, of the charter erecting St. Leonard's college, and which is dated the 20th of Auguſt 1512. The paſſage, too prolix for inſertion here, ſtipulates, in the moſt expreſs terms, that the principal of that college ſhall be "Per Priorem ejuſdem, perpetuis futuris temporibus, "ELIGI et NOMINARI *." Before the Reformation in Scotland, the Earl of Murray had been appointed prior of St. Andrew's; a circumſtance, which may ſerve to explain the ſource of Buchanan's preferment. On his arrival in Scotland, his chief reſidence, as Ruddiman tells us, was at St. Andrew's, in the family of his patron Murray; "Apud "patronum ſuum Moraviæ comitem." Whether his patron had nominally reſigned the title of prior, is a queſtion of little conſequence. Mr. Man affirms that he ſtill held that office, and whether he did or not, we may

* Cenſure and Examination, &c. p. 94. To this attack, Mr. Ruddiman replied, in a large and angry volume. As to the point mentioned in the text, he only obſerves that, "this has been "*fully conſidered* in my anſwer to Mr. Love's pamphlet." Anticriſis, or a Diſcuſſion, &c. printed at Edinburgh in 1754, p. 14. So ſlight a defence ſeems to imply a conſciouſneſs of error.

be certain, that he continued to exercise the full extent of power and importance annexed to it. To enjoy church revenues under a borrowed name, was, in that age, a frequent practice.

As to the pension of five hundred pounds Scots, it must be traced by candour, to the same source. When Mary first landed in this country, she found it necessary to temporise with the leaders of Reformation. In particular, she was under the direction of the Earl of Murray. But even independent of this evidence on the subject, it is certain that to Mary, a zealous Catholic, Buchanan must at all times have been an object of horror. At an early period of life, he had fled from his country, for composing an outrageous satire against the Church of Rome. Returning in triumph, he began his carreer by publishing, with the most hostile contempt of his sovereign, that very satire the source of all his former sufferings. About the same time*, he sent into the world, his FRATRES FRATERRIMI, a miscellany still more shocking to the ears of a Catholic. The slightest reflection must convince us, that the superstitious Mary, never would have preferred an apostle of rebellion and blasphemy, as a preceptor, a professor, and a pensioner. Yet the charge of personal ingratitude to his sovereign, has been incessantly chanted over, by a thousand bookmakers.

In the note, already quoted, Dr. Stuart objects to the terms of the oath sworn by the Scotch Commissioners at York, when attesting the authenticity of Mary's letters to Bothwell. He says, that as they did not pretend to have been present, when Mary wrote these letters, "and as "there was a possibility of counterfeiting very exactly her "hand writing, they could not be perfectly sure, that "they were genuine; and to swear most directly, of con"sequence, that they were so, was infinitely improper, e"ven on the supposition that the letters are real and au"thentic." To this objection, it is sufficient to answer,

* "Eodem fere tempore." Ruddiman.

that ſuch oaths are adminiſtered every day in our courts of juſtice. The evidence ariſing *Ex comparatione literarum* is known to every mortal. To this wanton charge of perjury, Dr. Stuart ſubjoins that of forgery. He affirms that it is more than probable theſe letters were forged by Buchanan himſelf. Mr. Whitaker, on the other hand aſſerts, that they were the ſole contrivance of Maitland of Lethington. Indeed, the groſs blunders in the tranſlations are to me a ſufficient proof that they were not written by Buchanan, the firſt ſcholar of a learned age. Dr. Stuart adds, "For theſe notices I am indebted to my much e-"ſteemed relation, Mr. Thomas Ruddiman, whoſe writ-"ings *ſupport* the literary glory of his country." To complete this part of my taſk, it is neceſſary to beſtow ſome farther notice on the conduct of Ruddiman, as an editor of Buchanan.

No queſtion was ever more impertinent or uſeleſs than that on which he has ſpent ſo much time, and from which he aſſumes ſo much merit reſpecting the period when Buchanan began to compoſe his hiſtory and *the order in which the books were written.* He has actually ſpent ſeveral pages * to prove that Buchanan wrote this hiſtory with a view to the Earl of Murray's obtaining the crown. Murray was ſhot on the 23d. of January 1570, and the hiſtory was not publiſhed till about thirteen years after, in September fifteen hundred and *eighty-two.* He would likewiſe perſwade us that the dialogue *De Jure Regni* was fabricated for the ſame purpoſe. Yet he cannot deny that this very treatiſe was not printed till the year one thouſand five hundred and *ſeventy-nine.* No human character could ſtand againſt ſuch torture. There is not a ſpark of proof that Murray intended to ſeize upon the crown of Scotland. The charge againſt Buchanan may be illuſtrated by a ſhort ſimilie. A. B. tells his neighbours that he has a pair of loaded piſtols. On this *evidence,* he is tried and hanged, becauſe his friend C. D. is

* Anſwer to Logan, p. 55, 76. et ſeq.

ſuſpected of having propoſed to commit a robbery ten years ago.

Another ſtory, fully as abſurd, is mentioned by Ruddiman; that Buchanan forbore to continue his hiſtory through Morton's regency, becauſe he hated Morton. It was with the utmoſt difficulty that Buchanan's infirmities permitted him to bring his work ſo far down as he did, and he actually expired about the time when the laſt ſheet was printed *. This is certainly a ſufficient anſwer. There can be no worſe mark of a writer than when he attempts to make a reader believe, *what he does not believe himſelf.* Mr. Ruddiman is ſometimes in this ſituation. Having noticed that Buchanan's hiſtory was printed when he was on his death-bed, and that it contains the ſevereſt reflections on Queen Mary, he would yet wiſh us to believe that the writer on that very death-bed *repented* of his animoſity to Mary. Dr. Stuart, who was more than once, a ſervile copyiſt, and a petulant declaimer, obſerves, "that the repentance of Buchanan has been affirmed "*with great probability.*" This is the mere echo of Ruddiman. After reading over what has been ſaid by Ruddiman and Whitaker, I have no difficulty in affirming that their evidence is altogether trifling. It is contradicted by direct perſonal teſtimony †, and is in itſelf abſurd and impoſſible. Nothing but a keen appetite for calumny, or the mere inſanity of Jacobitiſm, could have induced Ruddiman to prefix his name to ſuch an old woman's tale ‡.

* *Vide* Man's Examination, &c. p. 54.

† Mr. James Melvile, apud Man, p. 51, et ſeq.

‡ It has of late become faſhionable to ſpeak of Ruddiman in terms of the higheſt reſpect. Some of his co-temporaries muſt have entertained a very different opinion; for in the preface to his "Anticriſis," he tells us, that Mr. Logan, one of the miniſters of Edinburgh, had wrote no leſs than ſix different treatiſes againſt him; beſides which, he refers to a crowd of ſimilar publications. Of his volume againſt Mr. Logan, a great part con-

The accusations against Buchanan may be reduced to four heads, ingratitude, perjury, forgery, and rebellion. As to the first, I have proved that it is entirely unsupported; as to the second, the ground on which it is advanced by Dr. Stuart is ridiculous; as to the third, it is contradicted by Mr. Whitaker, who had made far deeper researches in the controversy than Dr. Stuart; and as to the fourth, it amounts to nothing, since the *rebels* were victorious, which ends the question.

Among other writers of inferior note, who have attacked our author's character, I have been advised to examine a book published in 1705, by David Crawfurd. After what has been already said, it seems to contain nothing which merits a farther answer.

In perusing the works of Buchanan, the first circumstance which strikes us, is, his uncommon fertility. Though the greater part of his life was spent in the task of teaching, a profession of which he bitterly complains, and though the history of Scotland, in which he has displayed such a profusion of excellence, might have exhausted a comprehensive mind, he has yet found leisure to write upwards of twenty thousand Latin verses, which are equal to three times the extent of the works of Horace. Of these verses, about one third are occupied in his translation of the Psalms, where he has wandered into twenty-nine different kinds of metre. In the variety of his numbers, therefore, he leaves every poet, ancient and modern, at an immense distance; and as if the genius of Rome had not sufficiently extended the limits of her language, he has employed five different sorts of verse, which are said never

sists of appeals to the Old Testament in behalf of the *Jus Divinum*, and on this topic it is remarkable, that he is constantly insinuating what he does not chuse to assert. James the First of England, he mentions, as "This good King, this truly just and "religious Prince," page 87. The execution of Charles the First was "the most dismal and wicked tragedy that ever was acted." Ib. page 110. Charles the Second, he terms "that good King." Ib. page 118.

to have been attempted by any former writer. He is conſtantly attentive to claſſical dignity of character. Good ſenſe predominates in every ſentence. He is not one of thoſe thoughtleſs compilers, in whom, to peruſe twenty pages of elegance, or wit, we muſt wade through whole volumes of bombaſt, or buffoonery. We can never ſay *Interdum bonus dormitat Buchananus;* for in the whole wilderneſs of his poetry, there are not, I believe, ten lines which his moſt judicious admirer could wiſh to be forgotten. I here ſpeak of the intrinſic merit of the verſes, without endeavouring to juſtify on every occaſion, either his panegyric, or his cenſure.

As an herald of civil and religious liberty, our author deſerves an ample ſhare of the gratitude of nations. Never did the "rights of man" meet with a more ardent partiſan, an advocate more acute, eloquent, philoſophical, and ſublime *. The truly virtuous characters of antiquity he mentions with the veneration they deſerve. But judgment never drops the reins to fancy. From his eye the ſplendour of conqueſt could not hide its deformity; and when there fell in his way a Cæſar, an Alexander, a Xerxes, or a Charles the Fifth, the moraliſt ſet no bounds to his ſcorn and deteſtation. When, in 1552, the emperor was repulſed, with the loſs of thirty thouſand men from the walls of Metz, our author addreſſed Henry the Second of France,

* On this head the public will liſten with reſpect to a writer who has lately deſerved and acquired their approbation. "The "firſt man at the revival of letters, who united elegant learn- "ing to original and maſculine thought was Buchanan, and he "too ſeems to have been the FIRST ſcholar who caught from the "ancients the noble flame of republican enthuſiaſm. This praiſe "is merited by his neglected, though incomparable tract, *De* "*Jure Regni*, in which the principles of popular politics, and "the maxims of a free government, are delivered with a pre- "ciſion, and enforced with an energy, which no former age had "equalled, and no ſucceeding has ſurpaſſed."

Vindiciæ Gallicæ, 2d. edit. p. 309.

in an ode, to which Horace cannot often produce a parallell. Where every ſtanza is excellent, ſelection becomes an office of delicacy. Having, with his uſual impetuoſity, reproached Charles as a monſter more hideous than the Gorgon Siſters, or the Hydra, having placed in the moſt ſtriking point of view, his barbarity, his ambition, and his power, he thus, in a tranſport of exultation, deſcribes the anguiſh of the defeated tyrant:

Tu bellicoſæ dux bone Galliæ
Sperare promtam cuncta ſuperbiam
Compeſcuiſti: tu dediſti
Indomito laqueos furori.

Quis vultus illi? qui dolor intimis
Arſit medullis? ſpiritus impotens
Cum clauſtra ſpectaret Moſellæ
Et juvenum intrepidam coronam.

Sic unda rupes ſævit in obvias,
Clauſus caminis ignis inæſtuat,
Hyrcana ſic tigris cruento
Dente ſuas furit in catenas.

In Engliſh thus,

"Thou worthy leader of gallant France haſt blaſted "that pride forward to hope for every ſucceſs: Thou haſt "fixed bounds to fury till now irreſiſtible.

"What were his looks? What agonies convulſed e-"very nerve? when his impotent haughtineſs beheld the "ramparts of the Moſelle *, and her intrepid band of "youth?

"Thus rages a ſurge againſt oppoſing rocks; thus ſub-"terranean fire ſtruggles for a paſſage; thus the Hyrca-"nian tyger champs his chains with his bloody teeth."

No reader will expect that the beauties of ſuch an ori-

* Metz ſtands on the banks of that river.

2

ginal can be transfused into a profe tranflation ; but it is better than feeble rhimes.

The poet proceeds to celebrate the gallantry of Biron and the French garrifon, who, difdaining the protection of walls, rufhed out, repulfed and difperfed the imperial army. Their rout he compares to that of inferior prowlers at the approach of the lion, and concludes by reprobating the defpicable cunning of Charles.

In the clofe of his ode on the capture of Calais by the Duke of Guife, he has defcribed, with ftriking circumftances, the abandoned fituation of QueenMary of England, who, by her bigotry and ambition, had become defpifed by foreign nations, and detefted by her own fubjects; and though then in the family of Marfhall Briffac, a Roman Catholic, he refers, with an excefs of indignation, to the flames of Smithfield. This ode, which extends to an hundred and eight lines, contains a variety of the fineft moral fentiments, and is diftinguifhed by a ftrain of the moft rational and exalted piety.

In his poem on aftronomy alfo, he has difplayed his deteftation of conquerors and tyrants, in juft and philofophical verfes. Having expreffed his regret that the names of the firft difcoverers of that fcience had not been tranfmitted to pofterity, he proceeds thus,—

At nos victuris potius committere chartis,
Barbaricum Xerxis faftum juvat, armaque diri
Cæfaris, et facta Emathii fcelerata tyranni:
At bene promeritos de vita hominumque falute
Negligimus Lethes tetra fub nocte jacentes.

" But we choofe rather to celebrate the barbarous pride " of Xerxes, the victories of the direful Cæfar, or the " execrable crimes of the Macedonian tyrant, while we " fuffer the benefactors of mankind to lie under the dark- " eft fhades of Lethe."

Another prominent diftinction in the literary character of Buchanan was an averfion to Popery. His innate abhorrence of monks, and his irresistible impulse to brand them with infamy, produced some of the principal misfortunes of his long and active life. The quarrel began by his writing a satire against the Franciscans, while in the family of the Earl of Cassilis. And being soon after appointed preceptor to one of the sons of James the Fifth, he, at the desire of that monarch, wrote some other pieces on the same subject. In one of these, which he calls a Palinode, a monk is brought forward, cooling his concupiscence, in a fall of snow, as the nearest nunnery was at too far a distance for the urgency of his occasions, and as he could not, in broad day light, walk into a bawdy-house. The female spectators of this exploit, shed tears at such a misapplication of the holy man's abilities, and the writer ends with some ludicrous comparisons, which decency must retain under the veil of a dead language. In another piece, he mentions the rage of the monks at his verses, and contrasts them with St. Jerome flogging his own shoulders, as a penance for the guilt of having read Cicero. As these attacks were too imperfect for the revenge of James, he undertook the memorable satire intitled FRANCISCANUS; which is probably, since the sixth Satire of Juvenal, the most beautiful and complete work of that nature which the world has ever seen. But with judgment to discover abilities, the worthless King had neither justice to reward, nor honour to protect them. Corrupted by a bribe from Cardinal Beatoun, he consented to the murther of the young poet. The priesthood anticipated the triumph of conducting him to the stake, and their black annals were never stained with the blood of a more illustrious victim. But Buchanan was reserved for a different scene of exertions and of sufferings. He broke out of prison and fled into England, where he addressed Cromwell, at that time Minister to Henry the Eighth, in a short but pathetic poem, describing the complication of disasters by which he was overwhelmed, "Look not" says Buchanan, "with a harsh countenance, on the humble advances of a man whose whole soul is devoted to

" your ſervice, who, a vagrant, an exile, a beggar, has " endured every misfortune which a perfidious world can " inflict. A ſavage hoſt of inveterate enemies purſue " him. The palace of his ſovereign reſounds with their " menaces. Over mountains buried in ſnow, through " vallies flooded with rain, I come like a fugitive to the " Athenian altar of mercy, and exhauſted by calamities, " caſt myſelf as a ſupplicant at your feet." Such entreaties, enforced by the ſweetneſs and majeſty of Virgil's numbers, one would think ſufficient to ſoften any heart but that of a ſtateſman, a being diſtinguiſhed in all ages, for beholding with indifference the miſeries of mankind. He likewiſe inſcribed to Henry himſelf an elegant copy of verſes, which conclude with perhaps the fineſt portrait of a great and good monarch that ever was imagined. His applications were unſucceſsful, and the verſes remain a monument to the diſhonour of the King and his miniſter. This experience of treachery in one ſovereign, and of ungeneroſity in another, may firſt poſſibly have inſpired Buchanan with that diſdain of royalty, and thoſe levelling republican principles which formed, as it were, the eſſence of his ſoul.

It is true that our author has produced many beautiful panegyrics on ſome of the moſt eminent ſovereigns of his time; but theſe are to be regarded rather as the ſports of imagination, as the labours of convenience or neceſſity, than as the offspring of voluntary choice *. He ſeems to have owed much of the happineſs of his life to the univerſal veneration excited by his abilities. No man, perhaps, ever enjoyed a more numerous, illuſtrious, and affectionate circle of correſpondents; and their attachment ſhows, that if he did not feel, he muſt at leaſt have exerted, in an uncommon degree, the ſocial virtues. Indeed, almoſt no poet has equalled him in diſplaying the ſenſibilities of

* We are indebted for the Ode on Alexander's Feaſt to the importunities of a Muſical Club. The Ode on the Siege of Metz is mentioned by the writer as a trifle obtained in the ſame way.

friendſhip, of gratitude, and of love. As a ſpecimen of his talents in this way, the reader may peruſe part of an ode addreſſed to a young lady.

Camilla, multo me mihi carior,
Aut ſi quid ipſo eſt me mihi carius,
Camilla, doctorum parentum
Et patriæ decus et voluptas:

Ni Gratiæ te plus oculis ament,
Ni te Camœnæ plus oculis ament,
Nex Gratias gratas, nec ipſas
Eſſe rear lepidas Camœnas.

Quæ virgo nondum nubilis, artibus
Doctis Minervam, pectine Apollinem,
Cantu Camœnas et lepore
Vel ſuperes Charites, vel æques.

"Camilla, much dearer to me than myſelf, or than "whatever elſe is dearer to me than myſelf:—Camilla, "the glory and delight of thy learned parents, and of thy "country;—

"Unleſs the Graces love thee better than themſelves, "unleſs the Muſes love thee better than themſelves, "I deny beauty to the Graces, or eloquence to the "Muſes.

"What virgin beſides thee has, at ſuch tender years, "excelled in learning Minerva, in muſic Apollo and the "Muſes, and in wit equals or excells the Graces?"

It is uſual to ſay that we can diſtinguiſh an author by the peculiarities of his ſtyle, but this rule cannot apply to the univerſal abilities of Buchanan. The beſt idea which can be conveyed of him to a mere Engliſh reader may be compriſed in five words, "Dryden always at his beſt." Indeed there is, in many points, a very ſtriking reſemblance, between theſe two poets. Both inherited from nature, in an equal degree, a moſt comprehenſive underſtanding, and a moſt ſplendid fancy. In variety of numbers, and facility of metrical compoſition, they ſtand unrivalled in the reſpective languages in which they wrote. Of wit, that faculty, in whatever it conſiſts of exciting laughter, both poſſeſſed of an ample ſhare; yet their proper element was the ſerious and ſublime. The ſmile of Buchanan is the ſmile of indignation; and as Dryden's taſte was much leſs cultivated, his merriment ſometimes degenerates into groſſneſs. For the ſtage both poſſeſſed abilities reſpectable, but moderate. They were by nature, or by habit, better qualified for the dignity of declamation than the vivacity of dialogue. Both have many paſſages truly pathetic, but tenderneſs is not the predominant excellence of either. Both had ſtudied human nature with cloſe attention; both abound with beautiful portraits of perſonal character, and the moſt inſtructive maxims for the conduct of life. But the profound learning of Buchanan, his habits of equality and confidence with men of rank, and his long reſidence in many different countries, afford him numerous advantages, in point of force, variety, and correctneſs. From the friend of Aſcham and Scaliger, from the preceptor of a prince, and the preſident of a college, productions more claſſical might juſtly be demanded, than from the playwright of a licentious ſtage, the tool of an uſurping prieſthood, and the reluctant hireling of a bookſeller. Both writers were long the poets of a court; both have left us an immenſe number of ſhort temporary pieces, deſigned merely to pleaſe, entertain, or vex a few individuals, but forcing themſelves on our laſting applauſe by the merit of compoſition. The Scottiſh poet, at leaſt, can hardly be ſtigmatiſed as obſcene; but both were ambitious of advancing to the utmoſt verge of decency. Both were by far the firſt ſatiriſts of their reſpective periods. Both poſſeſſed ſuch inexhauſtible talents for panegyric, and both were poetical tranſlators of ſuch ſupreme ſkill, that in either capacity they have hardly a ſingle rival in the whole records of literature. But the operations of the poet muſt always take an impreſſion from the manners of his age, and the temper of the man. Dryden ſeems to have been weak, indolent, and from levity almoſt incapable of principle or ſincere attachment. He is therefore often negligent, and whatever be his theme, he is in frequent danger of relapſing into a jeſt. On the contrary, his predeceſſor is grave, intrepid, impetuous, and implacable. He never attacks by halves. His ridicule darkens into rage. He combats not for conqueſt, but extirpation. From the pontiff and emperor, to the pedagogue and the monk, the victim of his deriſion is infallibly held forth not only as the dulleſt, but the vileſt of mankind. Every poſſible feature of vice and folly ſeems anxious to ſtart from the canvaſs. With the abrupt dexterity of a veteran familiar to victory, he at once cloſes upon his adverſary, tramples him, and tears him to pieces. Overwhelmed by a luminous burſt of thought, the mind bends under the graſp of his eloquence, while veneration and gratitude, for the artiſt forbid us to queſtion the juſtice of the likeneſs.—The dreadful annals of the ſixteenth century ſupplied inceſſant exerciſe for a mind glowing with every ſentiment of hoſtility and defiance. Buchanan was not only more ſteady in the exertion of his talents, but more fortunate in the objects of his choice. For the purpoſes of a laureate, Henry the ſecond of France, John third of Portugal, the two rival queens of Britain, and the memorable tyrant of the German Empire, were better adapted than the penſioner Charles, or the Jeſuit James. The foibles of the Preſbyterians preſent the mind with no image parallel to the ſcenes of impoſture and debauchery ſo copiouſly deſcribed in the Franciſcan. Even Monmouth and Shafteſbury were but pigmies of ſedition, when compared with the ſtupenduous atrocity of the houſe of Guiſe. In his addreſs to the Cardinal of Lorraine, compoſed after the maſſacre of Paris, Buchanan bids him ſurvey the price of his grandeur—a nation of widows and orphans—a country covered with blood and aſhes—and fternly affures him that to fuch a prodigy of guilt, hell muft be a defirable refuge from the curfes of mankind. "Yet even there," adds the poet, "you will be admit-"ted with terror, and watched with anxiety, left a foul "fo turbulent fhould fpread rebellion among the damn-"ed." Thefe fallies offend not our feelings, for they confift with truth, but they would have been utterly inapplicable to the heroes of Abfalom and Achitophel. On Ravillac or Felton neither Whig nor Tory would have endured an encomium, but no reader can be much offended when Buchanan refers with gratitude to the blunderbufs of Poltrot *. Dryden has marked as one of his fevereft effufions the portrait of Zimri. His provocation was an admirable burlefque on fome of his abfurd plays. He charges Buckingham with no deep vice or atrocious crime. He is fatisfied by reprefenting him as the moft thoughtlefs, frivolous, and defpicable of mankind. With what a contraft are we fometimes aftonifhed in Buchanan's "Mufe of Fire!" In what the writer calls an epitaph on Hamilton Archbifhop of St. Andrew's, he begins by informing us that our parent earth now breathes lighter fince delivered from the burden of fuch an abominable monfter; that all the angels of darknefs have been fatigued in preparing for his reception, and that every other department of perdition now ftands ftill, the whole tortures of Tartarus being devoted to a fingle victim.

Unius in pœnas, dum totus ruit Avernus.

After paufing with complacency on this charitable profpect, he concludes by profeffing his regret, that the Primate's carcafe had not been caft to the dogs. Hamilton had been executed as an accomplice in the murder of the Regent Murray, the friend and benefactor of the ferocious fatirift. The fervile temper of Dryden, is univerfally known, and in this part of the parallel Buchanan appears

* On the 24th February 1563, the Duke of Guife was mortally wounded at the fiege of Orleans, by John Poltrot, a French Proteftant.

with ſuperior advantage. The force of his mind was only to be broken, by the ſtroke that diſſolved its mortal exiſtence. At the age of ſeventy, when oppreſſed by the gout and ſtone, he publiſhed his tragedy of John the Baptiſt, which is inſcribed to his pupil with a tone of firmneſs and dignity worthy of his former fame. "If at any time," ſays Buchanan, "impelled by bad counſellors, or the licentiouſneſs of the kingdom, overcoming a virtuous education, you act amiſs, I intend this work as an evidence to poſterity, that the fault lies not with your preceptors, but with you, neglecting to follow their proper admonitions." The treatiſe *De Jure Regni*, is inſcribed to King James, in the ſame independent and manly ſtyle.

In the ſublime of Engliſh lyric poetry, Dryden has no rival, and in the crowd of modern Latin poets, the ſame honourable diſtinction may be claimed for our countryman. It will be difficult to produce an ode, which can be compared with thoſe on the ſieges of Metz, of Verceil, and of Calais, with that on the Kalends of May, with another on the conduct of the Portugueſe in Braſil, or with thoſe three inſcribed to Marſhall Briſſac and his lady, to the Chancellor of France, and to Queen Elizabeth of England*. Dryden wrote merely for money, to gratify his own paſſions, or thoſe of his contemporaries. His taſte had been early corrupted by the conceits of Donne and Cowley, and it was the ſummit of his ambition to pleaſe the audience of a play-houſe, or the concubine of a prince. Buchanan took his flight from higher ground. The greater part of his life was ſpent, not behind the curtain of a theatre, but in the retirement of a college. He held the ancients ever in his eye. On every occaſion, however triſling, he ſeems to have been mindful of fame and poſterity; nor did his meal depend on the caprice of a purſe-

* If the reader has an opportunity of examining the endleſs volumes of Italian verſe, he will diſcover, in this particular, the prodigious ſuperiority of our Author.

proud tradesman, capable of estimating his volumes only by their bulk. The distinction is easily discernible. Dryden is ever disturbing our tranquillity with a detail of his talents and his sufferings of persecuted virtue, and neglected merit. Buchanan, too proud for ostentation, never mentions himself or his writings, but in a tone of the most guarded propriety. His mind was superior to vanity or grimace, and yet more to that pitiful canting style, which pollutes the endless prefaces of the English laureate. To the Dunciad or Macflecknoe there is nothing correspondent in the satires of Buchanan. Of contemporary poets he often speaks, but always in the kindest and most liberal terms. Conscious, perhaps, that he was far above a rival, he celebrates with a profusion of praise, a multitude of writers whose names are now only remembered by their insertion in his verses. If he ever had any poetical enemies, the last traces of their existence appear to have been long since obliterated, for he never raised them into antagonists by condescending to revile them. This delicacy, which marks such a manly superiority to the petulance of some modern poets, deserves the higher praise, as we have seen that his passions were violent, his courage inflexible, and as he has left behind him full evidence that on every other topic from the civil wars of a kingdom, to the brawls of a bagnio, he was prepared and prompt for battle.

To write a regular criticism on the poetical works of Buchanan, or to give even but a faint idea of the wonderful variety of their contents and beauties would require a large volume. The reader may be amused by a short account of each of the principal sections, into which his original poems have usually been divided. It seems unnecessary to speak here of his Psalms, as they are in the hands of every school-boy.

I. It has already been observed, that, by the desire of James V. he began a poem intitled *Franciscanus.* After an exile of twenty-four years, he returned to his native country, " now," as he says, " beyond the hopes of all "men, happily delivered from the tyranny of monſters." His ſatire, left unfiniſhed for ſo great a lapſe of time, was publiſhed in the year 1564, with a dedication to his friend, the well known Earl of Murray. Buchanan was now at the age of fifty-eight; he had rambled over a great part of Europe, had ſeen, and ſuffered, and reflected much, and he poſſeſſed, in an ample degree, the proverbial ſenſibility of a poet. We are therefore entitled to expect a ſuperior monument of his abilities and his vengeance. The Franciſcan will ſatisfy our moſt ſanguine wiſhes. It extends to nine hundred and thirty-ſix lines, and opens by the author inquiring at an acquaintance, a Franciſcan noviciate, what he means by this ſudden grimace, and affectation of ſanctity in his appearance. He adjures him, in the moſt ſolemn manner, to ſpurn the trammels of vulgar ſuperſtition, to diſtruſt the pomp of the hierarchy, ſo much admired by the maſters of mankind, and examine Chriſtianity by the ſacred light of reaſon. He proceeds, in a vein of irony, to tell him that he himſelf had once indulged the ſame ſort of frenzy, but had been diverted from it by the ſage advice of his friend Eubulus. The author next repeats his admonitions, in the form of a harangue, from this imaginary preceptor, who goes on for a few ſentences in a calm, temporate ſtyle, with an evident deſign to gain the confidence of the reader. But ſuddenly, as if impatient to repair the loſs of time, Eubulus, or rather Buchanan, burſts out in a torrent of reproach. A literal tranſlation of the poem would extend to the ſize of a pamphlet. Every ſentence abounds with the wit, eloquence, and ſublimity of Juvenal; the copiouſneſs of ſentiment, the fluency of expreſſion, and the ferocity of contempt which diſtinguiſh the admirable, though neglected Claudian*. The Franciſcans are exhibited, in every point of

* Buchanan, with the taſte of a ſcholar, mentions this great author in the moſt reſpectful terms. Dryden raſhly and impertinently cenſures him. In many reſpects Claudian has a ſtrong reſemblance to the two moderns. Indeed, though much inferior

view, as vultures tearing out the vitals of ſociety. The writer deſcribes, at great length, their numberleſs arts of impoſing upon the mob, and eſpecially upon the weaker ſex. He tells, what we know to be true, that when a wealthy penitent was at the point of death, it was their practice to extort, under the terrors of eternal perdition, an extravagant legacy to their convent; and he affirms, what is ſufficiently credible, that by ſuch exactions, many families had been ruined. He enlarges upon their pride, ignorance, dulneſs, envy, hypocriſy, debauchery, and ſelfiſhneſs; their factious ſpirit, treachery, cowardice, and perſonal naſtineſs: their ſuperſtition, loquacity, and impudent affectation of taciturnity. He diſplays their progreſs in the various ſciences of ſcandal, pimping, treaſon, rebellion, ſeduction, cuckoldom, and ſodomy. He repreſents the various hazards they run of being gelded, and affirms that confeſſion, purgatory, and tranſubſtantiation are abſurd impoſtures. "An aſs," ſays Buchanan, "though "you clothe him in Tyrian purple, continues to be ſtu- "pid, and a tyger to be ſavage. Magpies will always "chatter, and vipers will always ſting." His inference is, that a Franciſcan has an invincible propenſity to every human vice. Having in ſhort, aſſerted their utter degradation below the reſt of the ſpecies, and having diverſified his performance with ſome ludicrous anecdotes, he concludes by telling the noviciate, that, upon the expoſtulations of Eubulus, he had renounced holy water, the girdle, the cowl, and the ſhaven crown, as ridiculous marks of diſtinction, invented for the moſt ſordid and infamous purpoſes. The whole work is worthy of Buchanan, the advocate and avenger of inſulted truth; and if conſidered merely as an animated and faithful picture,

to both, he approaches nearer to their general character than any ſingle ancient poet. There is far leſs nonſenſe in his text than we commonly imagine. Dryden has preſumed to condemn him for his bad taſte, and has, at the ſame time, left us ſix volumes of plays which contain perhaps an hundred tolerable pages.

must be highly curious and instructive. As a specimen of the spirit of this poem, it may be proper to extract a few lines, subjoining, as usual, a prose translation. After a long detail of the various circumstances which multiplied monastic vermin, he proceeds thus:

"Adjice præterea quos præceps alea nudat,
Quos Venus enervat, quos et potatio pernox
Ejecit patriis laribus, quos urget egestas,
Et quibus haudquaquam res sunt in amore secundæ,
Fastosæque inopes exclusit limen amicæ,
Quos scelus infamat, tutor quos urget avarus,
Huc, velut ad tutum cunctis est cursus asylum.
Hoc procerum e numero crescit generosa propago
Funigeri gregis: hi patres quibus ille superbit
Ordo sacer, seges hæc orbis moderatur habenas,
Quos metus, ira, furor, mens tarda, ignavia, crimen,
Ambitio, res adversæ, fastidia vitæ,
Durus amor, durus pater, implacata noverca,
Et mendax virtutis amor, collegit in unum.

"Namque velut quondam cum res adversa premebat
Ad laqueum, ad preceps, ad toxica, flumina, pontes,
Atque truces gladios, caligantesque fenestras,
Cursus erat, duram cupienti evadere sortem:
Sic modo cum sceleris pudor, aut formido severi
Judicis, aut gravior cunctis infamia pœnis
Urget, ad hunc scopulum Francisci in syrmate fune
Cingimur, et tanquam pariter cum vertice radi
Mens etiam scelerata queat: de sacrilegis et
De parricidis de furibus, atque cinædis,
Nos faciat cœli subitos rasura colonos."

"Add, besides those whom dice have hurled into ruin, "whom venery has enfeebled, or whom midnight ca-"rousals have driven from the inheritance of their fathers; "those whom downright beggary sweeps before it; those "disappointed in love, and against whom, for want of

" money, an infolent miſtreſs bolts her door; thoſe be-
" come infamous by their crimes; and thoſe who dread
" their puniſhment.—Here alſo there is a ſafe refuge for
" boys robbed by the rapacity of their guardians. From
" theſe worthy tribes are embodied the noble band of
" Franciſcans. Theſe are the fathers of whom this ſac-
" red order is ſo proud. This is the generation that
" ſteers the helm of the world; miſcreants whom rage,
" madneſs, and terror, dulneſs, lazineſs, and guilt, am-
" bition, poverty, and deſpair, diſaſtrous love, a ſullen
" father, an implacable ſtepmother, and a farcical pre-
" tence of godlineſs have confounded together.

" In former days a wretch diſtracted by misfortunes had
" recourſe to a halter, a precipiçe, a dagger, or a doſe of
" poiſon; or ruſhed into a river, or leaped from a bridge,
" or a high window, that he might avoid the ſhock of ad-
" verſity; but now, when the pangs of conſcience, or fear
" of a ſevere judge, or infamy more terrible than every
" other puniſhment purſues a criminal, he binds a cord
" about his middle, and takes refuge under the cowl of
" St. Francis. And, as if to ſhave the crown could ſtifle
" the agonies of guilt, the razor ſuddenly conſecrates a
" ſwarm of devotees, transformed from thieves, parri-
" cides, blaſphemers, and catamites."

This poem affords a fine counter-part to Dryden's Hind and Panther; and how much more honourably would he have been employed in turning it into Engliſh verſe? We cannot wonder that Buchanan was perſecuted through life by the blood-hounds of ſuperſtition, or that his memory has been loaded with a whole library of reproaches, the moſt unjuſt and incredible. I ſhall diſmiſs this article by the inſertion of threo lines, which may be read with pleaſure, but cannot be tranſlated with decency. In ſeducing a young girl, our author ſays,—

" Et pede tange pedem, dextram dextra, oribus ora:
" Sic, diis, rides, ſic molliter oſcula jungis,
" *Oſcula commiſſas inter luctantia linguas.*—

II. Another ſection of his works is intitled *Fratres Fraterrimi*, and conſiſts chiefly of ſatires, in various kinds of verſe, againſt the Catholic clergy of every deſcription, from ſeveral of the popes, one of whom he compares to Judas Iſcariot, down to the monks. The collection concludes with ſome of thoſe juvenile eſſays which the author compoſed againſt the Franciſcans at the deſire of the Scottiſh monarch. Several Engliſh poets have, at a mature age, affected to print pieces exactly as they had been written by themſelves when at ſchool. Milton, among others, has incumbered poſterity with this ſort of trumpery. In the works of Dryden we can eaſily diſtinguiſh that his ſtyle is gradually improving down to his tranſlation of Virgil; and the nobleſt ode in any language was itſelf the very laſt effort of his muſe. In the text of Buchanan no ſuch diſtinction is diſcernible. What he had written in youth he either committed to the flames, or improved into an equality with his later productions; and he is above the paltry vanity of telling us in the title of a piece, that it was written at twelve or ſixteen. The reader has nothing to do with the age of an author, but with the merit of his writings. From this digreſſion, I return to the *Fratres Fraterrimi*. This miſcellany conſiſts of thirty-ſix articles, with a humorous dedication to a man of letters. The worſhip of images and pictures, and tranſubſtantiation, the columns upon which Popery reſted, are here overwhelmed in a torrent of ridicule. An ode inſcribed to Queen Elizabeth, is written in the higheſt ſtyle of Horace, and contains an eloquent ſummary of the preceding glories of her reign; among which the extirpation of monkery ſtands foremoſt. There is a ſtrange dialogue between a painter and a baker, diſputing which of them could make deities ſooneſt. The painter founds his pretenſions on his profeſſion of drawing the pictures of the ſaints, while the baker boaſts that he can make ten thouſand holy wafers in an hour. The miſcellany begins with a poem at the expence of a rich abbot, whoſe life and conduct Buchanan contraſts with that of the divine founder of Chriſtianity. We have alſo a furious invective againſt the kingdom of Portugal, including a warm panegyric on the climate and people of France. One of the moſt remarkable pieces in this collection is an ode of eleven ſtanzas, upon the conduct of the Portugueſe in Brazil. He invokes the angel who deſtroyed Sodom and Gomorrah to hurl his thunderbolts againſt the execrable invaders; and concludes with an ardent wiſh that the earth may open and ſwallow them, or the fire of heaven blaſt them. In a word, it is the fineſt invective againſt the tyranny of Europeans in America, that the world has probably ever ſeen. From the peculiar boldneſs and rapidity of its ſtyle, a critic of learning would perhaps venture to ſay that part of this ode approaches neareſt of all poetry to the martial enthuſiaſm of Tyrtæus. Every line ſeems to flaſh from the heart of the writer.— There is, there can be nothing more awfully ſublime.

III. The next ſection is intitled *Elegiarum Liber*, and conſiſts of nine different articles. The firſt of theſe contains an hundred and ten lines, and deſcribes the miſerable ſituation of the teachers of literature at Paris. It is probable that at this time Buchanan was himſelf an underprofeſſor in the univerſity; for he ſpeaks with much aſperity of the profeſſors, and complains of the harſhneſs of their diſcipline in the moſt pointed terms. He obſerves that the plowman, and even the ſlave who works in fetters, enjoy at night an agreeable ſlumber; that the ſailor ſleeps in the midſt of the ocean; in ſhort, that all nature is at reſt, excepting the profeſſors and ſtudents in the univerſity of Paris. He concludes with a ſolemn peroration againſt Apollo, the Muſes, and the beggarly profeſſion of learning; and proteſts that Calliope would not have remained a maid till this time if ſhe had not been pennyleſs. The ſecond elegy is in a very different ſtyle, it is written on the Kalends of May, and exhibits one of the fineſt ſcenes of rural and paſtoral deſcription that can poſſibly be imagined: It extends to an hundred and forty-five lines. The third elegy is a ſtrange compoſition. It is inſcribed to one of the ſenators of Bourdeaux, and ought to have been intitled, A modeſt Defence of Fornication. How any man in the character of a public teacher, ventured to publiſh ſuch a performance, it is not very eaſy to conceive; yet we muſt remember that the manners of that age were much leſs refined than ours. There is, indeed, nothing in the poem poſitively indecent; but there is ſo much more underſtood than expreſſed, that we can hardly believe Buchanan expected its peruſal would invigorate the chaſtity of a young ſtudent. In this very piece, however, he declaims, in the ſevereſt ſtyle, againſt batchelors, and deſcribes, with the moſt intereſting eloquence, the tranſcendent felicity of poſſeſſing a virtuous and dutiful wife. The reader may perhaps imagine that ſuch diſcordant materials cannot compoſe a very coherent production: but there was nothing which Buchanan feared to attempt, and very little which he failed to perform. A ſhort ſpecimen may be agreeable to the reader; addreſſing the ſenator, he ſays,

"Cum mare, cum tellus homines populetur, et ignis,
Tot pereant morbo, tot fera bella necent;
Cumque hominum in pejus ſolertia callida ſemper
Inveniat cauſas in ſua fata novas:
Tun' prohibere audes veneris commercia? lenas
Si tollis, veneris commoda quanta vetas?
Tun' prohibere audes veneris commercia? ſola
Humanum poterant quæ reparare genus?"

"When land, and water, and fire, combine to deſtroy "mankind; when ſo many periſh by diſeaſe, and ſo many are butchered by barbarous war; when human invention, ever fertile in framing miſchief, is perpetually "pointing out freſh paths to deſtruction; dareſt thou to "forbid the commerce of love? By the expulſion of concubines how many of the enjoyments of love are de"ſtroyed? Dareſt thou to prohibit the pleaſures of love,

"the ſingle refuge left us to repair the ravages of the ſpe-
"cies?"

The poet proceeds to remind him that mankind cannot now be propagated like the Myrmidons from piſmires, or from clay and ſtones, as in the days of Prometheus and Pyrrha.

The fourth elegy is addreſſed to two of his literary friends, and contains an account of his ſufferings in ſevere illneſs. The fifth is inſcribed to the Chancellor of France, and is a petition in behalf of the ſchool of Bourdeaux.

The ſixth, which conſiſts of fifty-four lines, is addreſſed to a lady on her recovery from ſickneſs, and is, in point of tenderneſs, perhaps the maſter-piece of our author. It is one of thoſe happy productions which we can never tire of reading. The ſeventh and eight elegies are of a very different nature; they are inſcribed to a woman of pleaſure, on whom Buchanan diſcharges himſelf in a torrent of abuſe. The ninth elegy is in a ſuperior ſtyle.

IV. The next part of the collection is intitled *Silvæ*, and conſiſts of ſeven articles, all in hexameter verſe. The firſt is dated in 1539, and inſcribed in the name of the ſtudents at Bourdeaux to the Emperor Charles V. With great eloquence and dignity he touches on the principal events in the reign of Charles, and compares his condeſcenſion in viſiting Bourdeaux to that of Jupiter entertained by the Ethiopians. The Emperor had not yet, by the execution of fifty or an hundred thouſand of his Proteſtant ſubjects in the Netherlands, forfeited all pretence to the tenderneſs or eſteem of mankind *. The ſecond is inſcribed to a friend, whoſe abſence he regrets in a ſtrain of beautiful and pathetic poetry. The third is

* This trifling circumſtance has eſcaped the *comprehenſive* and *profound* reſearches of Dr. Robertſon. In the ſcience of *literary mutilation*, he perhaps is not inferior to any hiſtorian ancient or modern. The editor has been forced, for want of room, to leave out of this volume a review of his Hiſtory of America.

intitled *Desiderium Lutetiæ.* In this poem Buchanan laments, in affecting language, his absence from Paris, which he represents under the character of a mistress, whose charms had for seven years incessantly disturbed his peace. He concludes with the strongest protestations of fidelity.

"Et prius æquoribus pisces et montibus umbræ,
Et volucres deerunt sylvis, et murmura ventis:
Quam mihi discedent formosæ Amaryllidis ignes:
Illa mihi rudibus succendit pectora flammis,
Finiet illa meos moriens morientis amores.

"Sooner shall fishes be wanting to the sea, and the "mountains cease to reflect their shadows; sooner shall "birds leave their woods, and stillness attend the tem-"pest, than my passion for Amaryllis shall desert me. "She first kindled the flames of love in my breast, and "her death shall extinguish them for ever." The next article is an epithalamium on the marriage of Francis the Second with Queen Mary. In this poem, so different from the strains of a modern laureate, the genius of Buchanan shines in all its glory. To give a proper idea of a performance which extends to two hundred and eighty-seven lines is here impossible. The poet, after enlarging on the felicity of the young couple, and the joy that their union diffused over both nations, proceeds to give them a series of advices for their conduct in the exalted station which they were destined to fill. He begins with the French monarch, and after a profusion of compliments, proceeds in the most elevated language of poetry to remind him of the honours and advantages he derived from a consort so illustrious as the Queen of Scotland. He expatiates on the ancient independence of his country, and the valour of its inhabitants. Of this passage, which has been often quoted, one need only say, that it has hardly ever been excelled, even by our author himself: a few lines may ſerve as a ſpecimen. After having enlarged on the martial virtues of our anceſtors, he adds:

" Artibus his, totum fremerent cum bella per orbem,
Nullaque non legis tellus mutaret avitas
Externo ſubjecta jugo, gens una vetuſtis
Sedibus antiqua ſub libertate reſedit.
Subſtitit hic Gothi furor, hic gravis impetus hæſit
Saxonis, hic Cimber ſuperato Saxone, et acri
Perdomito et Neuſter Cimbro. Si volvere priſcos
Non piget annales, hic et victoria fixit
Præcipitem Romana gradum: quem non gravis Auſter
Reppulit, incultis non ſquallens Parthia campis;
Non æſtu Meroe, non frigore Rhenis et Albis
Tardavit, Latium remorata eſt Scotia curſum;
Solaque gens mundi eſt cum qua non culmine montis,
Non rapidi ripis amnis, non objice ſylvæ,
Non vaſti ſpatiis campi Romana poteſtas,
Sed muris foſſaque ſui confinia regni
Munivit: genteſque alias cum pelleret armis
Sedibus, aut victas vilem ſervaret in uſum
Servitii, hic contenta ſuos defendere fines
Roma ſecurigeris prætendit mœnia Scotis:
Hic ſpe progreſſus poſita Carronis ad undam
Terminus Auſonii ſignat divortia regni.

" Hence it was that when wars raged in every other " part of the world, when there was no country which " did not change its ancient laws and bend under a fo- " reign yoke, that A SINGLE NATION maintained its native " poſſeſſions, and its former liberty. Here it was, that the " fury of the Goths was forced to pauſe, here was check- " ed the dreadful force of the Saxons, of the Danes who " vanquiſhed the Saxons, and of the Normans who van- " quiſhed the Danes. If you do not bluſh to read the " annals of our anceſtors, here it was, that victori- " ous Rome ſtopped in her rapid courſe.—She whom nei- " ther the formidable Carthaginian repulſed, nor the hor "rid desarts of Parthia, nor the burning sun of Ethiopia, "nor the frozen Elbe, nor the Rhine could stop, was com- "pelled to pause on the confines of Scotland. This was "the only country in which the Roman empire was bound- "ed, not by inaccessible mountains, not by the banks "of a rapid river, not by the barrier of a forest, or by "an extensive plain, but by walls and trenches. While "by her arms she was driving other nations from their "native seats, or reducing them to disgraceful servitude, "here alone Rome was contented to defend her limits, "and protect herself by ramparts from the Caledonian "battle ax. Here, laying aside the hope of conquest, "Terminus, upon the banks of Carron, fixed the limits "of the Italian empire."—He proceeds in a style not very courtly, to remind Francis that the French nation had never, since the days of Charlemagne, performed any martial exploit of consequence, where the Scots had not borne away a full share of the honours of the field. He concludes by the usual predictions of prosperity and happiness. The next article contains a striking picture of the miseries of France, occasioned by the death of the young prince. Buchanan seems to have been fond of horsemanship; for we have a short but elegant poem in praise of the horse †.

The last piece in this division, is a poem upon the birth of James VI. He begins by anticipating the natural and happy consequences of an union between the two kingdoms, and expresses, in the language of a man who loved his country, his wishes that the royal parents may educate their son in such a manner as to qualify him for his exalted station. The rest of this performance consists entirely of a series of excellent moral lessons, of which it

* There is a foolish story of a quarrel, about a horse between our author and the Earl of Morton. Mr. Man, p. 33. et seq: has bestowed a refutation which it did not deserve. This fable is told at length by Ruddiman. Mr. George Chalmers of London, is at present writing his life, in which his treatment of Buchanan ought to stand foremost.

ſeems highly proper to remind the preſent generation. We have ſeen the mad prodigality of three or four individuals precipitate into bankruptcy the government of a great nation. We can have no doubt that, in other countries, the ſame conduct will, in due time, produce the ſame juſt and natural effects. Buchanan affirms that the manners of a people depend much leſs upon the laws of the ſtate than upon the example of their prince. He has not indeed inſinuated that his intended pupil, may one day become a jockey, a gameſter, a mendicant, the preſident of a beef ſteak club, or the arbiter of a boxing ſtage and a cock-pit. But he expatiates upon the ruin and infamy which attend an abuſe of wine or women. "What man," ſays Buchanan, "is not aſhamed of being drunk, when "he knows that his king is ſober?" He warns James againſt profuſion in his perſonal and domeſtic expences, and informs him that a worthleſs ſovereign is an utmoſt curſe of ſociety. Alexander, Nero, and Domitian, are brought forward as examples of the fatal effects of barbarity and deſpotiſm. In ſhort, the whole poem, except a few lines at the beginning, is a rigid lecture of which Hampden or Sully would not have been aſhamed; and for which he would have been ſincerely thanked by a Guſtavus Adolphus *, or a Frederick. He concludes with an advice to ſtudy letters and philoſophy, as the beſt ſchool for the art of government. "If in the buſineſs of life," ſays the poet, "he is attentive to theſe rules, he ſhall "be happy in ſwaying the ſceptre of his anceſtors." How oppoſite, how deplorable on the birth of a prince, is the language of Dryden, who compares the junction of three kingdoms in one, to the ſacred myſteries of religion. Dryden, however, would certainly, in our luxurious and ſer-

* Harte tells us that the Swediſh monarch, having, after an obſtinate ſiege, forced a town to ſurrender, to convince the inhabitants of their perfect ſecurity, entered firſt himſelf, without a ſingle attendant, and going into a bookſeller's ſhop, inquired for a copy of Buchanan's poems.

vile age, have borne away the palm of popularity and preferment from his cynical predeceſſor. Though he lived and died in the boſom of treaſon, rapine, and proſcription, Buchanan would have ſeen, with ſurpriſe, our modern ſtandard of morality. We call ourſelves a free people, and yet we have ſubmitted to hear, from the chair of juſtice, that *truth is a libel*, a doctrine which tears up the foundations of civil ſociety, and compared to which tranſubſtantiation, or even the divine right of tyrants, is a modeſt and reſpectable ſophiſm. With what indignation would the author of the treatiſe *De Jure Regni*, have branded the father and abettors of ſuch an execrable maxim? It is natural enough, that a barriſter, whoſe life has been employed in brawling, ſhould, in the end, diſtort his own mind out of all ſenſe of equity, and when HE mounts the ſaddle of authority, ſuch deciſions may ſometimes be expected; but what are we to think of thoſe abandoned jurors, who, ſporting with the truſt of their fellow citizens, have crouched under this utmoſt inſolence of juridical corruption.

V. The love verſes in this ſection have all the tenderneſs, elegance, and vivacity of Catullus. Some Engliſh imitators of Spenſer and Milton, have copied nothing but their faults. On the contrary, Buchanan improves upon his maſter. We are no where diſguſted by the licentious vulgarity of the Roman poet. The following elegant addreſs may ſerve as a ſpecimen of his ſtyle.

Quantum delicias tuas amabam,
Odi deterius duplo, ampliuſque
Tuam nequitiam et procacitatem,
Poſtquam te propius, Neæra novi.
At tu ſi penitus perire me vis,
Si vis perdite amem, et magis magiſque
Totis artubus imbibam furorem,
Sis nequam magis, et magis proterva.
Nam quo nequior es, proterviorque,
Tanto impenſius uror inquieto

Ventilante odio faces amoris.
Et lentas iterum ciente flammas.
Quod ſi ſis melior, modeſtiorque,
Odero minus, et minus te amabo.

" As much as I loved thy charms, twice as much more " have I deteſted thy pride and wantonneſs, after, O Ne- " æra! I knew thee better. But if thou canſt wiſh me ut- " terly undone, if thou deſireſt that I ſhould love to diſ- " traction, that madneſs ſhould more and more burn in " every vein, be ſtill more haughty, and ſtill more wan- " ton. For the more haughty and the more wanton thou " art, by ſo much more deeply am I inflamed with reſt- " leſs hatred fanning the torch of love, and again kind- " ling its decaying flames. Wert thou more modeſt, and " more worthy, I ſhould hate thee leſs, but I ſhould love " thee leſs."

We have alſo ſome ſhort and beautiful addreſſes to Theodore Beza, and other men of letters, which muſt have been infinitely pleaſing and flattering to the author's literary aſſociates. We cannot wonder, that wit, and learning, and valour, and beauty, whatever is amiable, or venerable in human nature, crouded into the correſpondence of a poet, prodigal of immortality. The laſt article in this ſection proves that Buchanan poſſeſſed the art of raiſing, into importance, a ſubject in itſelf trifling. It conſiſts of verſes on a diamond cut into the ſhape of a heart, and ſet in a ring, which Queen Mary, in 1564, ſent as a preſent to Elizabeth. To forbear their inſertion, is an injury to the author.

VI. *Iambon Liber.* This ſection conſiſts, like the laſt, of eleven articles. The firſt is inſcribed to Walter Haddon. The remainder conſiſt of four ſatires addreſſed to Leonora, a Portugueſe hoſteſs; four pieces of the ſame nature, inſcribed to a profeſſor in Coimbra; and two tranſlations from the Greek, one of which is the ſatire of Simonides upon women. This poem, the Spectator has pretended to tranſlate entire, but has omitted the laſt twenty-five lines, which, as the poet's parting blow, contain a furious invective against the whole sex. After this honest piece of management the Spectator praises the Greek poet for his delicacy in forbearing to cast out any general reflections against women. I return to Buchanan. His first address to Leonora begins thus:

Matre impudica filia impudicior,
  Et lena mater filiæ,
Vos me putastis esse ludumque et jocum,
  O Scorta triobolaria,
Sacrificulorum pauperum fastidia
  Relicta mendicabulis?
Vos ne videret gurgites, ne pasceret
  Vir filiæ usque ad ultimos
Profugit Indos: nec viæ longinquitas,
  Nec nota feritas gentium,
Nec belluosi rapida sævities freti
  Ab instituto terruit.
Nullum periculum, nulla monstri est vastitas
  Quam perpeti non maluit,
Quam vos videre duplices voragines
  Famæ reique prodigas.
Externa potius arma, quam domesticam
  Vult ferre turpitudinem.

"O daughter more impudent than thy impudent mother, and thou bawd to thy daughter, ye have thought me to be a jest and a sport, ye threepenny strumpets, ye detested leavings of the beggarly attendants of starving priests.

"Lest he should see, or support such whirlpools, the daughter's husband fled to the remotest Indies. Neither the length of passage nor the well known ferocity of the natives could fright him from his purpose. There was no danger, there was no savage monster whom he was not willing rather to encounter, than to behold "you, two gulphs abſorbing property and character. He "prefers foreign arms to domeſtic infamy."

The reſt of the poem, of which the above is a fourth part, is ſuitable to ſuch a beginning. The writer deſcribes with great eloquence, the deſtructive conſequences of Leonora's proſtitution, upon the ſtudents at Coimbra, and concludes by predicting that her debauchery muſt terminate in diſeaſe, deformity, and want. In another article he confeſſes, that ſhe had once enjoyed his utmoſt tenderneſs, and laments the infamy into which paſſion, or rather appetite had betrayed him, "My heart," he exclaims, "was not pierced by the dart of Cupid, but "blaſted by the torch of perdition. Ye avenging furies, "for what crime have I been ſcourged at your tribunal?" Even folly and vice are compatible with a ſpecies of dignity. Compare Buchanan frankly recording his faults and his remorſe, to Pope vamping four volumes of letters, with a catalogue of his headachs and his virtues.

The profeſſor is, if poſſible, handled with ſtill leſs ceremony, than the courtezan. "He knows," ſays Buchanan, "every ſcience except thoſe which he pretends to "teach; he is an excellent cook, weaver, huckſter, jockey, and uſurer. No butcher in the public market "ever excelled him at cheating with falſe weights."

I have already far exceeded the limits intended for this eſſay, and ſhall conclude by a few general remarks on our author's ſtyle.

No poet ever required leſs aid from critical illuſtration. In Buchanan we very ſeldom meet with thoſe ſudden tranſitions from one topic to another, ſo frequent in Horace and Juvenal; ſo diſtreſſing often to the learner, though ſometimes ſo pleaſing to the mature ſcholar. Whatever be his object, it is ever kept in view. From the FRANCISCANUS, for example, two lines cannot be abſtracted without evident mutilation. Perhaps his experience, as a teacher, may in part have inſtructed him to ſympathize with the difficulties of a beginner. No Roman author, now extant, exhibits ſuch a variety of ſtyle. There is hardly perhaps one claſſical word in the Latin language which may not be ſomewhere found in his writings. Yet there are very few difficult paſſages in Buchanan. As his ſubject requires it, he is alternately copious without prolixity, and conciſe without abruptneſs.

The remaining poems of this author conſiſt, *1ſt*, Of three books of epigrams, containing about an hundred and eighty-ſix articles. *2d*, His miſcellanies. This ſection which contains thirty-eight pieces, ſupplies us with ſome of his principal efforts in Lyric poetry. *3d*, His *De Sphæra*, in five books, perhaps the nobleſt didactic poem in the world, and unqueſtionably the moſt ſublime monument of the genius of Buchanan. *4th*, His four tragedies. *5th*, His ſatire on the Cardinal of Lorraine, and ſome other pieces not uſually arranged under any of the former ſections. Among theſe are his celebrated dedication of the Pſalms to Queen Mary, and a copy of verſes inſcribed to John Third of Portugal, which alone, had he compoſed nothing elſe, would have entitled him to the character of a great poet. It is aſtoniſhing to conſider what ſplendor of ſentiment, and luxuriance of imagery are compriſed within twenty-two lines.

It was my firſt deſign to glance over theſe remaining ſections, and hazard ſome remarks on their merit. But the taſk is arduous, and it becomes neceſſary to decline it. My chief intention was to excite a ſpirit of popular curioſity concerning Buchanan's original poems. For ſince Ruddiman's edition in 1715, they have not been republiſhed in North Britain.

This circumſtance is of itſelf ſufficient to refute the vulgar conceit of Scottiſh ſuperiority in claſſical learning. Of the people called men of letters, there are but a few who can read with facility the writers of ancient Rome. This ignorance at once accounts for the partial oblivion of a poet, who truly deſerves that title. In every condition of life, the deſponding ſtudent, the ſucceſsful ſtateſman, the philoſopher oppreſſed but not overwhelmed by the infirmities of age, he is always the ſame enlightened maſter of moral and political wiſdom, the ſame interesting painter of the ſcenes and characters of domeſtic life, the ſame incorruptible defender of the rights of mankind. On every ſubject his ſentiments are diſtinguiſhed by a ſuperior graſp of thought, his ſtyle by dignity, propriety, and ſimplicity. Since the death of Buchanan two centuries have elapſed, and his country, fertile in pleaſing writers of verſe, has not yet produced even the ſhadow of a rival *.

HORACE, LIB. II. ODE XIII.

THIS morning while I ſaunter'd round my fields,
Enjoying every ſweet which ſummer yields,
A more delightful day was never ſeen,
The corn ſo yellow, and the graſs ſo green.
The grape and orange cluſter'd in the grove,
Ten thouſand linnets tun'd the tale of love;
The amorous ſhepherd pour'd his tender lay,
While round his ſteps he ſaw his lambkins play;
And, through the roſes, the briſk bee purſue
Her pleaſing toil to ſip the ſhining dew;
The blue horizon not a cloud o'ercaſt,
The eaſtern ſun acroſs its boſom paſt;
In awful ſplendour up the Heavns he roll'd,
At ſuch a ſcene what ſongſter could be cold!
With health and innocence, my heart was light,
Nature's whole beauties burſting on my ſight.

* This article was drawn up at the particular deſire of the writer of the preceding Remarks on Engliſh Plays. To the ſame critic, it has been indebted for a variety of corrections both in the matter and the ſtyle.

There is a curious circumſtance reſpecting our countryman obſerved by Dryden, "That Milton's defence of the Engliſh people "is MANIFESTLY STOLEN from Buchanan, De Jure Regni Apud "Scotos."

But mark what hazards mankind hourly run,
Nor knows the wiſeſt all he ought to ſhun.
'Tis true, a ſailor fears the raging wave,
A hero fights for conqueſt, or the grave;
Thieves know their turn of Tyburn comes about,
And ſots, when ſober, can forſee the gout;
But Death far other fates may ſoon afford
Than ſtorms, or gouts, the gallows, or the ſword.
For while ſo cheerfully I mus'd along,
My boſom heaving with the future ſong,
Homer himſelf came ruſhing on my ſoul,
And the ſmooth verſe had juſt begun to roll;
Beſide an oak I ſat me down to reſt,
Where fifty rooks had hung their airy neſt;
When, (future ages tremble as ye read!)
The faithleſs log fell thund'ring o'er my head.
The rotten ſtem with ſuch a vengance broke,
Scarce could my ſpeed eſcape the craſhing ſtroke:
Ajax himſelf had ſunk with ſuch a blow,
And Hector haſted to the ſhades below.
Good Heav'ns! how nearly have I ſhun'd the tomb,
Where I and all mankind muſt quickly come.
Were Virgil's fine Elyſian fictions true,
What awful ſcenes had open'd to my view,
Where bards no more the flight of ſummer mourn,
Or dark December's terrible return;
No partial laws the wealthy rogue regard,
But Vice and Virtue reap their full reward:
No pamper'd prince, with ſalivations pale,
There ſquanders half his kingdom at a meal;
There the wrong'd widow ſhall no more complain,
There the ſad orphan finds his ſire again.
See Pœtus there his Arria's ſteps attend,
Brutus again embrace each long loſt friend;
Cato dictator in the bleſt abodes,
Horace recanting ſome obſequious odes.

I hear ſweet Sappho pour her plantive ſtrain,*
While keen Repentance racks her ſavage ſwain;
And thou, ſad Ovid, thy long exile paſt,
In happier regions haſt arriv'd at laſt.
What bitter pangs the baniſh'd wretch await,
The guilt of war, the madneſs of the great,
The fall of tyrants ſwell thy lofty ſong,
While to thy deep-ton'd voice the ſhades attentive throng.
Lo! fierce Tiſiphone to pity charm'd,
Of half her fury ſees herſelf diſarm'd;
Tityus no more his vultures ſeems to feel,
Enraptur'd Ixion reſts upon his wheel;
Great Julius, with each note forgets to groan,
And Nero vaunts ſuch verſes were his own;
While, ſunk in flames at hell's remoteſt bound,
The mean Octavius trembles at the ſound.

ON WINTER.

Though you nor gamble, wench, nor drink,
  And ſcorn to play the ſophiſt's tune,
You tell me you ſincerely think
  December juſt as ſweet as June.

Darkneſs, when debauchees deſire,
  The wiſdom of their choice we know;
And pedants, by a tavern fire,
  May laugh at cold, and froſt, and ſnow.

But were they wearied, ſhivering, wet,
  Behind the plow-ſhare, and, like me,

* Æoliis fidibus querentem
Sappho puellis de popularibus.

A natural topic for a female pen. The ladies have, in all ages been famous for MUTUAL ANTIPATHY, and Sappho's amours afforded food for ſcandal.

For coals and candles deep in debt,
The curſe of Winter they would ſee.

And though your pious blank-verſe bard
Thinks *admiration* ſuch a duty,
When Boreas in my face blows hard,
I bid the Devil take his beauty.

Rejoice with him in rattling ſhow'rs,
And tempeſts terribly ſublime;
But give me ſunſhine, graſs, and flow'rs,
And Summer bluſhing in his prime.

And ſhould a tertian or the gout
O'ercaſt your Chriſtmas with a gloom,
When May-day puts diſeaſe to rout,
You'll know the worth of nature's bloom.

A VIEW OF SOCIETY IN THE SOUTH OF EUROPE.

SOME Engliſh ſchool-boys who go there to dance,
Prefer the climate, language, taſte of France;
But who from Paris would not turn his back,
That recollects the Baſtile and the Rack?
There all the rights of mankind are a jeſt,
And truth and learning trampled by the prieſt.*
When others ſigh for Italy and Spain,
The ſame ſad ſtory may be told again;
The mildeſt ſky, the moſt luxuriant ſoil,
Can ſcarce repay the wretched peaſant's toil;
The tawdry nobles, a voracious croud,
And monks by millions feaſt upon his blood.
Nor in her marſhes would I chuſe to live
For all the gold that Holland has to give;

* Theſe lines were written before the late revolution, ſo pertly reprobated by an Iriſh orator.

Some bursting flood your villa may surround,
And half the nation in an hour be drown'd:
A second Louis may your province seize,
Or brutal Burghers crush you when they please.
When rage once kindles in their foggy brains,
Nor earth, nor hell, a madder mob contains.
The native charms of Greece we know by rote,
But every Bassa there may cut your throat.
The spirit of Lycurgus hath expir'd,
And all the wit antiquity admir'd;
And every vice corrupts the coward breast
Which meanness genders in a mind depress'd.
Nor dream of Sicily's delightful plains,
There Popish tyranny triumphant reigns;
Ferocious bravoes for your blood conspire,
And every mountain shakes with inward fire.
Where Carthage, Athens, Rome, for empire fought,
The poor remains of pomp need scarce be sought;
Majestic ruins o'er the desart spread,
Form a sad shelter to the shepherd's shed.
Let pettish Scots for Caledonia plead,
But freedom hardly ventures north of Tweed;
O'er civil pleas the sherriff nods alone,
In these the right of jury is unknown.
Each well contested point his lordship clears,
In five or thirty or an hundred years.
The man who takes a sheep must stretch a cord,
For him no mercy Justice can afford,
Though 'twas rank hunger forc'd the wretch to steal,
And five young beggars bawling for a meal;
But when some drab commits the foulest crime,
Which ever blacken'd the records of time,
Like Jason's far fam'd concubine, destroys
The guiltless fruit of all her former joys,
Then my Lord Advocate, his sense to show,
To some less baleful climate bids her go.
By every petty *Laird* at will opprest,
Can their pale pleasantry be counted blest?

Shoals wanting food, to ſeek ſome kinder ſky,
Like felons from a jail, their thankleſs country fly.
Then let us all be happy we're at home,
Nor ſeek repoſe at Paris or at Rome.
With one great truth contented we may reſt,
No ſtate on earth was e'er completely bleſt;
And, though we ſearch our ſcurvy globe around,
So fortunate a ſpot will ſcarce be found.
That England's deep in debt we don't deny,
Prelates and beggars tax us very high;
Each bankrupt gameſter to the *Houſe* may run,
And bid defiance to the boldeſt dun:
But ſtill our precious laws exert their power,
To prop the reputation of a whore:
And ſhould ſome parſon in due rev'rence fail,
The rogue muſt for a twelvemonth rot in jail,
And pay, beſides, the bluſhing fair a fine,
For daring her chaſte name to undermine!
Should Honour in his boſom make a ſtand,
And reaſon *linger ere ſhe leaves the land*,
Some brazen featur'd hireling bears him down,
And vindicates the virgin of the town!
By ſuch ſublime deciſions, who can wonder
When wives and maidens chance to make a blunder,
If our ſage legiſlators o'er and o'er,
Aſſert there's no diſtinction—leſs or more!
Who but muſt hear the fact with admiration,
And glory in deſcent from ſuch a nation!

HORACE, LIB. IV. ODE VII.

Returning ſpring the ſwain with rapture ſees,
Their lovely foliage opens on the trees.
The ſnows on yon bleak ſummit melt away,
Reviving nature hails th' extending day;
The teeming earth diſplays her verdant pride,
Within their banks the ſtreams decreaſing glide;

The froſt is ſoften'd by the weſtern wind,
Spring blooms, and Summer follows cloſe behind.
Anon—rich harveſt heaps the buſy plain,
And ſavage Winter ſweeps the grove again.
Theſe ever circling ſeaſons of the year,
Reminds us nothing is immortal here!
The moon repairs her wanings in the ſky,
But, we alas! when once our aſhes lye
Where kings and heroes ſink in endleſs night,
No more can viſit the reviving light.
And who hath learn'd, that Fortune ſhall allow
Another hour of life to me or you?
Then ſince the farce muſt quickly have an end,
Enjoy your wealth with each deſerving friend.
Your heir—nor wonder when you hear it told,
Will hardly thank you for the maſs of gold.
And when the turf is plac'd upon your head,
In vain would eloquence your pardon plead;
In vain to virtue, riches, fame, you truſt,
Not Rome herſelf can raiſe you from the duſt.
Monks may detail ſuch nonſenſe if they can,
But nature ſcorns to leave her common plan:
Not all his wit for Shakeſpeare could atone,
And fools muſt go where former fools have gone.
Brave Wolfe ſhall never burſt the bonds of death,
Nor England's tears recall her Howard's breath.

ON POETRY.

One reaſon why ſo many poets tire,
In quartos they ſuppoſe we ſhould admire,
Is, that while planning an immortal ſong,
They chuſe a theme too lofty, or too long.
What human bellows are not ſick to death,
Bawling three thouſand verſes at a breath.
That Homer often lags, his friends allow,
Ten poems muſt have charm'd us more than two.

'Twas pity he forgot the Golden Fleece,
And other famous feats of fighting Greece;
And all are sorry when his Iliad's done,
That Nell and Troy are neither lost nor won.
Why force Ulysses so far into vogue,
Six books might well have serv'd that vagrant rogue.
Lucretius chose a topic too sublime,
Which cannot be survey'd on this side time;
And mad assertion taking boundless scope,
Deforms the motely masterpiece of Pope;
The dullest of us all would laugh to hear,
That truth, in spite of *reason*, can be clear!
I wish, in sailing, to keep sight of land,
And shut a book I seldom understand.
Avoid with equal care the tragic school,
Where modern wits have also play'd the fool.
Unless you wish to be the common sport,
Above all points be certain to be short.*
A tale when drawn to more than common length,
Has fairly tir'd Herculean Shakespeare's strength.
Another fault too commonly we find,
That no connection captivates the mind;
Though splendid paragraphs perhaps appear,
They tumble in, no matter when or where;
What follows never usher'd by the past,
Since the first period might succeed the last.
In Horace, for example, you may see,
And more than once, one ode compos'd of three;
Of this, and every possible mistake,
Models from Dryden's storehouse you may take.

* Canute, the Danish conqueror, thought otherwise, and ordered a poet to be put to death for having dared to celebrate his valour in a SHORT copy of verses, " BREVES CANTILENAS." The author obtained a respite; produced, next day, thirty additional stanzas, and was rewarded with fifty merks of fine silver; a round sum in those ages.

See Warton's History of English Poetry.

For ſuch a fault no elegance atones,
To build is more than merely heaping ſtones.
Juſt the reverſe of many a modern bard,
Let reaſon occupy your firſt regard;
Nor with rough Churchill at your ſpecies ſcold,
Nor yet in panegyric be too bold.
Exalt no Cæſar to the bright abodes,
Or, if you muſt be damn'd, read Maſon's Odes;
Hark how he ſings, ſo admirably ſweet,
That common ſenſe falls charm'd at folly's feet:
To praiſe the poets of the preſent age,
Be ſure you never blot a ſecond page.
Nor ſeek by drawling epithets to ſhine,
Nor let *inverſion* bungle every line.
Reject that heavy turgid ſtrutting walk,
Compoſe with the ſame plainneſs that we talk.
Swift as an arrow ſhoots along the ſky,
So light, ſo rapid, make your verſes fly;
Let ſmooth familiar language be their boaſt,
That nobody may dream the toil they coſt.
Obſcurity's a rhymer's vileſt vice,
Mankind want time to read our trifles twice;
Correct each word, why ſhould we not compoſe,
With equal purity in verſe and proſe.
Yet while ſome Britiſh wits affect to ſoar,
Expiring grammar bleeds at every pore;
The patriot dean ſo claſſical and bright,
In pointing periods is not always right.
Nor croud like Pope, and him, your page with names,
In which poſterity no intereſt claims;
To tell the worth of every civil friend,
Or handſome wench, our feelings muſt offend;
Nor puſh your private quarrels into light,
Nor call that virtuous rage, the world calls *ſpite.*
Try, if you can, to make us good and wiſe,
For there the worth of compoſition lies.
Morality's a coin which cannot ruſt,
All ſhould be humble, merciful, and juſt;

And all to hear the ſermon are content,
And ſay their neighbours, not *themſelves*, are meant.
Nor into ſervile imitation ſink,
But for yourſelf on every ſubject think.
If * * * * has told ten thouſand Tory lies,
His faithleſs page take courage and deſpiſe:
No faſhionable name your ſtandard make,
The very beſt will frequently miſtake.
Some hours reſerve to ſtudy every day;
And hear on every point what both ſides ſay.
From any book ſome leſſons you may cull,
So rather than read nothing, read the dull.
For thirty years, that circle you may run,
And find the taſk of learning but begun.
Yet juſt to read, nor pauſe to underſtand,
Is merely caſting manure on dry ſand.
Reflect, if poſſible, both day and night,
The more you know the better you muſt write;
Extenſive knowledge when you want to chime,
Supplies a rich variety of rhyme.
The buyer thinks the volume cheaply bought,
And wonders where you found each happy thought;
But he who ſtudy never learns to prize,
Can hardly teach another to be wiſe;
We reap at once the harveſt of his brain,
And ſee the ſame dull joke return again.
Your trifles to a ſelect few rehearſe,
Who love and underſtand the charms of verſe;
When theſe condemn, be willing to believe,
Nor to deſtroy whole ſheets abſurdly grieve.
Compoſe with ardour, but correct with phlegm,
And rarely truſt yourſelf as far as them:
Nor vainly wrangle on the weaker ſide,
Embrace correction with a grateful pride;
Pore on each period, while your brains are cool,
Nor ſpurn good ſenſe when utter'd by a fool;
Compel each hearer frankly to adviſe,
Nor ſlight a hint from people you deſpiſe.

I want to ſhow you, in a ſerious light,
That 'tis no eaſy taſk to learn to write.
Before you can produce a ſingle page
Deſerving audience in a letter'd age,
Whole years in practice muſt have been employ'd,
Whole reams of raw eſſays in ſlump deſtroy'd;
So many great men have engroſs'd our praiſe,
No common merit pleaſes now a-days:
Or if caprice one winter makes us hear,
Profound oblivion hovers in the rear.
If Thomſon's Liberty was ever read,
'Tis long ſince number'd with "the mighty dead."
One-third of Waller, Denham, Wilmot, Prior,
Serve but to ſwell their volume's price the higher.
The lofty Mallet, marvellous to tell!
All ſuch admire as have his works to ſell.
In Maſon's praiſe before you raſhly talk,
Quite round his charming Garden try to walk.
Some yet with Francis doze their time away,
And bawl with tranſport the Norſe odes of Gray;
Or that profound, but lofty piece, the *Bard*,
Though John's Apocalypſe be not ſo hard.
Great Akenſide ſo deep in ancient rules,
Has ſoar'd a height beyond all former fools.
In almoſt all our poets, nay, the beſt,
Still there is room to pity or deteſt.
Thus Young, and Addiſon, (one ſcarce knows how)
To graceleſs Lords with pious rapture bow;
And every human virtue ſhrewdly find
In raſcals, the contempt of all mankind.

Ten thoughtful years may teach you to compoſe,
Till free of toil, each happy ſtanza flows,
Till rhyme and ſentiment ſo rapid riſe,
That even yourſelf muſt ſee them with ſurpriſe,
Till rival wits acknowledge your renown,
And all Buchanan's beauties are your own.
For though ſome folks of tuneleſs ears complain,
That rhyming is but dancing in a chain;

By practice you'll condenſe with perfect eaſe,
In any meaſure, every thought you pleaſe.
But what is the reward of ſo much pains,
A hero's glory, or a cobler's gains?
Do thoſe who love the verſes, love the man,
Or ſerve him as ſincerely as they can?
Your friends your merit ſelfiſhly approve,
And "ſhew the ſenſe of it without the love*."
Our critics have been paid, as well as read,
While half ourſelves expire for want of bread.
The hackney'd names 'tis needleſs to run o'er,
Since every ſchool-boy can repeat a ſcore;
Scorn, hunger, envy, all your toil await,
So bountiful the public and the great!
Poets who would not paſs for arrant fools,
Muſt mind œconomy's eternal rules,
Nor like ſo many ſongſters gift away
The borrow'd caſh they cannot hope to pay;
But hear a beggar with their patron's phlegm,
And ſerve the ſordid world as it ſerves them.
To common ſenſe and common feelings blind,
Maniacs may boaſt of loving all mankind;
But reaſons bids us tremble to embrace
Nine-tenths of what are call'd the human race.
A prudent man will venerate his pelf,
Nor to remount you, wade the mire himſelf.

EPITAPH.

IMITATED FROM BUCHANAN.

Below, the aſhes of a man are laid,
Who this, and every debt with pleaſure paid.
Unlike the world, he fancy'd it unjuſt
At once to purchaſe, and to ſell on truſt;
To reap a harveſt on raſh credit ſown,
Or hazard any fund, except his own.

* Pope.

By ſpecious talk he did not ſtrive to ſhine,
Nor pick'd your pocket with a pious whine;
Nor, by his intereſt, could his conſcience rule,
Nor forc'd a ſelfiſh bargain from a fool;
His wants and wiſhes were but very few,
He gave, and he exacted, juſt his due;
A failing friend was foremoſt to ſupply,
Nor won, nor ſav'd one ſhilling by a lie:
But rich and poor, in manhood, age, and youth,
His heart was Honour, and his words were Truth.
For him no hearſe with Sorrow's weeds was hung,
No coach was hir'd, no pariſh-bells were rung;
No multitude of mourners fill'd the road,
Three ſons alone ſuſtain'd their lonely load.
No Chriſtian brethren ventur'd to convene,
To grace the humble ſolitary ſcene;
No curate came through hackney'd forms to rave,*
He barely got what muſt he had—a grave.
No face aſſum'd the faſhionable maſk,
The very ſexton ſeem'd to ſcorn his taſk.
Perhaps you gueſs, he ſpurn'd the papal ſcheme,
And ſwore the maſs, a deſpicable dream.
But not for this we decent rites deny'd,
He was not worth a penny when he died;
We were not proffer'd a funereal feaſt,
Nor could his heirs have paid the prudent prieſt.

* Some years ago, the Captain of a ſhip in a ſea-port in the Weſt of England, cut his own throat: the SERVICE was read over his body at interment. When the parſon came to theſe words, "We thank thee, O Lord, for the HAPPY delivery of our brother "from this frail and mortal ſtate," a North Briton who was preſent looked about him to ſee if the audience were not laughing, but not a muſcle was diſcompoſed. Such farces are common in England. And is there any thing more ſtupid or indecent reported of Calmucks or of Hottentots?

THE FAREWELL.

FROM THE LATIN OF SECUNDUS.

What though by fortune forc'd anew,
My dearest Julia to depart,
And bid a long, a sad adieu,
To her whose anguish rends my heart.

Trust me, wherever I may rove,
Whatever alien charms I see,
The days of joy, the nights of love,
Which I've so sweetly spent with thee;

These, these I never shall forget,
My soul was form'd for thine alone;
I envy not the giddy great,
The miser's hoard, the monarch's throne.

'Tis not for Rodney's fame I sigh,
Nor yet for Shakespeare's fire divine;*
But his supreme felicity,
Who presses to a breast like thine.

'Tis not thy all-excelling form,
For that we know shall early fade,
Nor youthful passion's noisy storm,
That too hath long long since decay'd;

'Tis not thy ever-pleasing wit,
Intoxicates a stripling's brain,
But—'tis thy patience to submit,
Thy mild reluctance to complain;

That generous, that intrepid mind,
Which dares the darkest frowns of fate,

* In Secundus, the names are Dante and Charles V. This slight alteration will not, it is hoped, displease an English reader.

Whoſe humble innocence can find,
Solacement in its loweſt ſtate.

I chant not o'er a pedant's freak,
A dotard's or a ſchool-boy's dream;
But human languge is too weak
To tell my tranſports of eſteem.

FROM THE SAME.

Why, Julia, would you drown my heart,
With this inceſſant ſtream of grief?
Too well we know that human art
Alas! can lend you no relief.

Your anguiſh, if you can, allay,
By fond remembrance of the paſt;
How often were you wont to ſay,
Exceſs of pleaſure cannot laſt.

When that dear gentle ſpirit's flown,
How terrible the blank I ſee?
The buſy, gay, unfeeling town
Is but a wilderneſs to me.

Where ſhall I find a ſoul ſo ſweet,
Where all thy ſocial virtues ſhine!
Oh! in what boſom ſhall I meet
Such artleſs uniſon with mine!

FROM THE SAME.

Thrice happy the girl that's allied with a man,
Who ſtudies her comfort as far as he can:
Who ne'er like a tyrant endeavours to rule,
Nor fancies, like Paul, every woman a fool;

Who never at midnight patrolls up and down,
Nor values a fig any ſpouſe but his own.
A faithful companion, if ſuch a one meet,
With a judgment as ſound, and a temper as ſweet,
A wit ever watchful her huſband to pleaſe,
Without the keen edge that would murther his eaſe,
If happineſs ever be conſtant below,
That happineſs ſure ſuch a couple ſhould know.
Yet think not even theſe from adverſity free,
For all, ſoon or late, may be widow'd like me;
May endure the laſt pang which can tear a fond heart;
Be taught—what a terrible thing 'tis *to part;*
And ſigh o'er the turf which forever retains,
Of all they held deareſt, the mournful remains.

FROM THE SAME.

DARK is the night, and loud the wind,
The ſnow in heavy flakes deſcending;
And, like the friendſhip of mankind,
Beneath each blaſt my roof is bending.

An aching head, an anxious heart,
The levities of rhime diſdain—
Can ſounds tranquillity impart
To age, and penury, and pain?

Almighty Father! ſtretch thine arm,
In mercy o'er this trembling ſhed;
Our home hath loſt each humble charm,
For health, and peace, and hope are fled.

HORACE, LIB. I. EPIST. II.

WHILE you at London, my illuſtrious friend,
Intrepid Pitt from every foe defend;

Learn all the virtues of your chief by rote
And pour the partiot's melancholy note;*
The current week at Cambridge I employ,
With the great writer of the war of Troy.
With rigid wit the rules of life he taught,
With moral precepts every page is fraught.
Supreme o'er Tillotſon himſelf he ſhines,
Barrow and Clark, and twenty ſuch divines.
Their folio lectures nobody will read,
But Homer captivates the lighteſt head.
The fatal war from which his fable ſprings,
Diſplays the madneſs of contending kings.
Unhappy Paris ſteals the Spartan queen,
And half a world in hoſtile arms are ſeen;
All Greece now ruſhes to regain the prize,
The lover juſtice, and their force defies.
Antenor pleads the huſband's right in vain,
Paris replies, himſelf can never reign,
Nor Trojan power repel a foreign lord,
If lovely Helen be to Greece reſtor'd.
Thus ten long years, they ſteep the crimſon ſhore,
For who ſhall loſe or win a handſome whore.
But through the Greeks a ſecond quarrel ran,
As wiſe as that with which the war began;
Their chiefs a girl to great Achilles gave,
And luſtful Agamemnon ſeiz'd the ſlave.
Old Neſtor roſe their fury to aſſuage,
But one was fir'd by love, and both by rage;
And as wiſe doctors never take a pill,
But on the patient only try their ſkill,
So when the kings of Greece the madmen play,
'Tis the poor ſoldiers for their folly pay.
Atrides, to be ſure, would jerk the maid,
We're told Achilles on his fiddle play'd,
And ſaw with decent undiſſembled joy,
Impetuous Hector ſlaughter and deſtroy.

* This article was written in the year 1783, when Mr. Pitt was in the Minority.

Humane Patroclus lent a moment's aid,
But ſoon a corpſe by Hector's lance was laid;
Then wiſe Pelides was compell'd to go,
And Pallas, partial hag, betray'd his noble foe.
No pity or reſpect the victor feels,
The hero's body faſten'd by the heels,
Is dragg'd in triumph round the trembling town,
'Till wretched Priam pays a ranſom down.
In martial games the conqu'ring Greeks conteſt,
And every ruffian tries to cheat the reſt.
No age, or rank, or merit is rever'd,
When Trojan plunder tempts the ſelfiſh herd.
Such is the ſhocking tale. Our poet ſhows
What endleſs ills from rage and luſt aroſe.
His rapid eloquence ſublimes the heart,
And at his will compells a tear to ſtart.
But fifty vulgar ſermons ſhall be read,
And not one tear by prieſt or people ſhed;
Then may not one be pardon'd though he call
Majeſtic Homer far above them all.
When ſage Ulyſſes wanders o'er the main,
We learn what perils courage can ſuſtain;
The mighty man who vanquiſh'd Priam's race,
Now roams a fugitive from place to place.
In vain for Ithaca his followers mourn,
Vindictive fates prohibit their return.
The ſhatter'd fleet is caſt upon the ſhore,
Where the wild Cyclops thirſt for human gore;
Melodious Syrens captivate the ſoul,
And faithleſs Circe fills the fatal bowl;
Which had the hero ſwallow'd like the reſt,
Like them the ſage had grovell'd in a beaſt.
Misfortunes follow him in every form,
But ſtill he ſoars ſuperior to the ſtorm;
In every ſcene we never fail to find,
A juſt and curious picture of mankind.
A modern pilot with the utmoſt eaſe,
Would in ſix weeks ſail round thoſe very ſeas,

Where grave Ulyſſes loſt himſelf ſo long,
But ſtill we chaunt the venerable ſong.
In vain the pedant proves his crabbed ſkill,
The muſe of Homer leads us where he will;
We tremble with him in the giant's den,
We ſee his ſailors quit the ſhape of men.
We wander with him through the awful wood
Where Circe's ſolitary palace ſtood;
And every heart exults when Hermes tells,
How the bold ſtranger may diſſolve the ſpells.
Anon we liſten for the fatal word,
We ſee the victor wave his flaſhing ſword,
And all his comrades to themſelves reſtor'd.
We range together through Calypſo's grove,
Where Wiſdom riots in the ſweets of love.
At laſt the monarch gains his native iſle,
Our captive minds attends him all the while;
We hear what riſks Telemachus had run,
Who would not be the ſire of ſuch a ſon?
His faithful dog crawls forth the king to meet,
Gaze in his face, and dying lick his feet.
Ulyſſes now a beggar though at home,
With needful ſlaughter heaps the royal dome.
The ſage, the hero, huſband, father, ſon,
How many great men's merits meet in one!
Compell'd we ſmother an indignant ſigh,
To hear a ſoldier condeſcend to lie.
How charmingly the poet paints a wife,
In all the duties of domeſtic life;
As far above her ſex her genius tow'rs
As the brave man ſhe lov'd, illuſtrates ours.
So ſweet her eloquence, ſo humbly great,
That even the calmeſt cuckold curſes fate:
Though ſtill he fears no female e'er was made,
Who Virtue's impulſe to the laſt obey'd.
While thus applauding Homer to the ſkies,
Let us adopt his leſſons and be wiſe;

For you and I like many more ſeem born,
For little elſe than to conſume the corn.
We, like the ſwillers of Phæacian wine,
Think the chief end of living is to dine;
To the poor carcaſe pay ſuperfluous care,
But ſcarce a minute to the mind will ſpare.
Thoſe idle Greeks allow'd their time to roll,
In ſocial honeſt indolence of ſoul;
Pleas'd with their lot, they jeſted life along,
Enjoy'd their girl, their bumper, and their ſong.
But you, my friend, whom Chatham's glories fire,
Who give the ſon that aid you ow'd the ſire;
Reject the lazy pleaſures of the town.
Nor loſe your mornings on a bed of down.
All night the footpad ſcours along the ſtreet,
To rifle every perſon he can meet;
A watch at morning to the Broker brings,
And in a term or two at Tyburn ſwings.
And ſhall not you exert your utmoſt powers,
When Fortune's faireſt prize may ſoon be yours;
For ſhould your party in the Houſe prevail,
And ſurely ſo much *virtue* cannot fail,
The grateful nation will with raptures hear,
That you enjoy five thouſand pounds a-year;
And not a ſoul ſhall buy a pair of ſhoes,
Without advancing ſomewhat of your dues;
For 'tis a truth you hardly dare diſown,
The poor ſupply the bounties of the Crown;
Your ſtaunch exciſemen teach us how to pay
Five hundred thouſand taxes every day.
Then boaſt no more the ſplendour of the Court,
Conſider well who pays for all the ſport;
A generous heart the mendicant may ſhow,
Monarchs alone have nothing to beſtow;
And when they ſquander thouſands on a feaſt,
Their pooreſt ſubject ſuffers for the jeſt.*

* On a late birth-day a certain young gentleman appeared in a ſuit which coſt above eighty thouſand pounds!

You think, for certain, were the battle won,
And all a patriot pants for made your own;
Your pension fix'd beyond the power of fate,
Your party plump, though *toiling for the state*;
That then you'd be the happiest man alive,
Did all his millions purchase peace to Clive?
Nor fame, nor fortune could his qualms compose,
At length a pounce-knife ended all his woes;
For every crime determin'd to atone,
He did, for once, what justice should have done.
But had the British Cortez e'er possess'd
A social, feeling, philosophic breast,
At Glory's summit he had clos'd his days,
And Time's last accent echo'd all his praise.

SKETCHES OF CELEBRATED CHARACTERS,

ANCIENT AND MODERN.

The vulgar very often praise,
With stupid fulsome adulation,
Phantoms Philosophy surveys,
With pity or with detestation.
Their voice still stronger proofs arise,
Weighs not an atom with the wise.

And yet since gambling, wenching, drinking,
Turn'd marks of a superior spirit;
Since high-born dames forbore from thinking,
That decency's a female merit;
Why preach against this hopeful age,
Or drag her bankrupt jockies on the stage?

While every servile scribbler cries,
That all the great are wise and good,
And his whole wretched logic tries,
To render vice and folly proud;

Let us, revering ſacred ſtations,
Turn back to former generations:

Ere men of rank began to try
At cricket all their pimps to diſtance,
Ere half the peerage with a ſigh,
Suſtain'd the burden of exiſtence,
Beyond the kennel, turf, or ſtable,
The cock-pit, ſtews, or faro-table.

All ye converſant but with odes
Compos'd within theſe thirty-years,
Who fancy that a rhymer nods,
If common ſenſe her ſtandard rears;
Have mercy on a raſh beginner,
O'erhauling thus each ancient ſinner.

Troy's champion kindles our eſteem,
But doom'd Patroclus to his dogs;
With ſlaughter till your trenches ſwim,
Divine Achilles never jogs;
Ulyſſes, now alive, had got
Renown, by forging ſome bank note.

The bagnio had ſurely been,
At Athens a moſt hallow'd place,
Where fluent Socrates was ſeen,
To liſten for colloquial grace,
And his chaſte principles unfolded,
No queſtion why his yoke-mate ſcolded.

About his Dæmon thoſe pretences!
Quevedo's viſions were as true.
But was he perfect in his ſenſes,
To wed with an abandon'd ſhrew?
When fourſcore years had ſnarled by
No wonder he deſir'd to die.

Though Plato's morals are admir'd,
 An Engliſh jury ſhould have hang'd him; *
Carthage the virtuous Scipio fir'd,
 While Aſdrubal's dear ſpouſe harangu'd him.
His caſh, all-worthy Brutus lent,
So low as forty-five *per cent.* †

And when his debtors could not pay,
 He thruſt his dagger to their boſoms;
And pedants tell us every day,
 How pure his reputation bloſſoms.
I paſs in haſte that venal bully,
Loquacious chicken-hearted Tully.

Who thought himſelf ſublime and witty,
 By drawling forty words for four;
And while they kick'd him from the city,
 Snivell'd and ſobb'd like ſome young whore
When ſhirts or ſilver ſpoons are loſt,
And ketch has ty'd her to the poſt.

O'er Anthony's devoted name,
 He choſe in Billingſgate, to plead;
His reſtleſs tongue muſt bear the blame
 That Anthony chopp'd of his head; ‡

* This famous moraliſt aſſerted the right of parents to expoſe, that is, to murder their children. Decency forbids one to mention his ideas of love.

† Vide Cicero's Epiſtles.

‡ His vanity, which is of the groſſeſt kind, tranſpires in every ſentence. "Ego multa tacui, multa pertuli, multa conceſſi, mul- "ta ſanavi." Paſſages in this ſtyle occupy at leaſt one half of what we call his Orations. His ſcurrility is equally extravagant. In what has been ſtyled his Divine Phillipic, he reproaches Anthony as a Catamite, and a glutton, and tells the Roman ſenate how many hours he ſpent every afternoon, on a country excurſion, eating, drinking, and vomiting. "Quis interpretari poteſt, in "imprudentiorne, an improbior, an impurior, an crudelior!" &c. &c. &c.

Or did he dream that Cæſar's heir
The prompter of tyrannicide would ſpare.

A brief, if any counſel tries,
  With Ciceronian airs to read,
The court humanely will adviſe,
  The doctors both to ſhave and bleed,
And furniſh him, who rants ſo well,
The ſtraiteſt waiſtcoat, and the darkeſt cell.

Celeſtial Epictetus chatter'd,
  Till lo! his maſter broke his leg; *
How ſweetly ſhould their bones be batter'd,
  Who ſuch a piece of bounty beg?
Yet was the ſophiſt leſs a fool
Than thoſe who danc'd attendance at his ſchool.

For Trajan and your Antonines,
  Who pepper'd all our bomb-proof Martyrs, †
They—I appeal to ſound Divines,
  Were worſe than Wilmot, Wild, or Chartres.
Conſtantine, too, ſo great and good,
Was over head and ears in blood.

Though gracious till the world was won,
  What horrid carnage curſt his ſequel!
His friends, his wife, his gallant ſon!
  No—Tyburn never ſwung his equal!
Enough of Greek and Roman merit,
Which we ſo happily inherit.

The wits of this enlighten'd age,
  Who ſcarce peruſe a word of Latin,

* "Such another blow will break my leg," ſaid the Stoic. To ratify his prediction, he got a ſecond, and the limb was broken. N. B. He ſhould have held his tongue at the firſt.

† *Vide* REMAINS OF CHRISTIAN ANTIQUITY, publiſhed by LORD HAILES.

Upon the beauties of the ſtage
  Muſt be for ever, ever prating;
While many a farce, with which they flout us,
 Is not worth half a page of Seneca or Plautus.

Let ſome folks with a ſnuffling tone,
  Racine's enfeebled accents drawl,
And fancy that themſelves alone,
  On taſte and genius ought to ſcrawl;
Juſt as the frog in Æſop tries
To meaſure with a bullock's ſize.

But thoſe who read Horatian numbers,
  Majeſtic Juvenal admire,
Forgive arch Claudian where he ſlumbers,
  And catch a ſpark from Ovid's fire,
Muſt with peculiar tranſport, ſee
All Rome, rever'd Buchanan! ſhine in thee.

Whatever topic tempts thy muſe,
  So tunefully the dactyl flows,
That Vandals only would refuſe,
  'Tis worth a wilderneſs of proſe:
Such vigour braces every line,
That ſober Juſtice owns thy eloquence divine.

To paint a gormandizing drone,
  Fleecing his ſuperſtitious flock,
The guilty grandeur of a throne,
  The traitor haſting to the block,
The boldeſt flights of ſcorn and praiſe
Inſpire and dignify the lays;

While ſo much wit, and ſenſe, and learning,
  Such ſplendid burſts of mirth and rage,
O'erwhelm us, that there's no diſcerning
  What leading beauty ſhould engage;

What verſe pathetic or ſublime,
Eclipſes moſt the preſent ſons of rhyme.

Whether thy varied notes reſound
The feats of Guiſe, the fall of Charles,
Or ſoar the ſolar ſyſtem round,
Or ſtoop to ſketch thy petty quarrels,
Alike the mighty maſter ſhines,
And the whole ſacred art combines.

Butler's unbounded flood of thought,
Swift, ſimple, nervous, and ſevere,
The ſterneſt portraits Milton wrought,
And ſweeteſt Otway's Belvidere,
To thoſe thy text, who have not ſeen,
Afford a partial hint—of what thou once haſt been.

No wonder theſe enervate days,
Thy Attic volumes have neglected;
For operas vile, and viler plays,
Shakeſpeare begins to be rejected,
Though Garrick, to improve the Town,
So kindly ſtew'd and minc'd him down.

Our ſongs are innocent of meaning,
Our tragedies are wild bombaſt;
Since nothing here deſerves our gleaning,
From ſuch a deſart let us haſte.
But—Why does yon tremendous lumber,
Twelve rows in quarto deep, our bending ſhelves encumber?

Theſe brief abridgements of State Papers,
Atteſt a Queen may have amours,
That peers are liable to vapours,
Nay, ſometimes *bilk* their tavern ſcores,
As graceleſs, thankleſs Charles the Second,
Too ſeldom with his Antwerp hoſteſs reckon'd.*

* Vide ſome Letters from Clarendon, publiſhed in Dodſley's nnual Regiſter for 1787.

Though Clarendon had parts and confcience,
His brain was cramm'd with fuperftition.
With all his lofty loyal nonfenfe,
One doubts of Oliver's perdition.
We tire of his eternal pen,
Two pages might fuffice for ten.

What fignified a tyrant's head,
Unlefs fair liberty may thrive;
Moorfields could fpare a better breed,
Were all fuch bigots now alive,
Such baleful deputies of Heaven,
In one aufpicious blaft beyond the dog-ftar driven.

The mild, the venerable Locke,
Belies the nobleft works of nature,
Afferting parracide wont fhock,
In favage life a human creature,
That innate morals are abfurd;
Let fchool-men haggle on a word.

But does not every mortal fee
Tempers inherent in each child?
Young Shylock on his nurfe's knee,
Of plumb-cake cannot be beguil'd;
Foredoom'd to mortgage an eftate,
With puppies, Timon fhares his plate.

The fearlefs boy, whom nature forms
Flag-ftaffs and batteries to win,
At eight the cyder orchard ftorms,
Defies the maftiff and the gin,
Leaps headlong from the bounding horfe,
And drags the ftubborn falmon from his courfe.

The bending vine, the cedar tall,
When burfting from their parent feed,

One ſingle ſpecies to miſcal,
  With equal juſtice we may plead,
In ſwaddling clothes, while Newton lay,
Was his the ſame with Shakeſpeare's clay?
To underſtandings in the germ,
Innate ideas to deny, is quibbling for a term.

Though ſavage, the Mohawk diſplays
  Virtues unheard of in the college,
We need not very loudly praiſe
  Laborious Locke's unbounded knowledge;
His work, though one of Learning's wonders,
O'erflows with every ſort of blunders.

That Addiſon of port was fond,
  I neither prize him more nor leſs;
But then, for payment of his bond,
  His herald Dicky to diſtreſs—
Your charity till firſt I ſee,
The deuce may take your faith for me.

Had this church-trumpeter been poor,
  Selling Steele's bed-clothes I'd defend;*
But that apology his corps
  Of panegyriſts can't pretend;
Honour, did ever tool but he,
In Halifax or Wharton ſee.

Parſons his piety extol,
  His phlegm philoſophy miſcal;
A ſervile, ſordid, hen-peck'd ſoul,
  Is ten times worſe than none at all.
For him who tantaliz'd poor Stella,
What Tartar would have play'd his fellow?

* For this anecdote we are indebted to Dr. Johnſon, who ſtates the bond as being for an hundred pounds; and to Dr. Percy, who raiſes the amount of it to a thouſand. As to Wharton and Halifax, conſult the dedications to the ſecond and fifth volumes of the Spectator.

What ſerv'd tumultuous Dublin's noiſe
  His private happineſs to win,
Diveſt him of domeſtic joys,
  A Crœſus is not worth a pin.
Knocking Vaneſſa on the head,
Had been to Swift's abuſe humanity indeed.

For flattery, as a work of courſe,
  What mortal matches ſimple Young*?
Did Virgil or Boileau do worſe?
  He better, too, had held his tongue,
Than damn'd, with ſuch unchriſtian ire,
All but his own dear ſect to everlaſting fire.

Though ſcarce at ſermon twice a-year,
  Quitting tithe-pigs with ſcorn and ſorrow,
What has an honeſt man to fear,
  Should the laſt trumpet ſound to-morrow!
The glorious trades of King and Prieſt
Are ſadly on the wane at leaſt.

Some folks imagine pious Hume,
  Attain'd to Virtue's higheſt pitch:
They had been ſilent, I preſume,
  But that the writer died ſo rich;
The preſs, when that's the caſe, abounds
With "*dulcet and harmonious ſounds.*"

His lively periods may procure
  Attention to the end of time;

* "Fools laugh at God, O Wilmington! and thee," is a line which concludes one of the diviſions of Dr Young's Night Thoughts. This is fully as bad as a paſſage in Dryden's dedication of Juvenal, where he tells the Earl of Dorſet, that the Engliſh nation could almoſt as well ſubſiſt without GOD'S PROVIDENCE, as without—What!—Let the reader gueſs—without HIS LORDSHIP'S VERSES!

But will the world, for ſuch a lure,
  Forget chicanery's a crime?
This prince of ſceptics ſcarce could tell
Why *china* ſhiver'd when it fell!

A Bacon's, Dryden's, Shakeſpeare's praiſe,
  He weakly tries to undermine;
And, brilliant Martial to debaſe,
  Pretends he punn'd in every line; *
O'erlooks the great Preceptor's claims,
Yet ſtrives to compliment his ideot pupil James.

Behold, this precious Sage, adviſe
  Each peeviſh fool to cut his throat †!
And deeds of infamy diſguiſe,
  Coligni's murder rivals not!
Then, ſee him ſcruple to decide
Why Pym harangu'd, or Hampden died.

Ye ſacred and immortal names,
  Which Freedom's ſons with rev'rence hear,
When ſophiſtry your worth defames,
  And toils to taint the public ear;
With what indignity and ſcorn
Ought ſuch a libel to be torn!

What wit adores not Johnſon's taſte,
  Who wiſh'd Polybius had been dumb?

* The critic who ſeems never to have read Martial, affirms that he could not peruſe any of his Epigrams above once. As Mr. H—was always BREAKING EGGS WITH A HAMMER, he gives a metaphyſical reaſon for this important diſcovery. A great part of Martial's Epigrams have not, however, the moſt diſtant reſemblance to PUNNING. They are moral, pathetic, and ſublime. There are, indeed, in the end of his collection two entire books which bear no marks of his genius, and therefore may be deemed ſpurious.

† His Defence of Suicide was ſuppreſſed forty years ago by the Lord Chancellor of the day, but it is now publicly ſold.

To Salluſt and his paper-waſte
  Preferring Bunyan and Tom Thumb.
His wiſdom truſted every rogue;
His virtue hated a Whig Dog.

This far-fam'd Sage at all times ſaid,
  No man of common ſenſe would write,
Unleſs he on the nail was paid
  For every line that ſaw the light.
In *print*, the Doctor did not fail
At hireling garreteers to rail.

He told the Brewer's crazy wiſe
  How well he lov'd a ſtomach load,
And ſtay'd but once in all his life
  At home, when aſk'd to dine abroad;
Nay ſometimes reel'd about the cup
Till morning broke the ramble up,
For, 'twas his glory to declare,
The throne of human joy—a tavern chair.

When Hodge, his cat, fell ſick and blind,
  Nothing but oyſters pleas'd the elf,
Black Frank refus'd to be ſo kind,
  He therefore brought them home himſelf. *
Exciſe commiſſioners he ſcorn'd,
As footpads penſion'd and ſuborn'd. †

This deep philologer defin'd
  That *ſweet* is ſomething elſe than *ſour*,
That he who wants his eyes is blind,
  That three and one makes always four;
That thunder is *a rapid flame*,
And beaux and monkies not the ſame; ‡

*** For theſe particulars of the Doctor's private character, the public are indebted to Hawkins, Boſwell, and Piozzi.**

† Vide Idler, No. 70.

‡ His definition of man is—" Not a woman—not a boy—not " a beaſt!"

That ſucking infants are not *old*,
  That chamber-pots were made for cleaning;
That *long* and *ſhort*, and *hot* and *cold*
  Are words of very diff'rent meaning;
That virgins don't begin to breed
Till once you rid them of their maidenhead.*

For feats like theſe, ſagacious Bute
  Gave him three hundred pounds a-year,
And 'tis a fact beyond diſpute,
  He bought his wages very dear;
His book is large enough to crack
The ſtrongeſt Iriſh chairman's back.

In truth, as Parſon Horne obſerv'd,†
  His *Spelling-Book* is ſuch a *bore*,
As none half-learn'd, half-mad, half-ſtarv'd
  Gribæan ever hatch'd before.
Ah! Bozzy, Bozzy, ſhan't we ſee
Some wooden vacancy for thee?

How ſmartly might our ſchool-boys drive
  Their eggs about thy lantern jaws?
And toſs, if Hodge be yet alive,
  At that firm phiz her mangy paws?
While, with clench'd fiſt, ſtands Heſter by
To ſtamp the yolks on either eye.

Heav'ns! why has thy degraded name
  Provok'd my ſweetly temper'd pen?
Are we to blend thy brazen fame
  With that of thoſe illuſtrious men?
Compar'd to thine, thou literary wart,
Iſcariot play'd a manly part,
The cord atteſted ſhame could touch *his* heart.

* Virgin—"A woman, not a mother."
† *Vide* his Diverſions of Purley.

No ſon of Adam, not the beſt,
Acts juſt as conſcience would require;
Yet Locke, and Swift, and all the reſt,
What Goth would ſtickle to admire,
And candour cloſe ally'd to love
Will pity where ſhe can't approve.

ADVICE TO THE SEX.

Ye maids who are ſick of the title ye bear,
Five minutes advice condeſcend but to hear;
And if ye take notice, and follow my plan,
Your manners may pleaſe every ſenſible man;
And a cuſtomer quickly be found for the toy,
Which affords you ſuch endleſs vexation and joy.
One fault you moſt own tempts the patience of boys,
You make one and all ſuch a marvellous noiſe,
That if Death does not come to a huſband's relief,
The honey-moon trumpet may ſoon knock him deaf.
Ye would prate for the length of a mid-ſummer day,
And what is yet worſe, you have nothing to ſay.
You lively young virgins approaching fifteen,
Whoſe little fond hearts heave a ſigh to be ſeen,
In the name of decorum forbear to perfume,
Or a delicate noſe muſt retire from the room.
A healthy young laſs has a far better ſmell,
Than all the vile traſh that the ſtink-mongers ſell.
As ye value your lover, forbear to diſpute,
And if he's fond of talking, take care to be mute;
Pretend to believe what is certainly true, *
That all your admirers have more ſenſe than you.
When they ſeek your opinion be ſlow to decide,
'Tis becoming your ſex, and it pleaſes their pride.

* Dr. Swift, at leaſt, was of this opinion. See his Letter to a Young Lady on her Marriage.

But the plague of all is, your desire to be fine,
Which out of ten maids is the mischief of nine.
For every young wench, high and low, must be gawdy,
And rustle in silk, and set up for a lady;
While *Miss*, and *Dear Madam* commences the cant,
Her stomach should have, what her shoulders should want.
I don't recommend the detestable hags,
Who, as soon as they're married, go always in rags;
Your laureat would hazard his vast reputation,
Were he telling the fair to depart from the fashion.
He would only advise with a certain grave priest,
That ye try to be in it, the last, and the least.
He would likewise require, with the reverend Dean,
That your clothes and your persons are perfectly clean,
Though your features be tawny, yet shudder to paint,
So horrid a thought makes one ready to faint.
And O that the cockney had danc'd in a rope,
Who imported this freak from the Cape of Good Hope.
Though custom compels you to powder your hair,
Be as sure as ye can that no vagrants are there.
On this point forgive me for hinting a word,
The scandal is shockingly false and absurd;
'Tis your barbers, those rascals, tell so many lies,
B — I see the sweet blushes of innocence rise.
All the roses that bloom on a beautiful cheek,
If ye have not good nature, are dear of a leek;
And if you proceed, just as far as you're able,
In resounding the slanders of every tea-table,
Though love had erected his throne in your eye,
We dread the base tongue that delights in a lie.
This favour, at parting, I venture to beg,
As we smile at the glance of a clean taper'd leg,
Cut a quarter, at least, from the length of each gown,
And, as oft as ye please, make a garter slip down.
But let not your bosoms be jutting and bare,
Nor repay a fond peep with an impudent stare;
May ye all by kind husbands this evening be kiss'd,
Nor an hour after supper one virgin exist.

In the following article, an allusion is made to a Letter which gave occasion to it. For the sake of perspicuity, there is prefixed an extract from that letter, in so far as concerns the present subject.

" I sometimes think myself unlucky to have formed my " taste of English poetry on the writings of four great " masters, in different styles, Shakespeare, Milton, part " of Dryden, and Butler. They have not only the fire " of genius, a kind of inspiration, but a propriety and " force of expression, to which our flowery, figurative, " unmeaning, modern poetry has rarely any resemblance. " To this general censure, I do not think the pieces you " have just now sent me, are liable. I am really much " pleased with them. There is particularly in the second, " and in the last, an unaffected ease, propriety, and sig- " nificancy.

" Works of great original genius have yielded little " profit to the authors, though, in succeeding times, they " have enriched the dullest of critical editors and book- " sellers. Shakespeare made no fortune by his plays, and " Milton got less than twenty pounds for his Paradise " Lost. The ungrateful and worthless King Charles suf- " fered Butler to starve. In our times, quaintness and od- " dity have a better chance to make a thriving author, " than sense and taste."

THE PRESENT STATE OF PARNASSUS.

INSCRIBED TO A LITERARY CORRESPONDENT.

What rare felicity, a verse to write,
Which men of taste with fondness may recite?
More wit and skill are wanted to compose
One happy stanza than whole sheets of prose.
Departed health, an old excuse I plead,
For penning what, you'll likely scorn to read.

A ſick-bed does not ſuit the pleaſing ſtrain;
Forgive this final offspring of my brain.
Victorious Death! I feel thee coming faſt;
But let thy victim rally to the laſt:
Where med'cine fails, amuſement ſhould be ſought,
Though but to ſooth the miſeries of thought;
When one is juſt about to be a clod,
Cenſure may ſmile to ſee him lift her rod.
Since both in Arts and Arms the preſent age,
Impartial admiration muſt engage;
And, burſting Error's chains, the vigorous mind
Throws every former effort far behind,
You aſk, with ſeeming ſorrow and ſurpriſe,
" Why no ſuch bards as Butler now ariſe,
" To paint the follies of the paſſing day,
" And force moroſe enthuſiaſts to be gay?
" No modern rivals Milton's pure ſublime,
" Or Dryden's ſweet ſimplicity of rhyme;
" His happy boldneſs, great without pretence,
" His ſtrong inceſſant ſtream of common ſenſe.
" Our living Play-wrights likewiſe are confeſs'd
" To be but Shakeſpeare's ſhadows at the beſt.
" No Brutus dignifies their vapid page,
" Their phantoms but exiſt upon the ſtage;
" The language of the ſtews, perhaps rehearſe,
" Or elſe out-bedlam Bedlam in blank verſe."
Thus ſtands the fact, but then we muſt allow
Numbers were never leſs eſteem'd than now;
And thoſe who bear the patron's boaſted name,
Of taſte, a ſolid ſhare can ſeldom claim,
A juſt conception beauties to diſcern,
Knowledge to teach, or modeſty to learn;
And pedantry and quaintneſs oft obtain
That praiſe Buchanan might demand in vain.
But words, alas! are all the great can ſpare,
As if a poet could ſubſiſt on air.
Artiſts, dear Sir, in every other trade,
For every piece of work are duly paid.

What but bad verſes ſhould the world expect,
When riſing worth is ſure of groſs neglect?
What harveſt would the richeſt acres yield
Did not the farmer cultivate his field?
And who but madmen would manure a ſoil
Which cannot promiſe to reward their toil?
Yet 'tis a vain young rhymer's common fate
To burn his bundle, and be wiſe—too late.
When ſix fond prattlers for their food exclaim,
What ſire would take the gift of Virgil's fame.
Domeſtic eaſe our happineſs muſt found,
For all beſides is nothing but a ſound.
  Old, peeviſh, poor, we to the duſt deſcend,
Without one veſtige of a generous friend.
But thoſe who, living, would not ſpare us bread,
Illuſtrate, publiſh, and admire the dead.
Some reverend Doctor, with his long tail'd notes,
And damn'd corrections, each plain ſentence blots:
Drench'd in his critic's filth, a writer lies,
From twelves diſtorted to the folio ſize.
Then ſordid widows, as a work of right,
Expoſe what never ſhould have ſeen the light;
Our cloſet-ſweepings to low printers ſell,
And Memoirs next the precious cargo ſwell.
  Yet, though in life our proſpects are o'ercaſt,
All other human labours ours outlaſt.
An actor's efforts with his breath expire,
And colours from the canvaſs muſt retire.
Of Roſcius we juſt know what Tully ſays;
No portraits of Appelles reach our days.
The fiddler who ſtands foremoſt in renown,
Succeeding fiddlers in their quavers drown;
But Pindar's ode outlives the Doric lyre,
Yet ſtern Tyrtæus ſets each nerve on fire,
Warns the bold youth "his country's wrongs to feel,
"And ruſh undaunted on the reeking ſteel,
"To war's embattled van his front oppoſe,
"Nor ſhrink one foot-ſtep from an hoſt of foes:

"But, breaſt to breaſt, repulſe the warrior's ſhock,
"Cleave the broad ſhield, and give the ſhorten'd ſtroke."
His laurels, yet unfaded, Homer wears,
Freſh from the havock of three thouſand years;
And ſhall, when Afric freezes at the Pole,
And Hecla's flames between the tropics roll.*
Of all the fatal viſions ere poſſeſs'd
A ſcholar's mind, 'tis wilder than the reſt,
To graſp each man of letters as his brother,
To dream the ſpecies truly love each other,
And fancy that the friend who ſees your worth,
Will frankly try to draw each talent forth.
Though, otherwiſe, he ſhows an honeſt heart,
Reſiſtleſs paſſions at this project ſtart.
Pride views all mankind with malignant eyes,
And Envy ſickens at a rivals riſe.
"What! ſhall I puſh this upſtart into view,
"Who knows my ſervice nothing but his due?
"A dunce, for certain, ought to be preferr'd,
"Whom titles cannot raiſe above the herd."
Forward to purchaſe an immortal name,
And hear their bounty fill the voice of fame,
The days have been when every rank of men
Were proud to patronize a claſſic pen.
Thus Milton's toils the great Protector paid;
Dryden, from Dorſet, found a father's aid:
His friend Southampton, Shakeſpeare's wants ſupply'd;
A Templar buried Butler when he died.
But now the fit of patronage is paſt,
And Spite and Scorn the budding poet blaſt.
Let us, to Pity ere we ſhall pretend,
Forget poor Chatterton's indignant end.
Truſt not that thoſe who Walpole's meanneſs mourn,
Will be one jot more generous in their turn.
That Grub for certain ſhocks with worſt neglect,
Who moſt of all your merit ſhould reſpect.

* Philoſophers compute that twenty thouſand centuries are requiſite to accompliſh this revolution.

On a ſmall eminence by fortune plac'd,
With not one ſpark of underſtanding grac'd,
Obſerve yon book worm—who a chaiſe has got,
By vending two trite quartos which he wrote.
He quarrels with old madam twice *per* hour,
And thruſts his gray-hair'd ſervant to the door,
(A man, with whom he ſpent his ſchool-boy days)
As too infirm to drive the new-bought chaiſe.
Will ſuch a cold hard-hearted coſtive thing,
O'er infant Genius ſtretch a parent's wing;
His grace, whom endleſs ſupplications ſteel,
Has neither time to think, nor ſenſe to feel.
'Tis really ſtrange, for what capricious ends,
A vulgar man of wealth his income ſpends;
Where no true pleaſure, profit, or renown,
Can tempt the fool to throw his money down.
By heaping ſtones, one, eager to be great,
To build a palace, ſquanders an eſtate:
Another on his ſtable caſts away
The caſh, a third, ſtill worſe, conſumes in play:
For game-cocks, hounds, and girls, another ſighs,
Each cobler's vote the borough-member buys,
Sneaks through night-cellars with a fawning face,
And, if a patriot, rails at rogues in place;
Bears the groſs belch from every porter's lungs,
And groſſer outrage of ten thouſand tongues.
Others, by law, their ſenſes undermine,
While ſoakers, to the glaſs, felicity confine.
But theſe, and all the reſt, alike refuſe
To ſhed ſubſtantial comfort on the Muſe:
When half their barber's wages would preſerve
The wretch they flatter—ſtill that wretch muſt ſtarve;
Or, ſome proud bookſeller's inſulted ſlave,
Place his laſt dream of hope beyond the grave;
From ſtale exiſtence drain the vileſt lees,
And envy every beggar whom he ſees.
Yet, when he views Old England's preſent ſtate,
No more he marvels at injurious fate;

He learns that ſenſe to folly bows her head,
That rank corruption hath our iſle o'erſpread;
That, of Auguſta's cits, not half a ſcore
Who get a wife, can want one bed-mate more;
That half their ladies well deſerv'd the ſtocks,
That half the town is rotten with the p—;
That, as for virgins with unſhatter'd ware,
The ſphynx and unicorn are ſcarce ſo rare;
At dice that ſtateſmen condeſcend to cheat,
A prince with jockies joſtle for a ſeat;
That peers, for bruiſing butchers, form a ring,
And prelates preſs to hear an eunuch ſing;
That dutcheſſes canvaſs from ſtreet to ſtreet,
And ſink five thouſand guineas on a treat;

* * * * * * * *

* * * * * * *

The caſe explain'd, no longer you'll inquire
For Satan's dignity or Richard's fire;
Cecilia's Odes unrivall'd ſhall remain,
Nor Butler's Quixote pound the bear again;
The wiſe apply to more auſpicious ſchools,
And leave the field of poetry to fools.
Then wonder not, my friend, that I reſign
All correſpondence with the tuneful Nine;
With me the days of vanity are paſt,
Oh! that my firſt attempt had been my laſt.
The approbation of the learn'd and great,
Each bard's experience proves a bitter cheat.
See them admire, eſteem, avoid the man,
And then ſuppreſs abhorrence if you can.
Moſt happy he, foredoom'd to hold his plows,
To plant his cabbages, and feed his cows;
Who glad to ſeize one moment for his own,
Along the moſſy turf can lay him down;
And, as his lambs are ſporting by his ſide,
Smiles at the littleneſs of letter'd pride.
While honeſt ſcorn provokes me to deſcribe
The wonted baſeneſs of the patron-tribe;

One worthy man is deſtin'd to remain,
To whom misfortune never ſu'd in vain;
In whom good ſenſe and tenderneſs conſpire,
And cool reflection fans the nobleſt fire.
He, to ſupport the poor, ſpends all his days,
Envy, for him, is prodigal of praiſe:
He did true Genius ſtrike an orphan bard,
Hath taſte to feel, and juſtice to reward;
While ſome ſage friends of learning ſcarce allow
A monthly breakfaſt, and a civil bow.
  Might he with theſe unhappy verſes bear,
My proudeſt wiſh is but to ſuit his ear;
T' amuſe the landlord of my little farm
Would force exiſtence, though in age, to charm.
—Weak Hope, adieu! theſe nerves convulſe with pain,
And mortal ſickneſs ſhoots through every vein;
By cares, infirmities, and years oppreſs'd,
The long-toil'd intellect retires to reſt.

INTRODUCTOTY VERSES TO THE FRANCISCAN:

FROM THE LATIN OF BUCHANAN.

Why knit your brows, dear Frank, in ſuch a frown,
As if you thought one glance would knock us down;
What mean you by that grave affected ſtalk,
That drawling, dull, ſolemnity of talk!
No jeſt, no adage, animates your ſtyle,
Have human follies ceas'd to make you ſmile?
Go pare your nails, and clean your face from dirt,
And comb your hair, and buy a decent ſhirt:
You ſay race-horſes ſhould be taught to plow,
And cocks on dung-hills die in peace for you:
Nor can by dice your ſaintſhip be delay'd,
Nor bear the prattle of an amorous maid,

Nor in the ſalmon's murther feel delight,
Nor for the pheaſant ſtrain your aching ſight,
Nor from your greyhound force the hare to fly,
Nor ſhoot the hawk, that Nimrod of the ſky,
Nor pierce the boſom of the bounding deer,
Nor turn the tyger's terrible carreer.
To Paradiſe you take the ſhorteſt way,
You ſcourge your back, and faſt, and preach, and pray,
You ſnore on ſackcloth, on a herring feaſt,
How pleaſant, how ſublime to be a prieſt!
Who but muſt murmur at this ſcene of ſtrife,
This dark and deſpicable farce of life;
Where ſilly hopes, and ſilly fears, alike
At the frail baſis of contentment ſtrike;
Where hours of joy embitter years of pain,
And genius toils and virtue ſoars in vain:
Where dear bought wiſdom warns us all to trace;
A knave, or fool, in every ſtranger's face;
Where few or none pure innocence can boaſt,
For what the head acquires, the heart has loſt;
Where men of ſenſe will ſeldom dare to ſay,
Their laſt night's friend continues ſuch to day.
When in my fancy theſe trite truths combine,
This worthleſs world I purpoſe to reſign;
And huſband what remains of precious time,
To make amends for every former crime.
My earlier tale, with honeſt grief I hear,
And many a frantic feat demands a tear.
Oft I for trifles into fury blaz'd,
Some fools I flatter'd, and ſome raſcals prais'd;
My levity has told a thouſand lies;
Still more reflection, more remorſe ſupplies.
But ah! how calm and happy ſhall I be,
From all terreſtrial cares for ever free;
When belted with a cord, I ſhave my crown,
And, on the ſordid great, look ſourly down;
When under your directions I retire,
And feel each wiſh for wealth and fame expire;

In counting beads each morning hour beſtow,
And hear at eve celeſtial anthems flow;
Bend the bare pious knee before a ſtone,
Or kiſs the fragment of a martyr's bone.

CONCLUSION OF THE FIRST BOOK DE SPHÆRA.

FROM THE LATIN OF BUCHANAN.

Observe yon ſun whoſe beams enlighten all,
How far his bulk exceeds our earthly ball!
Yet while he rolls above the wint'ry blaſt,
Even he ſo mighty, luminous, and vaſt,
Appears, could we depend on mortal eyes,
Hardly to fill twelve inches of the ſkies.
But if his everlaſting ſource of light
Fades to ſuch ſcanty limits in our ſight,
Could Phœbus to our care, as Ovid feigns,
For one adventrous day reſign the reins,
When glancing from on high, how ſmall a clod,
If viſible to all, would ſeem our own abode?
The huge abyſs round which cold Saturn's driven,
Is but a ſpan in the expanſe of heaven.
Our globe is like a molehill to the ſun;
Himſelf but faintly ſees how wide his planets run;
And the whole ſyſtem, as they ſweep along,
Form but an atom in the ſtarry throng.
How narrow at the moſt our parent earth,
Which gives to man, to beaſts, and birds, their birth!
Even of this orb we vainly call our own,
How large a ſpace unfathom'd oceans drown!
Through the firm boſom of Gibraltar's rock,
With what tremendous force the ſurges broke,
When firſt on Libyan ſhores the deluge hurl'd,
And ſever'd from our own the Southern world.
Add that which beats around Arabia's coaſt,
And the wide wilderneſs Columbus croſs'd.

Here Sodom's lake a deadly ſtench exhales,
There Holland's marſhes bury half her vales;
Now the fierce Danube tears whole woods along,
Then bids in noiſome bogs, his billows throng.
O'erflow'd or undermin'd on every ſide,
Like a ſmall iſle aſſaulted by the tide,
Or ſolitary cliff, the land remains,
While the flood revels o'er unbounded plains.
Even of thoſe ſhatter'd fragments undeſtroy'd,
How vaſt a ſhare preſents a frightful void?
Clad in eternal ſnow, an Alps aſcends;
An ice-bound waſte from either pole extends.
A Zaara's fiery ſands in waves ariſe,
A Siam's rich domain an uſeleſs deſart lies.
The verdant tree preſents her poiſon'd fruits,
From flow'ry beds, the ſavage tyger ſhoots;
The bear, th' embattled wolf blockades your way,
The giant crocodile arreſts his prey.
Here from green ocean, while the ſhark invades,
There the fell ſnake ſweeps through the ſylvan ſhades;
Lo! the red light'ning furrows up the ground,
Down yawning earth deſcends the rocky mound.
Diſeaſe embodied in ten thouſand forms,
Each tortur'd nerve of fainting nature ſtorms.
Inceſſant agonies exhauſt the mind,
And leave a ſage the hindmoſt of his kind.
To ſwell the mad profuſion of a crown,
By ſloth, and luſt, and luxury, o'ergrown;
To clear a jockey's or a fiddler's claim,
Or deck a ducal ſyren for the game,
Our rights to bribe a ſenate to deſtroy,
Or whet the vices of a bankrupt boy,
Lo! *Dæmons* of *Exciſe*, a ghaſtly band,
Like Egypt's locuſts deſolate a land;
While blaſted penſioners their progreſs write,
And tugging our tithe-pigs with all their might,
While pamper'd prieſts aſſure us black is white.

Disastrous truths! too known to be deny'd,
How piteous then the farce of human pride!
How short the lapse of years, how strait the bounds
Through which ambition hunts for empty sounds;
Fear trembles, discord rages, sorrow mourns,
And thankless wealth dependent friendship spurns;
Law, physic, pestilence, and fire and sword,
Church, gauger, king, o'erwhelm a planet's puny lord!

THE END.

ERRATA.

Page 7, line 15th from the bottom, read *your* party.
Page 30, line 2d from the top, read an occasional *epilogue*.
Page 147, line 16th from the bottom, read *taste or* capacity.
Page 156, line 7th from the bottom, read *other* quacks.
Page 160, line 7th from the bottom, read in this *poem*.
Page 161, line 3d from the bottom, read serious and *comical*.
Page 162, line 5th from the bottom, read scriptores.
Page 167, line 18th from the top, add, *particularly in these two plays*.
Page 195, line 14th from the botom, read *on every*.
Page 209, line 3d from the bottom, read this venerable *writer*.
Page 273, line 2d from the bottom, read sic *dicis*.
Page 286, line 3d from the bottom, dele the words *of life*.

CONTENTS.

TO THE PUBLIC.

Buchanan is one of thoſe few happy writers of verſe whoſe power of pleaſing remains undiminiſhed by the lapſe of ages. Yet while the Engliſh nation are inceſſantly publiſhing the moſt elegant and ſplendid editions of their immortal Shakeſpeare, it is painful and humiliating for a North Briton to reflect that the original poems of Buchanan, the favourite, not of this country alone, but of Europe, have remained unprinted in a Scottiſh preſs for ſeventy-ſix years. This neglect ariſes not from our want of money, for we are daily printing whole libraries on every ſubject. It ought not to be from our want of taſte, ſince we have deafened both ourſelves and our neighbours with volumes of metaphyſical criticiſm. The cauſe of this partial oblivion has already been mentioned [p. 286.], and the Editor begs leave to ſuggeſt an eaſy and effectual method to remove it.

The Reader has already had opportunities of obſerving how the poetry of Buchanan appears in the dreſs of Engliſh proſe. A complete tranſlation of his original poems, on this plan, would render the Latin text perfectly intelligible to the moſt careleſs ſtudent. A few notes might be convenient, though to an author ſo remarkably perſpicuous, they could not be termed neceſſary. Theſe, together with the text, and propoſed verſion, might be compriſed within two octavo volumes of about the ſame ſize with that elegant edition of the poems of Oſſian, lately publiſhed by the printer of this volume. On this ſubject he has already had the honour of converſing with ſeveral gentlemen who have agreed to ſubſcribe on the moſt liberal terms. But before he engages ſeriouſly in an undertaking ſo laborious and expenſive, he wiſhes to learn the general opinion of the public. He is aware of the difficulty of producing a popular work of this nature *; but if ſuitable encouragement ſhall be offered, his ſubſcribers may depend on the ſincerity of his wiſhes to deſerve their approbation, and the vigour of his exertions to acquire it.

* *Vide* an Eſſay on the Principles of Tranſlation, lately publiſhed, a performance which contains both curious information, and uſeful inſtruction.

www.ingramcontent.com/pod-product-compliance
Lightning Source LLC
Chambersburg PA
CBHW021120270326
41929CB00009B/965
* 9 7 8 3 7 4 4 6 8 9 4 0 3 *